Eudora Welty and
Walker Percy

ALSO BY MARION MONTGOMERY

John Crowe Ransom and Allen Tate:
At Odds About the Ends of History and the Mystery of Nature
(McFarland, 2003)

Eudora Welty and Walker Percy

The Concept of Home in Their Lives and Literature

MARION MONTGOMERY

McFarland & Company, Inc., Publishers

Jefferson, North Carolina, and London

LIBRARY OF CONGRESS CATALOGUING-IN-PUBLICATION DATA

Montgomery, Marion.
    Eudora Welty and Walker Percy : the concept of home in
their lives and literature / Marion Montgomery.
        p.   cm.
    Includes bibliographical references and index.

    ISBN 0-7864-1663-7 (softcover : 50# alkaline paper)

    1. Welty, Eudora, 1909–2001—Knowledge—Manners and
customs.   2. American fiction—Southern States—History
and criticism.   3. Percy, Walker, 1916–1990—Knowledge—
Manners and customs.   4. Authors, American—Homes
and haunts—Southern States.   5. Authors, American—
20th century—Biography.   6. Southern States—In literature.
7. Welty, Eudora, 1909–2001.   8. Percy, Walker, 1916–1990.
9. Home in literature.   I. Title.
PS3545.E6Z777   2004
813'.52—dc22   2003020302

British Library cataloguing data are available

Cover photograph ©2003 Clipart.com

Manufactured in the United States of America

McFarland & Company, Inc., Publishers
    Box 611, Jefferson, North Carolina 28640
    www.mcfarlandpub.com

Table of Contents

v

Introduction

A preliminary note to any reader of the pages that follow: here are two short books or long essays, betwixt and between. Each was written independently, with no planned conjunction in mind. But once written and twice revised, they emerged as complementary of each other. Here are two Southern writers, Eudora Welty and Walker Percy, rather close friends but as fiction writers widely differing. Still, each is aware of responding to place as relating to their made things, their fictions. Is place in relation to their art a mystery? A problem to be solved? How interesting that, as writers, they respond with intense interest to the relation of place to fiction, out of the same neck of the woods so to speak— out of the Deep South, both of them claimed by Mississippi. That place appears more a problem for Percy than for his friend Eudora, for whom Jackson is reassuring and comforting to her as a writer. Covington for Percy is most comfortable in being a "noplace," as he will say.

Percy was the more acutely aware of a considerable difference between them, perhaps relating as difference in each's philosophical perspective. There were differences in the habits of their lives, not unrelated to differences in their fictions. For Percy *place* is a nagging problem, and because nagging becomes the more a personal problem to him as *homo viator;* man on his way. Place, he keeps discovering, involves much more than a technical concern in the making of novels, a concern for setting a fiction—a backdrop. One may talk endlessly about *place* in relation to art, a considerable library having now accumulated on that relationship, reaching back to Homer as homeless. There has been especially a considerable recent critical interest in the question in relation to the practices of "Southern" writers of the 20th century—poets and novelists and short-story writers and essayists. Indeed, William Alexander Percy, Walker's "Uncle Will" at home in Mississippi, writes the celebrated *Lanterns on the Levee* in which Southern place is shown to be central to both his poetry and his prose reminiscence, his Stoical vision of his South.

1

The relation of place to art: inviting to critical theorizing 'til the cows come home; but of a central and increasingly personal seriousness to Percy. What is the relation of my "self" to any "place" or to a particular "place," at any "moment"? The term *place* becomes a pivotal one for him. Is he a "Southern" writer, as the growing critical attention to his novels speculates? If so, then he is Southern in ways differing from those evident in Eudora, just up the road from Covington. Percy knew that his friend Eudora had been a long time at home, comfortably settled at 119 Pinehurst in Jackson, Mississippi. He, on the other hand, had been born in that phenomenon so much reviled and celebrated, defended and deplored during part of his lifetime in the second half of the 20th century—the suburbs. Specifically, he began life in the vicinity of a country club, with its golf course, in Birmingham, Alabama, a city prospering as a New South industrial center at the time. These circumstances Percy would reflect on often, though there is not much suggestion that he remembered in mundane detail that very early beginning. It was rather like an inherited omen, foretelling a world he must enter and become a *part*, though not always a happy *member*, of. Eudora on the other hand had been born in Jackson, had lived within the ambient air of a small town grown out of country ways, so to speak, and felt herself very much a member. Older than he, she was born, lived, and was to die there in Jackson, though she died after Percy did.

Hers was a culturing climate to her sensibilities. She breathed more comfortably the cultured air he also knew while living with Uncle Will. For he is more Mississippian than Alabamian or Georgian or Louisianian. He was by circumstances a wanderer, in his formative years wandering the South. From Birmingham as a child, he was gathered (out of family tragedy) to live with his grandmother in Athens, Georgia, for a while. Then, more significantly, he went to live with a cousin, "Uncle Will," that Stoical patrician who was rather more at home on a Mississippi "plantation," given a Stoical comfort in place, than young Walker could be. There Walker spent his formative adolescent years, followed by college years in North Carolina (where he majored in chemistry). And there was the summer interlude in the 1930s, spent as student wanderer in Germany. It was an experience that would prove more resonant in its meaning for him much later. He witnessed idealistic youth raising Nazi salutes of "Heil Hitler." He sensed a whole people mesmerized by a concern for "living room," belligerently declaring themselves denied "place" they insisted was rightly theirs. Here was at work, through political power invoked by magic, a growing dream summoned out of mythical history, transforming a people in a threatening restlessness about *place* thus mythologized. Theirs was a myth hardly compatible with the sense of myth Walker would discover in Eudora Welty much later, in the stories of *The Golden Apples* for instance. In retrospect, he would engage those differences, dramatized especially through the figure of Father Smith in his last novel, *The Thanatos Syndrome*, and in relation to Dr. Tom More, a Southern native who found himself strongly homeless. The Nazi adoption and distortion of place was to be revealed to Tom More by Fr. Smith, that world wanderer, to some comfort to Dr. More's sense of homelessness. This was radically at odds with the vision Percy would encounter in Eudora Welty, especially summarized in her "Place in Fiction," an essay published five years before he published his own first novel, *The Moviegoer,* in 1961.

From life with Uncle Will (some of that life reflected in Uncle Will's *Lanterns on the Levee,* which everybody seemed to know), to North Carolina, then up East to medical school. Then an internship in Bellevue, in the Cook County Hospital up in New York State, far from his youthful journeys in the South as very much alone though in the loving keep of family (Georgia, Mississippi, North Carolina). In New York he found himself very far from home indeed, as Faulkner's Quentin Compson found himself to be in Massachusetts as a student in that refuge from the South, Harvard. In the course of his internship, Percy contracted tuberculosis, an accidental infection that brought him to a shocking arrest. Recuperating in upstate New York, he began to read: Kierkegaard, and some of St. Thomas Aquinas, and then Dostoevsky and Camus and Sartre. There followed further recuperation in the Southwest. But then, where? He turned back "home"—not to Alabama or Georgia or Mississippi, but at last settled in Covington, Louisiana, south of Eudora's Jackson.

Getting to know Eudora Welty led him to reflect on what seemed a great advantage to her as a writer: she had been long settled in a place. It was not that she had been confined to Jackson, or if so it was in some respect by grace confined. After school at Mississippi State College for Women, she had ventured North to the University of Wisconsin, then to Columbia University's School of Business. There had been for her no accident forcing her home, unless (as she may have on occasion at least considered) the necessity to come home to care for aging parents in Jackson. After her return there followed much traveling—for brief days—as she became a "famous Southern" writer. From Percy's perspective, however, she seemed almost a homebody in Jackson, accepted by her local community in the place where she had been born. She was accepted as a *member*, not as a *part*, of the community, in contrast to that growing decay of community whereby persons are reduced to parts in a mechanism called a city, only partially escaping the mechanism by a suburban retreat. Of course, she began to write stories at home, an activity that perhaps made her somewhat exceptional on the local scene. But what is a daughter to do, caring for elders in a small town? Apparently, the diversion was not held against her by those closest to her: *closest* in respect to geographical proximity in a neighborhood. In coming years there would be more and more activity at 119 Pinehurst. Pilgrims from afar showed up in Jackson, perhaps knocking at a neighbor's door for directions to the house; itinerant intellectuals like those Percy had known earlier who sought out his Uncle Will's plantation.

From a neighbor's perspective, then, Miss Eudora, though a writer in that place, was certainly not so peculiar a presence among them as Bill Faulkner was to his neighbors over in Oxford. And so, quietly at home, a friendly presence on the local scene, she took her photographs and wrote her stories. Years after, some of those pictures would be collected and published—after she had become famous in far countries as a writer. The pictures reveal to a careful eye (to the eye of a diagnostician such as Percy, for instance) how comfortable she was with the subjects of her art and, as importantly to that sense of longing in Percy, how comfortable they were with her. As for the writing which had made her famous, increasingly it made her a tourist attraction in Jackson. Critics from distances away began remarking her literary sensibility in remote journals, perhaps from hints she may have given along the way in her own essays. They ventured into the South, out of curiosity stirred by her art, to see whether *place* might have anything to do with that art. As a writer she seemed closer to the distant world-famous Russian Anton Chekhov, at least to some curious critics, than to her writer-neighbor now himself world-famous, William Faulkner. How odd, such juxtaposition of literary genius in a country held mythically to be at best "provincial."

Eudora Welty was very much aware of Faulkner as a literary giant living rather close at hand. She speaks of him very comfortably as reassuring to her in her attempts as writer, a sheltering "mountain," in one interview. She was to hear increasingly her own name yoked with his, and then later in tandem with other Southern writers, especially those of a younger generation, Flannery O'Connor and Walker Percy. Not a very comfortable position for a writer, especially in being yoked with that Nobel Laureate from next door almost. Walker Percy's Georgia friend, Flannery O'Connor, hearing herself paired speculatively with Faulkner as Southern writers, doesn't find Faulkner a protective mountain: "Nobody wants his mule and wagon stalled on the same track the Dixie Limited is roaring down."

Faulkner's South, as Welty and Percy and O'Connor knew quite well, was not their South, nor was the South as seen by each of them the same for the others. The differences in their seeing, however, were somewhat slow to emerge from the critical yoking that forced them into the comfortable category of "Southern Novelists," which had given rise to essays and books and even to academic courses on their work. Miss Eudora in Jackson would, of course, see herself as undeniably somewhat closer to Faulkner, since the "local" grounding of their fictions shared actual place. That common geographical place urged critical quests for similarities buried in the common history of the place. The country "informing" Faulkner's Yoknapatawpha County (his "postage stamp" place, as he reckoned it) was in the fiction dependent, hung from, the place from which Miss Eudora's own little world depended. Theirs was a shared real place with a real history, though (as evident to them) it was seen by them with quite different eyes.

If we look at the intricacies of family entanglements that are of interest to Faulkner and Welty as makers of stories, we hear echoes of that common community, but recognize it as peculiarly different. Miss Eudora provides for her gathered stories, *The Golden Apples* (1949), a preliminary orientation for her reader under the title "Main Families in Mac-Lane, Mississippi." The Morgana of *The Golden Apples,* she advises, is a "fictitious town in a fictitious county, MacLane, Mississippi," as Jefferson is the fictitious county seat of an imagined Yoknapatawpha County for Faulkner. But neither is substantively fictitious insofar as it depends from an actual local place and borrows the actual history of that place for the geography and history of the fiction. The *selectivity* from generally common ground as actual is unique to each. When Malcolm Cowley edited *The Portable Faulkner* in 1946, just before Faulkner's Nobel Prize, Cowley persuaded Faulkner to contribute at least a brief history of that intricate family of Compsons, and Faulkner's response appears as an appendix entitled "The Compsons, 1699–1945," with its famous concluding line: Following his mere naming of the Compson servant Dilsey as a last entry, and having previously noted the other blacks "TP, Frony, and Luster," Faulkner concludes, "They endured."

A common ground; common substance to the necessity of "in-forming" fictions; but of very different imaginative visions. We need only read at a sitting, for instance, Welty's "A Worn Path" from her baker's dozen of stories (*Thirteen Stories*) and Faulkner's "That Evening Sun" to become quite aware of at least their differing literary sensibilities. Each is intent upon quite different imaginative projections of a more or less common matter, an "incarnating" in imaginative fiction of the local. One sees in Welty's story why she invites comparison to Chekhov, and especially so after reading her essay in tribute, "Reality in Chekhov's Stories." But despite a kinship of sensibilities as persons who are writers, her perspective yet differs from Chekhov's. We do not sense in her work, for instance, that restless, troubled energy of Chekhov out of his own concern for a place in which he might rest from circumstantial impositions

upon him as he is slowly dying of tuberculosis. He seems hardly content
with that accident, as Percy becomes content in believing it to be a gift
to him. Nor is there in Welty that other species of restless energy we find
in her neighbor Faulkner, in his pursuit of history's consequences upon
this place, upon whose history he so much depends. Faulkner's restless
energy spills out in the large fictions which make that "Dixie Limited"
roaring down the track to the new literary frontier country labeled
"Southern Fiction."

Closer to Chekhov in delicacy of sensibilities, Welty nevertheless
does not in her fiction suggest Chekhov's uncertainties as a person who
is never quite comfortably at home in any place in this world. For
Chekhov is touched with a Keatsian melancholy which she does not
share. As for Percy, there might be said to be in him a similar kinship to
Chekhov in respect to restlessness, differing as a restlessness from any
kinship with Faulkner. What Percy and Faulkner share, setting them apart
from Welty, is an intensity of concern for ideas. Faulkner's ideas engage
social and political history and its consequences. Percy's concern for history is rather for the "history of *ideas*" themselves as affecting his inherited "Southern" sensibilities, which are yet to be defined as he pursues
his new calling as novelist. Faulkner, of course, looks wider than to Mississippi or the South, a delayed discovery to some critics who at first
took him to be provincial in his concern for history. We find him discovering kinship with quite other Russians than Chekhov. He is rather
akin to Tolstoy, and, to a lesser degree, to Dostoevsky. Similarly, given
Percy's increasingly engaged concern for the spiritual relation he discovers in ideas—from which he cannot exorcise the South—he will find
Dostoevsky companionable. Percy finds himself especially drawn closer
to Faulkner by his appreciation of Faulkner's Quentin Compson, arguing Quentin exceptional among Faulkner's characters.

Such comparative suggestions as we have been making here among
these Southern writers, especially in turning to 19th-century Russian
counterparts, help us understand each writer's concern to discover the
limits of literary gifts as dependent upon a country too easily called the
"South." As writers, troubled or less troubled by ideas, they find themselves required to engage place or to avoid that engagement. That is a
concern appearing and reappearing especially for Percy, enough no doubt
to make him envious of his friend Eudora, so comfortably settled as a
writer in a place. In contrast to Faulkner—or to Percy or O'Connor—
Eudora Welty in her arresting stories is a Southerner less troubled by the
South, it would seem. But she also seems enigmatic if we attempt to
parse her fiction by social or historical measure as has become the dominant concern of what is still called "literary criticism." One evidence of
just how enigmatic her fiction is was the shocked surprise to our "social

consciousness" when she wrote that story, "Where Is the Voice Coming From?" following the assassination of Medgar Evers. Her presenting a disturbing character, the white lower-class assassin, makes that story seem more nearly Faulknerian, her protagonist somewhat like Faulkner's John McLendon in "Dry September." Given "Where Is the Voice Coming From" as exceptional in Welty, the critic with social and cultural concerns has better prospects to mine in Faulkner than in Welty. The difference is to be discovered in a contrast between Welty's "A Worn Path" and Faulkner's "That Evening Sun," we suggest. It is no accident that the central sensibility in Faulkner's story is that of Quentin Compson, who puzzles the ostensible protagonist of the story, Nancy, the Compson servant. We discover that it is Quentin who proves to be the protagonist, baffled by experiences unresolved in his responses to his family and its place on the one hand, and to Nancy and her place in the small social world of Jefferson on the other. Quentin, we anticipate, will not "endure." As for Welty's Phoenix Jackson, how seemingly she is at one with Welty herself, as Welty will suggest.

Her own likenesses and unlikenesses to that comforting "mountain" in her neighborhood, Faulkner, are of interest to Welty, but we do not discover any concern in the things she says—in essays and in interviews. He is different, but he is not that "Dixie Limited" to her. She knows very well, and celebrates, Faulkner's rich textural matter, which is so close in origin to her own recognitions of place, delicately gathered to her uses in a more "Chekhovian" than a "Tolstoyian" manner. Not that it isn't sometimes a thick matter, perhaps at times even lumpy, in Faulkner, in the fiction itself; handled with Chekhovian delicacy only on rare occasion. Then, too, there is some difficulty, especially for "foreign" readers, to discover any recognizable worn path through Faulkner's Yoknapatawpha County as reassuring to the reader in his progress through a Faulkner fiction. As Welty remarks (in "Place in Fiction") Faulkner is nevertheless particularly rich in "social fact" as it bears upon his dramatic moment. And not many readers are as attuned to social fact in its local history as is Faulkner—or Welty. Such fact enriches by his very complex sense of the history of place made culturally manifest in his fiction, but the richness requires mining and refinement. It is an actual history more intimately known to Faulkner than to most foreign, and sometimes even local, readers. So, too, Welty's own enrichment as well; but how different her own response to "social fact." On that point, we need only compare her *Losing Battles* to Faulkner's great Tolstoyian and Dostoevskian novel, *Absalom, Absalom!*

Faulkner, then, through Quentin Compson, may be said to have cast an additional obstacle before Southern writers. Percy finds a close kinship with Quentin as much in reaction to Faulkner as in approval of

Quentin's interest in ideas. It is reaction at a personal level as it were. Tell me about the South, Quentin's Harvard schoolmate from Canada begs, setting Quentin on that way to a suicide far away from his South, a South which Quentin swears he does not hate. As Percy will suggest, Quentin is on the way to becoming an "ex-suicide," a kinship Percy shares with him. Only late does Percy find comfort in his own South, resolving his own love-hate as Quentin could not, and enabled to do so because he himself has become an "ex-suicide."

Such ambiguous complications of "place" as disturbing to a "self" do not trouble Eudora Welty, quietly at home there in Jackson and not besieged by unresolved "ideas" such as those Percy struggles with. As for the *mystery* of place, rather than the *problem* of place as for Percy, we may be more confident that she would have been found—would have found herself—adaptable to place wherever circumstances might have dropped her in this world. Or so she suggests indirectly (as if to her self-evident and requiring no assertion) in remarking her much-admired fellow story writer, Katherine Mansfield, who in England carried New Zealand comfortably with her in her blood as it were—without the sense of homelessness that so haunts Walker Percy's fiction, we may add.

From the outside, then, as perhaps viewed by an itinerant Southerner come home and yet suffering a sense of homelessness, how different Welty is from her neighbor Bill Faulkner of Oxford, Mississippi. The local stories were numerous—about how he took delight in dressing peculiarly to stir local gossip, took pleasure in that self-epithet of "Count No Account" of Oxford. Faulkner might thus keep his curious neighbors at some distance—especially perhaps any locals fascinated with having the world-renowned writer in their midst. He did so on occasion with shocking pronouncements and actions. Nevertheless, venturing west to Hollywood to write film scripts for much money, he was miserable until he could escape back home to Mississippi and to Rowan Oak, his "suburban" Oxford home.

When Percy at last finds himself more or less comfortably at home in Covington, he writes an essay called "Why I Live Where I Live" (1980), with a wit perhaps echoing Welty's story, "Why I Live at the P.O." Covington is "a pleasant nonplace," unlike New Orleans for instance. It is a South he loves, but it is not his by birth, as are Oxford and Jackson for Faulkner and Welty. For him, it had been "necessary to escape the place of one's origins and ghosts of one's ancestors but not too far." Preferring to live in the South, "but on my own terms," it would be less difficult to insert himself into that community at Covington "in such a way as not to succumb to the ghosts of the Old South or the happy hustlers of the new Sunbelt South." Here he finds a settled community, but a *nonplace*, its members rather indifferent to him as writer (though, because they are Southerners, no doubt curious about this stranger among them). Indeed, the general indifference to his peculiarity—his being a writer of novels—was one of Percy's pleasures of citizenship in that nonplace, a pleasure which he will speak of from time to time. From within his own concerns, his is a definite advantage of place over Faulkner's; perhaps even over Welty's.

What was remarkable to Percy about his neighbor up the road at Jackson was that Eudora was untroubled by being at home, underfoot in community. Hers was a serenity beyond the easy label of "Southern" to explain it. Hers was a contentment unlike his own experience on returning "home," a return which only exacerbated his sense of homelessness. She was not haunted, he recognized, by any intellectual dislocation from place like that which so troubled him. He, on the other hand, must engage his own deracination as a malady, an infection of mind by a false idea. It was almost a relief to discover it as having become a worldwide Cartesian disease of mind and so not attributable to the accident of his having been born in the South. That idea itself becomes a repeated matter to his fiction—that Cartesian malady. He addresses it with concentrated attention in essays, particularly in "Diagnosing the Modern Malaise" and "The Fateful Rift: The San Andreas Fault in the Modern Mind." And still that disquieting contrast to himself of a serene Eudora, just up the road. Meanwhile, his own symptom of that malaise, as if a fever "struck in": his sense of being homeless wherever he found himself, a symptom of an intellectual deracination to which Eudora was apparently immune.

The theme of homelessness runs through Walker Percy's fiction, and we discover it born out of his personal experiences of dislocation, whether he finds himself in or out of the South. As diagnostician, he engages the malady initially through philosophy, set on his intellectual journey by Kierkegaard into French writers. He is wary of the epithet "philosophical novelist," more so than of "Southern novelist," one suspects. He is rather, as he insists, a diagnostician, a "physician as novelist." Nevertheless, his concentrated concern for *ideas* as the center of his fiction makes it difficult to avoid philosophical aspects of ideas. That ideas may allow dramatic rendering he reports having discovered, to his relief, in French writers like Camus, but especially in Sartre. But in response to them, he is inevitably drawn into philosophy's arena. In contrast (as she observes again and again), Welty's point of departure for a story lies in some person she has observed, an actual person in motion in an actual place. And it is the place in its immediacy to her observation that provides the means of her making a character incarnate in fiction's mode. Place provides as well an enveloping situational arena to a story. That is a point allying her to Henry James. (Faulkner, too, is "Jamesean" in this respect.)

Percy unlike Welty is drawn to *idea* as his point of departure, a response to an idea as it impinges upon his own consciousness in an interesting, troubling way. Lest he become too much a philosophical novelist, however, he depends initially upon his own intellectual gifts as scientist, a more comfortable country of mind to him. And so as diagnostician, as opposed to metaphysician or poet, he develops an intense dramatic concern for the endemic sickness of mind inherited and spread by the intellectual triumph of Modernist philosophy, that philosophy having itself become servant to science, especially to Positivism. In that combination (philosophy subservient to Positivistic science) the intellectual ground had been prepared over a few centuries, whereby *science* becomes at last *scientism*, as he recognized. Scientism is quasi-science, he will argue, and as such it becomes for Percy a principal antagonist as an idea in his fiction.

To clarify the point somewhat of this considerable separation of Percy and Welty as Southern writers, we might say in counterpoint that for Flannery O'Connor—like Percy a "Southerner" and a "Catholic" writer—not idea but doctrine believed affects her sense of place. Her principal antagonist (one not to be overcome) proves to be an active but hidden presence whose mode of action is a constantly threatening grace. It acts as agency to her protagonists, offering a possible resolution as love, always threatening to overwhelm the self-love of the protagonists. The contention at issue in O'Connor's drama is in *this* character as surrogate person, specific in fictional manifestation but always standing for actual man. As an intellectual creature, that figure of man (her protagonist) is pulled by the possibility of grace on the one hand, while on the other he resists with an intention to self-autonomy through the power of self-will. We see dislocated *will* in O'Connor, then, as opposed to dislocated *idea* in Percy, though Percy's dislocated ideas speak, for O'Connor as well, as an accurate symptom of dislocated will intent upon an intellectual autonomy, as if autonomy were man's ultimate end. We discover that the intellectual and spiritual circumstances of O'Connor and Percy bear close parallel.

A recognition of difference from O'Connor is at least hinted at by Percy when he demurs from her insistence on the actuality of the agent of evil, the Devil, the subverter of man's will. For O'Connor it is not enough to simply concede that evil exists, as Eudora Welty will do. In one of Jan Gretlund's conversations with Welty, Professor Gretlund remarks, "You do not seem to be interested in the concept of 'sin' or in the idea of 'evil.'" Welty responds in her own defense: "I am, though. Not in 'sin'—not from a Roman Catholic point of view like Flannery O'Connor because I'm ignorant of that religion. But I do believe that there is 'evil.' I believe in the existence of 'evil,' or else your reaching for the 'good' could not mean anything.... I thought there was 'evil' in Fay in *The Optimist's Daughter.*" For Flannery O'Connor, evil exists very explicitly "from a Roman Catholic point of view" as an effect of diminution of the good. It does so, she believes, as encouraged by the human will seduced by an Evil Agency, by the Father of Lies. And so, O'Connor emphatically insists, "we need a sense of evil which sees the Devil as a real spirit who must be made to name himself, and not simply to name himself as vague evil, but to name himself with his specific personality for every occasion."

The Devil as a reality, she argues, has been denied through that intellectual malady which Percy diagnoses in the Modernist mind. That mind has, through reason's calculations toward self autonomy, proved successful in the denial of any actual agency of the Devil through carefully structured rationalistic denials, making a belief in the Devil a quaint vestigial idea, evidence of a provincial isolation. The evidence to O'Connor of the Devil as actual is that symptom Percy labels the San Andreas Fault in the Modernist mind, now become dominant even in the popular spirit of the age no less than a treasured property of the detached intelligentsia. Ever since Descartes, sin has more and more been set aside as an illusion, a residue of a human failure of will to the perfections of self-autonomy. Meanwhile, autonomy is aided through the progressive emergence of rationalistic science, especially that science so troubling to Percy himself at last—psychology practiced as scientism. If psychology goes astray through *scientism* in Percy's view, for O'Connor the same distortion allows a subtle intellectual advantage to that intellectual creature without rival, Lucifer the "light-bearer," bent upon turning light toward darkness in pursuit of his own "self" as godhead: Lucifer become Satan. O'Connor's position in this question, then, is closer to Dostoevsky's than to Percy's, though Dostoevsky is an inescapable mentor to Percy again and again on the Modernist malady.

The Devil's banner of revolt is *non servium.* Thus *I will not serve* becomes the buried principle upon which is built the illusion of the absoluteness of intellectual autonomy—the exploitation of which by the Modernist "spirit of the age" is proving widely effective. The Devil's subtlety of "indirection" (a virtue of mode as writer which Percy embraces as novelist, warning us that as novelist he is deceptive) is succinctly put by Baudelaire in a preface to his *Flowers of Evil.* In our world, Baudelaire says, measured from Adam down to the present, "it is more difficult to love God than to believe in Him." But in the world since the Renaissance it has become "more difficult for people nowadays to believe in the Devil than to love him. Everyone smells him and no one believes in him. Sublime subtlety of the Devil." Convinced that he does not exist, O'Connor would say, we worship him in the image of our "self" as autonomous, as ultimate. And so effective is that strategy of deception—so O'Connor suggests—that our violence in resistance to grace erupts out of this disorientation. Such violence, for instance, as that in the story Welty finds of much interest, "A Good Man Is Hard to Find."* O'Connor's Misfit, no intellectual in his command of "Percyian" ideas, nevertheless reacts to a world which denies the existence of evil in order that such a world may establish the "idea" of the good as but relative and therefore dependent for any goodness upon the intentions of autonomous man. It is not surprising (from O'Connor's perspective) that the Misfit reacts by defending at least the reality of his own evil against such denial. This implies that he is (in her view) still hungry for a good denied him by social, economic, and political determinations that reduce the good to the convenient, hence making good relative and dependent upon the power of civil enforcement in the moment.

In his progress through this world as *homo viator,* Walker Percy will move closer to O'Connor's reading of the signposts to intellectual circumstances inherent in the Modernist mode of a new post–Renaissance "tradition." We see this, for instance, in *The Thanatos Syndrome* and in his late essays. And one of the accompanying effects of this change of emphasis in relation to idea will be Percy's growing comfort in place, somewhat alleviating that old gnawing uncertainty—his sense of homelessness recognized increasingly as a signal of a true spiritual desire. That sense of deracination will be discovered to involve an inner action deeper than intellect itself—as if the sense of homelessness were spoken to consciousness by conscience. Indeed, it would seem very much so to O'Connor, since for her—and increasingly for Percy—deracination speaks less of our being lost in the cosmos than of our having lost a right way through the cosmos toward an ultimate end. It is a signal of a spiritual exile self-induced, which neither geography, nor the traditions of a family long settled in place, nor an idea evolved in justifying autonomy, can sufficiently alleviate. But what is nevertheless required is an even closer relation to place itself than at first realized. We are to recover the experience of created things actual and also here and now. This is, indeed, a Thomistic recognition of the spiritual significance of (a *signifying* by) things in a place to the person in transit of this world toward a proper, ultimate end.

*Welty remembers first learning about Flannery O'Connor's "Catholicism" at Converse College (South Carolina) when Flannery delivered her lecture "The Catholic Writer," as Welty says in an interview (*Bloodroot,* Grand Forks, ND, Spring 1979). Her interviewer asks which of O'Connor's had been read in Welty's "class" at Converse. There was especially "A Good Man Is Hard to Find," which, Welty agrees with her ex-student and interviewer (Tom Royals), was "a tremendous story" needing no knowledge of "Catholicism" for an initial impact. But Flannery's talk, Welty adds, concerned with "grace and redemption and all of that," proved to be "so much more deeply rooted in her fiction, enhancing her stories more than I had realized because I didn't know much about the church itself."

O'Connor's and Percy's Church teaches this in both its philosophy and theology.

What we would suggest is that Eudora Welty herself recognizes as much, but she does so intuitively. She does not (as she says) "know much about the church itself," meaning the Roman Church. But her essay "Place in Fiction" has implicit in it this very recognition, never consciously formulated in words. Percy must himself have recognized as much in praising her wise quietness in Jackson. As Percy comes to understand more and more, it is evident in her response to things and persons, here and now—in this place. It makes of Welty's fiction a healing and restoration from that San Andreas fault within the Modern mind which seeks refuge in its own nonplace. How aptly Thomistic, then, Eudora Welty's commentary on her story of a "Worn Path" faintly echoing Dante's path to love. The story reveals what she calls "the deep-grained habit of love," dramatized as it is possessed by old Phoenix in her story. Phoenix repeatedly rises from the ashes of a moment's spent life through an openness of love toward the realities of creation itself, here and now, in this next moment. And how appropriate as well (and reassuring to a Percy or O'Connor as "Romans") that in closing her essay "Is Phoenix Jackson's Grandson Really Dead?" Welty concludes that "old Phoenix's way might even do as a sort of parallel to your way of work if you are a writer of stories," since the writer who is "like Phoenix" has "to assume that what you are working in aid of is life, not death." Such is the conclusion Percy will come to himself in a last essay, "The Holiness of the Ordinary," putting Welty's hope as writer in theological terms: Percy affirms the world itself as real and therefore sacramental in its presence to us beyond any Cartesian doubts and uncertainties. It is by its very existence an offering to us by Love, requiring as our response a lifting up of things to that Love in the actions of stewardship.

If place is for Percy a problem, it is for his fellow Southern Catholic O'Connor a mystery. But to the contrary of both, place for Eudora Welty is neither a *problem* requiring the analytical services of science in pursuit of an epistemology, nor a *mystery* to be accommodated through philosophy and theology. Place is where she is, now. Responding to her own gifts as poet, responding intuitively, she will speak of her deportment as a poet in a place, as revealed in her parable of the writer, the journey of Phoenix Jackson in "A Worn Path." The lesson learned by the poet and celebrated through her characters is a recognition she believes shared with Chekhov, remarking him as so fully given to the realities of human nature that "It was not in Chekhov to deny any character in his stories the dignity and purity of singularity. He would have found it not only alien to his art but morally unjust to slur over a man ... as only an example of his class or sex or calling in life."

Such is the "idea" we shall briefly explore as Eudora Welty's centering concern. It makes her a writer comfortable in a place, in that situation somewhat envied by her friend Walker Percy. As writer, hers is an exploration concerned with what O'Connor and Percy (as *Catholic* Southerners) might understand as a deportment through which obstacles to grace are removed, allowing a blossoming of her intuitive response to actual persons and things in Jackson, Mississippi. It is a response out of her love of persons in the "dignity and purity of singularity" proper to them. Hers is, then, a celebration of a habit of love which seems a deeply-grained habit in her, allowing her a comforting vision within her own place. She seems to have considered this as perhaps partaking of mystery, perhaps somewhat stirred to that reflection in response to those younger Southern writers in whose company she finds herself increasingly gathered in the growing body of criticism about Southern Literature. Such reflection seems deeply implicit in the words of her "Place in Fiction." Nor does she shy from the *personal* in her essays, though the *private* is a quite different matter. The aspect of the personal is revealed with some more direct intention in two of her rather late works more than before: her series of lectures in 1983 gathered as *One Writer's Beginnings* and the late novel which is unusual in that it depends upon private correspondences between herself and her parents as modified to serve the incarnating of her fictional characters in family circumstances. The good of the work itself arises out of the personal, but not at the expense of the private. I mean of course *The Optimist's Daughter* (1972), which earned her the Pulitzer Prize.

In our concern for this distinction between the personal and the private as a confounding difficulty to writers in the 20th century, we propose an analogy to another "personal" poet, now remembered as St. Augustine of Hippo, who in his *Confessions* unhesitatingly reveals both the personal and the private in witnessing his failures as a sinful man, and who as *homo viator* reaches an impasse requiring his turning. The *Confessions,* indeed, prove something very like a "Modern" novel, as Percy will recognize. St. Augustine experiences an epiphany quite other than Percy's discovery that *idea* may be dramatized. For St. Augustine, it is a moment's vision of actual things in an actual place, an act of grace opening his eyes and ears in the occasion, and by his very rescue rebuking his long neglect of the habit of love that has separated him from things and therefore from God. The things of creation speak to him: "I asked the whole fabric of the world about my God" in that moment of turning. It is a point of turning which Percy might call a movement whereby a *person* becomes an ex-suicide. That whole fabric "answered me," St. Augustine adds: "'I am not he, but he made me!'" The recognition comes: "My question was the gaze I turned on them; the answer was their beauty."

By that intuitive vision of things, we suggest, St. Augustine experienced a vision which has a parallel in Eudora Welty's recognition of that "deep-grained habit of love" she celebrates in Phoenix Jackson, a "natural Augustinian," we might say. In consequence, Welty could be comfortably, serenely, at home—in place, to the wonder of the early Walker Percy, but to his better understanding at last as revealed in his late essay, "The Holiness of the Ordinary."

From what we have been saying here, a reader will know in advance that the pages ahead are not "literary criticism" in any formal manner, but rather suggestive of a possible recovery whereby we may share the vision of two superb craftsmen as makers of fiction. It will be, grace allowing, a recognition as well of the importance of their differing visions occurring within a shared world. And perhaps it will allow a reader of the fictions themselves a more proximate perspective from which to respond to the richness of their various testimonies to the possibilities of beauty such as might otherwise go unrecognized.

Beyond these two small books (my long essays?) I anticipate a more complex engagement of Flannery O'Connor's vision as Thomist, out of which (grace allowing some aid) a next work may prove more revealing as well of this present question of place in respect to matter serving art. As such, foreshadowings anticipated sometimes prove also after-lightings still helpful to acceptance of paths already trod. Perhaps there may even be some deepening of the grain of love in intellect itself, toward an openness to things in whatever place we may find ourselves on the way, even in such works as these as signposts. If so, we may discover that the "Southerness" which was and is of much critical concern in both social and literary matters proves always more surely grounded within our own given nature as *homo viator* than in any geography or geography's accumulated local history in any place. The reality of place seems now threatened by a dissipation, through cultural concerns increasingly turned antithetic to our existences as each *this* person in *this* place, egalitarian distortions which disallow at last the "dignity and purity of singularity" in the interest of abstract identity. The hope of recovery from that blind deconstruction of our reality as persons in places—each *this* person in *this* place—must be kept alive. We may do so by a feeding of intellectual wonder out of love itself as the first principle of art, but dependent always upon a love antecedently the first principle to life, the life of *any* person in *any* place.

PART I

The Swift Bird of Memory, the Breadboard of Art: Reflections on Eudora Welty and Her Storytelling

It is memory that is the somnambulist.

Laurel, in *The Optimist's Daughter*

1

Greater than scene ... is situation. Greater than situation is
implication. Greater than all of these is a single, entire human
being, who will never be confined in any form.

—Eudora Welty, *One Writer's Beginnings*

I owe a special debt to Jan Nordby Gretlund for his Eudora Welty's Aesthetics of Place *(Odense, Denmark: Odense University Press; Newark: University of Delaware Press, 1994). Given his extensive and intensive analysis
of Welty's fiction, which he makes in response not only to that fiction but also
to the considerable body of historical and critical work that has been done
on it, Professor Gretlund establishes both a scholarly and a critical context
upon which my speculative concerns depend. It is in the light of his study
that I have written what follows, intending to bring to the support of our
common concern for literature a metaphysical dimension of concern which I
believe appropriate to literary criticism.*

Eudora Welty has understood from the beginning a responsibility
to the truth of things in response to the wonder and delight she is granted
by life itself, and both the delight and the responsibility have governed
her deportment in creation as person and as artist. Her long remembering of that deportment, in celebrating existence as fiction writer, she
gives us in her Massey lectures at Harvard in April of 1983, published
as *One Writer's Beginnings*. She recalls that, "beginning to write stories
about people, I drew near slowly, noting and guessing, apprehending,
hoping, drawing my eventual conclusions out of my own heart." As artist,
concerned with imitating the actions of human nature—the possible or
probable—she was from childhood shyly aware (as she would put it) of
her own participation in humanity that requires a certain deportment as
person, but also as an artist presenting simulacra of persons through her
special gift as artist.

Now because piety requires a recognition of limit by the artist as
both in himself and in the attendant complex of existence upon which
his art depends, *place* becomes of considerable importance. Fiction in
particular is an "incarnational" art, requiring from nature a substantiat-
ing presence in the artist's signs, lest abstraction reduce the fictional "persons" (the simulacra) and the enveloping world they inhabit to the
two-dimensional, an old complaint against lesser fictions. One wants the
three-dimensional in a persuasive imitation of the action of nature. That
is the issue touched upon when we speak of fiction's art as *incarnational.*
Nor is this necessity to dramatic making any the less, however stylized
the made thing may be. *Oedipus Rex*, surely, echoes a three-dimensional
nature—man's nature—despite masks and high shoes and formal cho-
ruses. And the subtlety of Chekhov's art is possible because Chekhov

19

(one of Welty's favorite writers) is himself so closely (in a physical sense) attuned to proximate reality—to persons and their complex circumstances in nature. It is in recognizing this dimension of Welty's art that Jan Gretlund writes so persuasively of her in his *Eudora Welty's Aesthetics of Place.*

From the beginning, then, Welty, long before she realized her calling to be that of the poet—the maker of imitations of human nature through words—recognized as already under way a feeding of her heart by place, by things "at hand" as we say. The world impinging upon consciousness does so only in a *place* and at this *present moment.* That means that the encompassing world is first of all *local.* It is within the immediate range of our senses as they mediate to consciousness the mystery of creation itself. And further, it is a mystery of *limit,* without which no thing could even exist, not even the most gifted artist. For even by that superlative title (artist), we name limit. Many of our most gifted writers in the 20th century struggle long to discover place and the limits of place that make art possible. We especially find the struggle in those writers fleeing Puritan distortions of our proper response to contingent reality. Remember Ezra Pound in exile, who as artist insists that "art is local." Or remember T. S. Eliot in his flight, who asserts in concluding the body of his own poetry that the whole journey has as its end that we return to the place from which we set out and "know the place for the first time." Or remember that other Southern writer, Walker Percy, who after much wandering returns to place, settles into it, and is only with difficulty lured away from his settled place in Louisiana to New York or Washington, D.C.

Eudora Welty was blessed in knowing at once the importance of the proximate to her as person and artist. She remarks the point in *One Writer's Beginnings,* and elaborates that fundamental recognition through her memory, summoning her childhood. Her art, she says, constitutes a recovery of the "discoveries" she has made, which "all begin with the particular, never with the general," with local circumstances and situations which persons willy-nilly must respond to as proximate locality— in *this* place at *this* present moment. The witness of her fiction and of her talks and essays carries the humor of acceptance of her own limit as person, the "self" as only allowed existence *in locus.* The person experiences the proximate circumstantial world of place as *current* to consciousness itself in a figurative sense that at last may prove more actual than the figurative. It is by the acceptance of these conditions to her own nature as person that she celebrates existence out of lessons learned in her "beginnings" as a child. It was then, before discovering her calling and required commitment as poet, that she touched the limits of existence in place through awe and wonder—before the dawning in her of responsibility to such marvelous gifts of existence.

How wise her memory: "Children, like animals, use all their sense to discover the world. Then the artists come along and discover it the same way, all over again." That is a wisdom Eliot came to late, closing his poetry in *Little Gidding* with his own "beginning." In that late poem he recalls once more the "voice of the hidden waterfall/ And the children in the apple-tree." Welty makes similar recovery through memory, recalling her delight in discovering the power of the word as the word touches truth through senses in her response to a local place. Hers is neither a Cartesean alienation from reality nor a Kantean abstractionism. "Held in my mouth," she says, "the moon became a word. It had the roundness of a Concord grape Grandpa took off his vine and gave me to suck out of its skin and swallow whole, in Ohio." It was a moment of actual, not fictional, epiphany, in which a confluence of like epiphanies occurred. What is of conspicuous importance to note here is that this necessity of the local, of place, is not determined by history or geography—even though those old *moments* in old *places* are brought together into a vivid presence.

The truth discovered is discovered again and again by the child becoming adult, whether the place be Jackson, Mississippi, or Logan, Ohio. We are here affirming an encounter with truth, but not in respect to any enlargement of geography, broadly drawn on maps, in relation to which those temporal points of knowing in reality are accumulated by memory in a sweep of epiphanies from childhood down to now, designated abstractly. Such is that species of abstraction as we more usually understand *biography*, ordered by the calendar and literal road maps. But hers is a truth out of experience, recognized as a continuing truth held in an active intellectual confluence of events in memory itself. In such confluence the past is in presence, in relation to the immediate contingent reality of *now*, regardless of abstract namings. In such confluence, past feeds the present. It is this mystery of memory as agency to fulfillment of our personhood that is the central fictional concern of *The Optimist's Daughter*, a novel complementary to *One Writer's Beginnings*.

In this present local place, and now, and through piety, a person may reach an accommodation to existence with thanksgiving in joy beyond solemnity. For out of such piety of deportment rise signals to the self of its own hope of fulfillment as person. If one catches such a moment in an incarnational way in art, one may well become such an arresting artist as Eudora Welty. No wonder, then, that in her memory of coming to a sense of responsibility to words through the child's untrammeled awe and wonder toward existence, she recognizes as well that her responsibility to her calling as maker depends necessarily from limits of time and place and most especially depends as artist in the limits of herself as person. That is the recognition that any person, artist or other, is a maker and not a creator. And so no wonder as well that we hear her quote the Gospel of St. John: "In the beginning was the Word"; creator preceding all human makings.

As for the necessary deportment, it is properly called piety in response to the presence of complex creation, in respect to both persons and to the things of nature—flowers and trees and birds. In response to lesser creatures, piety is less difficult to maintain than toward the mystery of human persons as encountered just at hand. That piety is no less required toward one's own self than to the world of persons contingent to that self, or to lesser creatures in creation. Because this pious deportment in creation requires first of all that a person recognize the *limits* of any presence to the consciousness so deported, attendant as well upon the limits of consciousness itself—whether a presence to oneself or to whatever *other*—the manner binding in this deportment we call *humility*. That is the manner making any community possible to consciousness, whether with a flower or bird, or with a person. *Piety, humility*: how much these concepts suffer from the excess of a Puritan fear of limit, which leads to a false humility whose expense to such a Puritan spirit is the loss of awe, wonder, joy, curiosity, and especially the comic mischief of response to existence which we may inevitably develop in recognition of our own limits as persons.

It is no accident that in the literature of the 20th century we are more likely to discover an *ironic* deportment in writers, born out of and in revolt against their Puritan inheritance. But in a conspicuous and celebrated contrast, there is an additive, *humor*, in certain writers who seem obliged by nature itself to take delight in existence, and especially in response to that most curious presence of all in nature, human persons. Such an obligation to humor, which includes wit and even irony but is yet larger than both, appears characteristic of the so-called "Southern" writer, whether we mean William Faulkner or Walker Percy, Flannery O'Connor or Eudora Welty—however diverse their responses to existential reality. And so here I intend celebration of this Southern writer, Eudora Welty, whose virtue of piety is so conspicuous in her art.

Now I am quite aware that Eudora Welty keeps a distance between herself and what she calls "organized religion" as she encountered it in Jackson. She applies the phrase in remembering her childhood experiences with the Baptist, Methodist, and Presbyterian churches in Jackson. She remembers that church life of her youth with a humorous participation that maintains nevertheless a careful distancing such as she argues necessary to the writer—what she calls the "distance of the observing eye." But in that careful distance, there is no condescension. For as we discover in the witness she bears by turning her writer's observing eye upon herself as a person emerging in the concrete circumstances of

Jackson, hers is a spiritual deportment in place. She maintains a reverence for existence, which includes a reverence for herself as a child encountering place with a child's developing curiosity about existence as now remembered. Supported through the continuous love of her close family, hers is a response of spirit beyond any possible *determinisms* of place or time in any technical sense of the term.

It may well be that the continuity of community, the sustaining presence of love constituting the community called family, allows a person a larger enfolding which affirms the obligation of the particular spirit to its own existence in those local circumstances, an obligation unaided by any "formal religion." There may be made possible thereby an openness to the institutions of a particular place—the Baptist, Methodist, Presbyterian churches of Jackson, Mississippi, perhaps—that does not require one's formal submission to those institutions in their particularities. Put another way, if one is so fortunate as to live among families beyond one's own house—families who, by intuition and custom as reflected in manners, share a common obligation as community—then the place of that community may become a particular locus to celebrations of community beyond the merely civic virtues of community. Such a deportment partakes of the religious, even if only vaguely or raggedly and intermittently understood as touching upon a person's "religious" obligations of love active in this particular person.[1] Even so, it is wrong to suppose that place—or history of place—determines a person's spiritual deportment, because in truth it is the other way around. This, despite the insistent conclusions of generally deterministic sociology acting as a "theology" of the secularized civil community. That is a truth which our actual experiences as persons in a place will show us, if we ourselves are attentive through an active awe and wonder before the mystery of existence itself. For existence is intellectually irreducible to abstract formulae as the essence of existential reality, and most especially as forced upon the person contingently active in place, upon for example Welty's "entire human being, who will never be confined in any form," either by science or by art.

What is of interest to the poet, as opposed to the social or political historian committed to a pseudo-scientific reading of communities in time and place, are those failures of obligation by specific persons, traditionally evidenced to a person, unless distorted as obligation to creation (natural and social), in his resistance to conscience. In Eudora Welty in particular there is the recognition of this human inclination to distortion as the ground rich for fictional tensions among her imagined persons and communities. Out of that tension, her characters respond to existence, seeking a sustaining love even as they violate it. There is as an instance of such distortion in the actions localized in Mount Salus in *The*

Optimist's Daughter, especially evident among Laurel's aging "brides-maids," who are not wrong insofar as they have a concern for local tradition but rather misunderstand and so distort the proper uses of memory in sustaining community. In this respect, their counterparts are the outlanders who invade Mount Salus when Judge McKelva dies. Even Laurel, the Judge's daughter, seems strangely an outsider to the "bridesmaids," requiring them to rescue her. Such fictional strategy, then, reminds us that a right obligation of a person to community, through memory rightly taken, is a governing vision for Welty, both as person and as artist. In this recognition we discover her to be a religious writer, though she eschews organized religion. The center of her vision is the primacy of love in response to existence itself, and she affirms this commitment in a moving passage in her recollection of her beginnings as writer—as poet.

"I painlessly came to realize," she says, "that the reverence I felt for the holiness of life is not ever likely to be entirely at home in organized religion." Let us emphasize that what she is speaking of here as *organized religion* are those manifestations of the institution in Jackson, Mississippi. In the South in particular, churches tend to so anchor themselves in the discrete place as to give an impression at least that this particular church is a spiritual vortex independent of, though circumscribed by, a world that seems often to threaten it with intrusions upon the local through external power as opposed to open love. Outsiders often experience their own "otherness" in such circumstances in the cautious response they receive, confusing because Southern manners nevertheless obtain. One may be a newcomer to a community for a generation, while being an active member of that community. Probationary status differs from community to community. I myself have lived for over thirty-five years in the "old Blanchard house," which earlier was the old "Little house," 'till those more ancient members of this rather old community died out at last. One hardly needs to say that there are both advantages and disadvantages to such tradition, though the advantages are less and less valued now. Meanwhile, especially from "outlanders," alarmed cries rise more and more about the disadvantages. (For me to say those alarms are sounded by a world outside community, intrusive upon it, is perhaps a sign that our home is well on its way to becoming "the old Montgomery house.")

As for those advantages, in relation to local organized religion, a person's presence as outlander is somewhat ameliorated if he brings a letter from a church in another community, a rite of passage to the new community. But such a letter bears only residually, through the long erosions of community history, an authority of *sacramental* testimony. One may be certified as "baptized," but more nearly on the authority of local waters than of holy water. In respect to organized religion, rites of passage tend to partake more of the civil dimension of community order than of sacred community, and that has been one deleterious effect of Welty's local bodies of organized religion. This is an aspect of her experience that one must recognize and see in relation to discoveries she makes beyond a merely local ground of love, to which local ground she continues nevertheless devoted. She adds, having remarked it unlikely she would ever be "entirely at home in organized religion":

> It was later, when I was able to travel farther, that the presence of holiness and mystery seemed, as far as my vision was able to see, to descend into the windows of Chartres, the stone peasant figures in the capitals of Autum, the tall sheets of gold on the walks of Torcello that reflected the light of the sea; in the frescoes of Piero, of Giotto; in the shell of a church wall in Ireland still standing on a floor of sheep-cropped grass with no ceiling other than the changing sky.

What she is recognizing are those signs which have been made by the person as *homo viator*—pilgrim man in the world. Those signs are left in testimony to a common recognition of the "holiness and mystery" of a local *presence* which is intuitively known as *presence* beyond time and geography. And what we may also recognize is the descent of a holiness into the local matter as celebrated by her own art, whether in her photographs or her fictions. Her summoned memory of encounter with holiness beyond Jackson, Mississippi, stands in her words as recalled epiphanies, encounters of "holiness and mystery" which she has already known in her own experiences from childhood on. In that sustaining confluence of epiphanies called memory, Welty recognizes that her obligation as artist is to witness to the holiness of life, a witness which requires an openness to immediate place, whether lingeringly spoken by a decaying church wall in Ireland or the mysterious state capitol in Jackson through which as a child she passed to the library in pursuit of viable signs suited to her devotion to the holiness of existence. In her recalling that experience, we hear echoes of her actual, present passing through that vaulted space, which is still standing just down the street and around corner from the house in which she must have sat on a morning summoning memories of her beginnings as writer, put on paper before making the long journey up to Harvard to share her memories.

We in turn are obliged to see that in summoning the illusive (and in our own experience sometimes erratic) bird of memory to witness to the holiness and mystery of existence, as in *The Optimist's Daughter*, her witness is continuing in community with Piero and Giotto and with the anonymous builders of that deserted church ruin in Ireland. Her witness in praise of "the presence of holiness and mystery" is her gift out of confluent memory, feeding anew awe and wonder beyond whatever limits of her art. We recognize this as true if we are fortunate enough to have seen in person, as we say, the liveliness of her eyes as she looks at creation, including our own self present in an occasion, in an event in time and place. In her eyes we gain some rescue of delight in creation itself, that necessary support of hope which a community *in things and persons* supplies to our uncertain consciousness. (We speak here particularly of a "communion" of persons, being reminded of that ancient assurance that the eyes are the seat of the soul.) Her art is a gift to us, in part effected through our own recovering and gathering memories in a devotion sustaining the holiness of life itself. That *reminding* gift is ours from her marvelous stories, which bear presence to us through artful signs recalling permutations of the human spirit. Such is a resonant presence to us in her quietly unpretentious witness of *One Writer's Beginnings* no less than in her fiction.

It is worth saying of Welty, as we might of Augustine or Aquinas on this point, that she refutes the Manichaeans in celebrating the goodness of the immediate world. We shall pursue that analogy of visions presently, but here we first look at the witness of her memory as made "incarnate" through her gifts as artist given us in *One Writer's Beginnings*. There is, for instance, the formidable presence to the small child Eudora of her teacher, Miss Duling, with her "high-arched bony nose, her eyebrows lifted in half-circles above her hooded, brilliant eyes ... the long steps she took in her high top shoes." Out of such memories, including that shortcut to the library through the Mississippi State Capitol on bicycle or skates in quest of a word as palpable as *moon*, that we recognize her spiritual nature, as she has recognized it all along. That recognition is summoned from long ago as she talks to us of her gradual discovery of her calling, her writer's *confessions*. She was fascinated by the grammar of Latin in her first year of high school. Through that grammar she discovers "words in continuation and modification, and the beautiful, sober, accretion of a sentence." This is an enlargement upon that earlier epiphany with the word *moon*, which proved so like a grape as held and voiced by the child. "I could see the achieved sentence finally standing there, as real, intact, and built to stay as the Mississippi State Capitol at the top of my street, where I could walk through on my way to school and hear underfoot the echo of the marble floor, and over me the bell of its rotunda." Her witness to the holiness of existence through art's signs echoes anciently, though through the immediacy of her witness it bears a local habitation, a *presence* that is *here* and *now* to us.

It is with this community of witness, a confluence of presences through signs celebrating the holiness and mystery of existence, that I should like to engage Eudora Welty as a spiritual classicist, in no wise intending thereby to appropriate her to such organized religion as she experienced in her Jackson childhood. There is nevertheless in her witness an order in relation to limit, through signs, so that we may safely conclude her to be member of a larger spiritual community beyond the limits of either the time or the place which we associate with her as her biographical record. How this may be so is my concern, signaled to us in the titles she gives her Harvard lectures: "Listening"; "Learning to See"; and finally "Finding a Voice" in her beginnings. We recognize the central theme of her lectures (the William E. Massey, Sr. Lectures in the History of American Civilization) to be an unfolding of herself in an openness called love, a more profound undertaking than the defining title of the lecture series can account for. A confluence of epiphanies in her led her to recognize that a deportment through *love*—a piety and humility before limit—was unfolding to her a gradual discovery of her special calling in the world as artist. It is this concept of *love* that we must clarify, for it has become confused in our careless invocations of it.

2

The eyes see better when guided by love; a new dimension of "seeing" is opened by love alone! And this means contemplation is visual perception prompted by loving acceptance!
—Joseph Pieper, *Only the Lover Sings:*
Art and Contemplation

Eudora Welty as a young woman was able to travel farther than on her repeated childhood journeys to West Virginia and Ohio, where her mother's and father's families lived. Those were exciting expeditions for the child, especially to West Virginia, where she experienced the closeness of a family delighted in its accommodations to and by the surrounding mountainous countryside, in contrast to the more reserved and pragmatic Ohio family. The images of her recollections carry an immediacy for her many years later, especially of her sense of being in tune with the world about her, delighted not only by an uncle's playing country music but by the hovering mountains and the flowers and birds to which she became so personally attached that her respect for accuracy of detail from such personal encounters with things remained with her always. Such experiences prepared her for Italy and Ireland later, from which traveling she returns always to Jackson, reassured in an enlargement of her devotions to the holiness and mystery of existence. She understands a commonness of places thereby, a commonness larger than the artist's (let alone the philosopher's or scientist's) signs can ever *contain*—arrest—as is the temptation to hungry intellect. What she understood is that the artist (or philosopher or scientist for that matter) must use signs, but without despair from his recognition that the best used signs are limited in relation to the holiness and mystery of existence itself. There is a subtle distinction between *comprehension* and *understanding* required of intellect, the evidence of understanding being that deportment to existential reality we have called *piety*.

In a reflective moment, concerned with understanding herself but sharing that understanding, Welty says: "I found the world out there revealing, because ... *memory* had become attached to seeing, love had added itself to discovery, and because I recognized by own continuing longing to keep going, the need I carried inside myself to know—the apprehension, first, and then the passion, to connect myself to it.... The outside world is the vital component of my inner life.... My imagination takes its strength and guides its direction from what I see and hear and learn and feel and remember of my living world." An apt formulation, this, of a person's experiences of life, the confluence of which is held by memory. And we must take seriously such terms as *love* and *passion* here, as they are related to the actual experience of the action called *living* as carried into consciousness and held by memory out of the senses themselves. For *love* and *passion* are much decayed as concepts in our day, having been far removed from our spiritual natures and left as if only residually in the senses—as if the appetitive dimension of human existence were ultimate. As if animal nature defined the limits of human existence and consciousness itself to be reduced to biochemical formulations.

What we require is a recovery of the complexity of love as *eros*, witnessed through the senses. Thus a deportment of love as *eros* is more inclusive than the "sexual," which has been increasingly the prescribed limit of *eros*. Our sensual response has thus been reduced by biology and psychiatry in the 20th century so that we are conditioned to see sexual implications even in the deportment of a child as he strokes a kitten. Our several senses, let us say, allow us to respond to the actuality of the things we encounter. Nor should we forget Thomas Aquinas's insistence that our first movements toward Perfect Love—toward God—are through the senses. There is a range in our sensual openness to creation to which a reduction to the biochemical limit of being is inadequate. Indeed, it is in our initial opening to existential reality through love as *eros* that wonder and awe first stir in us. Through wonder and awe, in response to the "presence of holiness and mystery" of existence itself, we are moved beyond the mere *knowledge* that we possess our experience through memory ... as if experience were a subjective property only, though in this view as abstract as our bank account. Knowledge, the province of the variety of sciences, is inadequate to the desire raised in us by that knowledge, desire moving us beyond the possessiveness of knowledge. For what we desire is understanding, which is possible at last out of a confluence wherein love carries *eros* beyond itself into a higher incorporation of consciousness and existence in that love we call *agape.*

The movement is that of the self in its willed openness. Thus consciousness knows itself to have experienced and to continue experiencing contingent realities beyond consciousness itself. This changing "self" we used to call the soul, from which a love proper to the senses is not to be excluded. For that exclusion will ultimately mean a separation of the self from community in existential reality through a gnostic contentment with mere knowledge. Thus we describe in the aberration a Puritan gnosticism, now dominant in community, which is not simply that of our Puritan fathers, many of whom had much difficulty coming to terms with sensual existence. The immediate descendants from this Puritan inclination into gnosticism give rise to our current religion of secular scientism, to which we owe the now-dominant reduction of both the mystery and holiness of existence itself: the mechanical or chemical or psychological base in biochemistry as both the ground of human nature and the outer limit of human existence. If we do not rescue *eros* from such reductionism, through which the sensual as ultimate is dictated as the limit of our sensual nature (and out of which pornography, incidentally, currently flourishes), we shall be hard-pressed to defend even art itself as anything other than a means of satisfying appetite. That has been a tendency in aesthetics which parallels the rise of scientism since the 19th century.

Art self-evidently is depended to consciousness and depends upon consciousness through the senses. An aesthetic which denies the body is meaningless. That was a troubling point in both philosophy and aesthetics for Plato, who struggled to come to terms with the poet. It is a troubling point in the interval down to us, the history of the artist increasingly reflecting the artist's discomfort with the relation of art to theology. It leads, among its other effects, to repudiations by artists of their own works, from Chaucer to Tolstoy. But only in our day has art become thoroughly relocated to the province of science, with results less than encouraging. Increasingly, an artist such as Welty, whose devotion is to the holiness and mystery of existence itself, tends to suffer a disfranchisement from community far other than that disfranchisement Plato attempted in the *Ion.* The concern for a separation of church and state as a popular political issue has a popular corollary, though not one clearly defined because the underlying issue, unstated though programmatically advanced, is that there must be a separation of art and religion. The consequence of that separation will not be the triumph of art over religion, however, but rather the triumph of gnosticism over art. That love proper to the immediacy of art (*eros*) will have been relocated to the province of science as opposed to the province of philosophy, whether that province be called Political Science or Biological Psychology.

Eros names a god presiding in the senses, or so the Greek mind suggested. That is a recognition not out of consonance with Thomas Aquinas, though Thomas puts the point in another way. Through *eros*, there is an initiating opening of the self toward its own potential fullness which encompasses and includes erotic love. A person does not set erotic love aside in fear, as our Puritan fathers were inclined to do. Nor is the erotic reduced by gnostic secular puritanism through formulaic reduction of abstract analysis, abstraction always being the enemy of art. Eudora Welty's fictions, she insists against this tendency, rest in "particulars" which "all begin with the particular [as experienced in reality], never the general," never that reductionist accumulation of particulars to the formulaic. The love she exercises through art is in celebration of particularities. Either species of gnostic puritanism, on the other hand, in a response to existential reality through divided sensibilities, intends an escape from the continuity of our actual experience of creation. It would interpose concept between the experiencing self and that which the self experiences here and now according to its nature as an incarnate consciousness. Thus science and its sibling art would be made to depend upon the mechanical, whether actual machines or the formalized methods of theory—the "machine of existence" reduced to aesthetic blueprint. (The poet's seeming necessity to justify himself as philosopher-theologian by methodical theory is a significant assumption of authority since the Renaissance.) Concept as thus understood by the new scientist and the new poet tends to become the *sign* as an empty symbol which must be supplied meaning by subjective intellect. Thus concept serves as a shield against reality and especially against the endangering uncertainty of awe and wonder.

What Eudora Welty recognizes is that desire, moved beyond mere knowing in an enlarging and fulfilling of consciousness, discovers its ordinate relation to memory. What we are describing here, even at some risk of abstraction, is the dramatic parabola of Welty's *The Optimist's Daughter*, to which her *One Writer's Beginnings* serves as a commentary. In both works, the sign as an imitation of the action of nature brings a presence to us just as art may do the incarnate person—Eudora Welty or her personae. In both works, the poet's (Welty's) concern is to recover an ordinate openness to the seeming disorder of existence itself as experienced by *any* person in whatever particular time or place. That is so because every person possesses a sensual nature through which that person responds to the mystery and holiness of existence, in an openness to it or in some degree a closure away from it. This is the openness of love, Welty's primary theme as poet. If we explore the parallel between one writer, Eudora Welty, and the central agent of one of her fictions, Laurel McKelva Hand, what dawns upon us is the dramatic unfolding discovery, in both poet and agent of love, of a proper deportment through piety toward that uncertain and mysterious world which is *to* consciousness *through* the senses. Just as importantly, that love may be maintained as a continuing evidence of life itself in and out of the confluence of epiphanies of experience as served by the mystery of memory.

3

What I do make my stories out of is the *whole* fund of my feelings, my responses to the real experiences of my own life, to the relationships that formed and changed it, that I have given most of myself to, and so learned my way toward a dramatic counterpart.

—Eudora Welty, *One Writer's Beginnings*

There is a stillness of spirit in Eudora Welty which is a sign of love's depths in her, and perhaps that is what we ultimately value in her, through our responses to her made things, her stories. We respond in wonder, if not in awe, that such is possible, given her rather sheltered life in what appears to us, partly through her fiction, a Southern country town the capital of a popularly notorious state, Mississippi. The stillness of love is what she is speaking of in her Harvard lectures, though ostensibly speaking of her beginnings as a writer. What she says of the virtues of "listening" and "seeing" toward discovering her own "voice" as writer are incisive at the level of what is now popularly called the "creative process." But she knows all along—knew intuitively as a child even—that such a term violates the reality of the witness that is the proper response to the holiness of existence itself, vouchsafed us by the very gift of life.

The witness she makes as a writer is to our human nature as gift, to be perfected by labors of love that do not degenerate into sentimental pretensions about our actions of love, as if by that pretense we might assure our own salvation or the salvation of others. It is a resonant witness because it is prophetic: It stirs in us known but forgotten things about our own nature as persons. What she knows is that neither our limited human love, nor its opposite human deportment, *power*, are sufficient to absolute rescue. For there falls always the shadow of death upon our actions, whether actions of love or of power. She talks of these high matters in *One Writer's Beginnings*, as if she were talking of the "creative process." And she effectively dramatizes her understandings of responsibility to community as person in *The Optimist's Daughter*.

If we seek correspondence between the two works then, as I suspect she intends that we should, we might begin by observing a fullness of perspective in her lectures, whereby she recovers to us, and to herself, engaging detailed memories of her own childhood and young adulthood. Hers is a wise position which Laurel McKelva Hand will come to see only in the final two or three pages of the novel. But Laurel's late recognition is one already certified by Laurel's dead husband, Phil Hand, who is never directly present in person, but as person sustains Laurel at last. The position is one Laurel knows intuitively but does not understand until she reacts to the shadow of death that closes upon her and lingers after the death of her father, Judge McKelva. The beginning of her understanding is a series of epiphanies centering in that house of memories in Mount Salus, the empty family home. Laurel's love is at first perversely niggardly in the reflections she makes, though she conducts herself for the most part publicly as required by the community. In the present time of the novel, she is oriented by memories of her father, especially of his last days, until at last she comes to recover the proper witness to love out of memory of her dead husband. Thus she becomes enabled in the present through Phil, though he is now long dead. That supporting love, out of memory, begins to move her beyond merely private memories such as might turn her back into herself and away from the larger outer world in which she lives and breathes and has her being. She must learn to embrace that larger world, consenting to its immediate presence, in spite of its disturbing particularities, one of which is the always present shadow of death falling across persons in time and place, suddenly engulfing them or slowly dissolving them out of place in the drainage of time.

In *The Optimist's Daughter* Welty dramatizes through Laurel what she would term "a dramatic counterpart" of her own "responses to the real experiences of my own life." Laurel of course is not a mirror image of herself, but an imaginative version of the possible or probable in such fictional incarnations of person through art's making. It is made on the authority of Welty's own experiences of life. We notice, for instance, that both Phil and Laurel are artists: Phil was an architect; Laurel is an interior decorator. By such a selection of human nature's possible callings, our poet-maker deploys witty parallels between herself as maker and those fictional agents. What our poet and her agents have in common, out of the reality of human existence, is the "house" of memory and a responsibility for memory's proper appointment and order in relation to the "neighborhood" of general existence of that person so housed intellectually and spiritually. This is the most difficult art of all for Laurel to master. The prospect of ordering her own "house" through an ordinate response to present circumstances as supported by her remembered experiences opens slowly to her. She begins to *anticipate*, recognizing contingent implications by her immediate circumstances, specifically the circumstances of her bidding a final farewell to Mount Salus at the novel's end.

Implication, as Welty knows so well as artist, is proper to the art of storytelling. The contrary supposition by lesser artists is that by art the possible or probable may be finalized as if art thereby were given the authoritative role of history. The poet is no more capable of encompassing contingency than the historian, which is why in sober moments he remembers (as cautioned by Flannery O'Connor on the question of art's relation to human finalities) that you cannot *prove* anything with a story. Dramatic resolution in a poem or story, in relation to reality itself, proves always tentative, because art not only depends from a reality larger than art itself but also depends for the form of its being upon the finite gifts of the poet.

With such reservations in mind, we may avoid entrapment by the seductions of analogy between art and nature. Mount Salus is only a dramatic counterpart of Jackson, Mississippi, or a suburb, as Phil Hand and Laurel are dramatic counterparts of Eudora Welty. History's proofs of the authority of art are not at issue, but rather art's ordinate dependence from the nature of reality, in relation to the truth of things themselves as enjoined by the finite, limited, gifted maker (the poet) who would in-form a thing he makes in consent to the implicit limits. And so implication, governed by possible or probable actions within possible or probable contingent circumstances, is the life of fictional art. And because fiction as a counterpart of actual life echoes life in haunting ways, commentary on the ambiguous relation of life to art is tempting to rational intellect in its pursuit of understanding.[2]

Thus self-cautioned, we may come more and more to understand and value this quiet lady from Jackson, through exploring parallels between her thoughts about herself, expressed at Harvard, and Laurel's reflections about herself stirred up by her return to Mount Salus. We shall not confuse the two as identities, but perhaps begin to recognize the truth of Aquinas's distinction concerning art's relation to reality itself. For art, he says, is not an imitation of nature (as if Laurel McKelva Hand were a mirror image of Eudora Welty), but an imitation of the action of nature; that is, art involves the contingencies of the possible or probable as distinct from the actual.

This is the ground, in the person of the artist, where his experience of things in their actualities feeds a matter into his making, into form ordering matter in the act of making. And it is in this ground as well that the poet must discover the truth that by his own nature he is maker, not creator. The poet's virtue (out of which rises his "virtuosity") is limited to form, which he draws forth by intellectual action in response to a precedent existence of which he is not the cause. For he is incapable of "creating" the matter required in relation to his enacted form. He is the maker of a particular thing, his poem, but not creator of a world. On this point one recalls a late Romantic poet struggling against this limit, James Joyce, who projects himself as poet more conspicuously into his young artist Stephen, for whom the achievement of a thing made perfect by art would be (he insists) the creation of a "world" obviating the world of reality itself. Joyce is sufficiently versed in the intellectual tradition, of course, to recognize in such a pretense by his young poet that old revolt, and he puts Satan's words in Stephen's mouth: "*non servium*."

There is a parallel here between Eudora Welty's approach to the limits of art and Joyce's, but with a difference to be made emphatically. Joyce practices, with his considerable intellect, an anarchy against nature, committed to an intensity of perfection of form itself so considerable as to provide the poets who follow him with recognizable techniques of the sign in service to intentional form. If we were content to reduce his contribution to the simplicity of "influence," we would say that Joyce's own art must be considered an "influence" on Eudora Welty's, as is Chekhov's or Flaubert's. But that is to recognize certain accidents of art, in contrast to the presiding essence of art as limited to the person as maker in the actual thing he makes, lest identity become our critical concern. As we speculate on the kinship between Joyce and his Stephen, we may also speculate on the relation of Eudora Welty to her Phil Hand, to more profitable conclusion. And if Joyce is properly celebrated as a sophisticated wit in his deployment of such parallels, Miss Welty herself proves quite witty in her fictional deployments. Thus while Phil Hand is from broad-shouldered Chicago, hog-butcher to the world, and Eudora Welty is from a quiet country town in Mississippi, they share a vision of existence and of art's relation to existence.

There is a wit in the disparity, to which we must be attuned. The disparity lies in accidents of place (Chicago as contrasted to Mount Salus or Jackson). What is revealed to us by this disparity is that place does not determine vision, an implication in Miss Welty's art which is counter to the usual determinism that has shadowed art since the turn of the century. What is implied concerning the nature of art is the obligation of the maker to the good of the thing he makes (Phil his houses—or breadboard; Miss Welty her stories). In order to fulfill that obligation the artist must surrender his made thing to the ravages of nature and history at last. That is the principle in art which is contradictory of our arguments that nature and history are *deterministic* in the philosophical sense of the term. Hence, though circumstantial accidents of nature and history help reveal essential natures (and especially the nature of persons, the poet's central concern) those accidents are neither themselves of the essence of, nor the causes of, essential nature. Only in a gnostic intent to power over being itself may that false principle flourish.

Phil Hand as *donne* bears witness to this truth about the poet's relation to creation, a truth to which Welty subscribes. And in relation to this principle, there is an added dramatic playfulness to her making. In this novel, which turns on love's rescue of Laurel from the closing death of the soul, Phil Hand as agent to that rescue is dead long before Laurel's journey "home" to Mount Salus. By Phil Hand's steady witness to love in its relation to art, Laurel is sustained in her gradual unraveling of the mystery of her own memory. She reaches a point of encounter at last with a viable presence of love, her recovered memory of Phil. Laurel at first feels herself entombed in the house that belonged to her parents but which now belongs to Fay, that flitting and disturbing presence in Mount Salus society, the second wife of its principal citizen, Judge McKelva. For to Laurel, the old McKelva house seems very much a ravenous grave. It is most difficult for her to reconcile this present experience with her vague memories of life in it as a child. She is so suspended in this conflict as to appear destined to become the house's victim, urged to self-victimization by her local friends, who want her in residence as a convenient substitute for her father. As for contingent implication, should Laurel succumb to that pressure, we might imagine her thirty years later, an old woman thoroughly entrapped in the house as tomb, as Faulkner's Emily Grierson is in "A Rose for Emily." The McKelva house, for Laurel, is haunted by vague memories, to which Welty's fictional strategy applies an old metaphysical conceit subtly submerged by art: The actual historical house (in its "fictional" aspects as concretely described) lies as a parallel to Laurel's consciousness, the house of memory.

Perhaps we have by now sufficiently presented our critical perspective: The parallels between the life of the maker of this story and the lives of her agents—between Eudora Welty and Phil and Laurel Hand—are undeniable. Literal details from Welty's own life, as related in *One Writer's Beginnings*, appear in modified ways in her novel, and we might even conclude that because those details are such vivid memories out of her own experiences, they contribute authoritatively to a persuasive "incarnation" of characters in her fiction. But the literalness of correspondences between the history of Eudora Welty and the art of *The Optimist's Daughter* is at most of secondary interest to us. We might exhaust these correspondences in a catalogue of them, for the novel's rich texture of concrete imagery and dramatic argument is tempting to such an academic exercise. But our concern is other than with a specific poetry's (this novel's) analogies to specific life (Welty's), in a critical exercise pursued as if to establish scientific aesthetics. Such a pursuit might prove of a limited—if secondary—virtue, though becoming a vice if reduced to an ultimate critical end rather than a most limited means to under-standing. Pathological comparisons of microscopic slides are useful only toward recovery of life beyond pathological dead ends.

For Eudora Welty herself, by her art she witnesses to the obligations of love transcending the always intimidating shadow threatening any making, the shadow of death. And in that witness she moves beyond the merely "personal" in the popular sense of that term. If through art there is a rescue of her own person, the witness of her art is that such rescue may be possible to all persons through love. The concern is not, there-fore, that of a limited dependence between "biography" and "art," by which limit of attention one freezes both art and biography as trophies in the ravenous grave of memory itself.[3]

All art, we might say, plays love against the shadow of death, though there is an infinity of play for the mind between the tensional poles of love-death to consciousness. Those tensional poles feed a ravenous art, which supports also a ravenous criticism of art—even such as this under-way. In our own ravenous—or perhaps more acceptably, passionate—concern, we might juxtapose a beginning and an end, in relation to the "history" of our art as it loses its ordinate concern with the possible and probable, properly understood as an imitation of the *action* of nature rather than an imitation of nature itself.

I have in mind the live presence to us of Michelangelo as artist, in contrast to the deadened presence of J. Alfred Prufrock at an afternoon tea party, where the women move about the room, "talking of Michelan-gelo." The women's own emptiness (from Prufrock's failed perspective) haunts Prufrock's consciousness, echoing his own. Through Eliot's art the poem develops an old conceit: the little world of consciousness in relation to the larger world of creation contingent to consciousness. But in Eliot's deployment, there is an insuperable chasm between the worlds, at once lamented and defended by this consciousness we remember as Prufrock. One of Eliot's concerns as poet is with what we might term psychological pathology, a projection, through signs, of a consciousness self-isolated by self-love. What a falling-off there has been since Michel-angelo in Prufrock, who smolders in the bathos of self-pity. He is so knowl-edgeable that he cannot love, understanding having eluded him.

In this poem Eliot dramatizes a dead end to consciousness, and one which he himself seems rapidly approaching as person. If we think of Prufrock as failed poet, we discover him more a failure as a figure of a person than as poet. Still in the signs we accept as his, which give a slight movement of his peculiar consciousness, there is evidence of a consid-erable artfulness learned of poetry's tradition in the West, especially that poetry which at the moment is of such interest to Eliot, who has just come upon it (circa 1910, the time of his poem): English Metaphysical poetry. As dramatic agent, knowledgeable in such sciences of sign, Prufrock uses his science to shield himself against the larger world, content with memory arrested. As intellectual, as he almost sees in a famous metaphor in the poem, he is very much a pair of ragged claws scuttling in the silent seas of memory, thus self-protected somewhat from the outer and larger world which requires of intellect acts of love counter to self-love. He can talk very clearly, no doubt, about Michelangelo, categorizing and arresting that lively soul, pinning him to consciousness's wall as one specimen of art and history, an intellectual trophy. But Eliot's art is heavy with irony, to such an extent that, through allusions, the life of an intellectual community larger than that arrested by Prufrock is summoned to a presence in the poem. Michelangelo as actual person, responding in the world to his calling as artist, is very much such a presence, even as is Dante, and, by the implication of allusion, as is Eliot himself.

By juxtaposing such counter-presences as Prufrock and Michelangelo, of Eliot and Dante, we may enlarge the matrix of our concern and perhaps discover interesting parallels between Eliot-Prufrock and Welty-Laurel. We anticipate, suggesting that Eliot as person and as poet is slowly moving toward an epiphany himself, which will be reflected in his *Waste Land* a decade after "Prufrock." He comes to it through his labors in answering his calling as poet. Let us say that what the poet attempts is truth, raised by perfections of his gift as poet in the making of his poem, even if that raised truth be as limited as that emptiness of self-love in a persona such as Prufrock. Yet what Eliot may well discover, through his obligation to the good of the thing he is making, is that his art itself may be raised by the very pursuit of the good of the thing he makes. There is, in that pursuit, already a self-sacrifice, his love of the thing he makes, though he may not recognize it as self-sacrifice. Indeed, to recognize his action of making as an action of love is to risk turning back toward the self and away from the good of the thing being made. (The self-importance of the artist is sufficiently notorious.)

By such reflections, we may come the closer to that continuing and lively presence to us out of the 15th and 16th centuries, Michelangelo, who as artist accomplished an effect beyond self-consciousness as artist through his makings. For the art of making in pursuit of truth proves reciprocal, art thus perfected by truth. This consent to labor for the good of the thing made—its truth as the thing it is—we may value as a cause of a certain perfection of the person of the maker. That is a rebounding effect of love turned outward and away from the self; that is one of the mysteries of *becoming*. The maker himself may reflect upon it as a *beginning*: not a *new* but a *renewed* beginning, cumulative beginnings affecting this present moment of his action of love turned outward from the self. We yet treasure Michelangelo's own words so richly implicit with the argument, his saying that as sculptor he would release the figure lying in the stone before him. We are drawn to such figurative testimony because it reveals a central truth seen by the maker and intuitively recognized by us. What Michelangelo affirms are the limits of the possible or probable as he would formalize it—as he would execute form released from the stone. By his words he acknowledges the mutual dependence of the artist as maker, in response to the reality of the given, specifically this given stone awaiting chisel and the sculptor's capacity to make.

What is arresting in his words, then, is this maker's recognition of limits, out of which by love he moves toward the limits of gift. Such is openness to the good of the thing he would make in celebrating limit through love. The stone bears in it limited possibilities of the form which is the poet's (i.e., the maker's) own virtuosity of form.[4] (As cause of the made thing, the maker is limited to form alone.) The impatient maker will at times of course revolt against such limit, and we cited Joyce's dramatization of this revolt in his *Portrait of the Artist as a Young Man.* But as our living sculptor knew centuries ago, his own "genius" is not reduced but transformed through piety by his recognition of and acceptance of limit. How inevitable, then, given circumstantial contingencies, that Michelangelo should create that arresting work, his *Pieta.* An epiphany in stone, in which glows forth Love transforming all love.

How inevitable as well that he should find in stone another arresting presence to us, King David, a centering presence not only to civil community, but as poet ordering perceptions of nature in the "light" of the Cause of nature. King David in the Psalms sings not only as an agent of order in community, but as servant to the Cause of community and nature and so as steward to both. What is celebrated, beyond limits of understanding (David laments that he is insufficient in understanding), is the goodness of creation itself, whereby any making by a person—as poet or as king—must be consecrated to the good. The absence of the good, denied to either creation or to man's social deportment, is the haunting pain of Eliot's Prufrock. What is lost to him in his world is love, and the pathetic recourse is self-love, which is a turning toward emptiness.

We have not gone so far afield as may appear in this measuring of Prufrock and Stephen Dedalus against Michelangelo. For Eudora Welty bears evidence of similar recognitions of limit, through her piety. From the beginning, as a child, she knew herself a "privileged observer," and later, traveling farther than West Virginia or Ohio, and intellectually traveling further than the word *moon* on the tongue, she discovers a commonness in existence; she discovers the holy descending "into the windows of Chartres" and into the "stone peasant figures in the capitals of Autun" and into the "tall sheets of gold on the walls of Torcello."

4

The memory throws up high and dry
A crowd of twisted things; ...
Rust that clings to the form that
    the strength has left....
The moon has lost her memory....
Memory!
You have the key....
    —T.S. Eliot, "Rhapsody on a Windy Night"

The art of making, under the obligations of love and in recognition of the lingering shadow of death: That is our concern beyond academic formalisms in praise of Eudora Welty. And it is a concern turning upon the mystery of memory to the existential consciousness, a presence to consciousness which not only makes possible our actions as artists—as makers—but in which we discover as well the actual, personal obligation of love in any making. Such is the desirable deportment to this present confluence of circumstances in our present place. In this respect, we are sustained in this present moment *out of memory*, so long as we have not succumbed to *an arrest of* memory. That is the shocking recognition to Laurel when, in her final encounter with Fay over Fay's sacrilege against Laurel's memory arrested, Laurel at last sees herself "in irony" as reflected in Fay. Fay "desecrates" Laurel's memory of her father and mother by rejecting all past experience in her ravenous intent upon the present moment—in the name of some ambiguous future for herself. She does so in particular actions against Laurel's treasured—i.e., arrested—memories. What we recognize in Fay as cause of such desecrations (Laurel's term) is Fay's terror under the shadow of death. In Laurel's view, Fay has caused the Judge's death, a view seconded for Laurel by her father's attending nurse. Fay had attempted to force the Judge physically out of his hospital deathbed. But as she says to Laurel, when they come to a physical confrontation over the breadboard in their final encounter, she was only "trying to scare him into living!"

As for Laurel's recognition of ironic likeness to Fay, hers is a terror of response to death no less than Fay's. But she has been tempted to a perverse defense, and only in the novel's last moments is she prepared to see this. In Allen Tate's phrase, Laurel would set up the grave in the house. It is with maenadic fury—to Fay's bafflement—that Laurel attacks Fay over the breadboard and almost uses it as a literal weapon against Fay. "You desecrate this house," she cries out. The evidence? Fay has damaged the "perfect" breadboard by cracking black walnuts on it with a hammer. Laurel's discovery of this desecration is confluent with summoned instances of Fay's numerous desecrations, most of them as seemingly trivial as this. For a while, Laurel's attention to Fay's gauche transgressions has forestalled her recognizing her own more subtle species of desecration of the house of memory. And we ought to remark here an aspect of Miss Welty's wit and wisdom. For at the level of fictional spectacle, we again and again deal with trivialities of social confrontations and engagements, as if this novel were a comedy of manners. Beneath the spectacle, however, lies a fundamental truth independent of comic or satiric magnitude of spectacle, the obligation to love in making, whether one makes a garden or a simple breadboard or a commodious house or a carefully structured story. Spectacle is signal of the reality of action, but one may put off the significance of action through a concern for the magnitude of spectacle itself. That has been a considerable complication to the artist as maker since Dante.

With a careful artistry appropriate to Modernist conditions, but without submission to those conditions, Welty has prepared us for Laurel's self-recognition. The chimney swift, blown down from its chimney haven, flits from room to room in front of Laurel, who reacts in terror though she is drawn by the erratic trapped creature. From the hall, to Laurel's childhood room, to her parents' room which is now Fay's. The "jackleg" carpenter, capable of responding to spectacle but not with a suitable deportment, says the swift is only an accidental presence. It is not trying to get in but to get out, as wild things do. Laurel remembers that "Birds fly toward the light," and so attempts to drive it toward the outside world. The family maid, Missouri, sees it as nothing but "vermin" suited to cat fare. Laurel, recovering her courage in response to the maid's and carpenter's bored responses, captures the small creature and takes it outside to release it. In doing so, she feels her cheek struck by air from its wings. She watches the swift's erratic flight as a "tilting crescent drawn back into the sky."[5]

The suggestive event, whose implications Laurel has not yet absorbed, is followed by decisive action in destroying memory's dusty fragments in the house. She brings out her father's letters to her mother, her mother's old cookbooks, a West Virginia residue her mother brought to Mount Salus from her childhood home. Laurel burns this detritus that has so tempted her to set up the grave in the family house, as if a home could be made by turning it into a museum. All along she has been urged by her "bridesmaids" to arrest memory, but this is her first action in response. It is not a rejection of memory, but toward recovering memory to its life in her present moment, though Laurel is not fully aware of what is happening. She too is presently to take wing herself for Chicago, out of the chattering temptations of her bridesmaids. (Incidentally, the cardinals and their actions on the periphery of the afternoon gathering of the bridesmaids for a farewell tea in Laurel's [Fay's] garden provide flitting counterpoint to them.) Laurel's action is to be, not a continuing desecration of the house of memory, but a cleansing of memory and thereby its restoration into a new living presence. That will be a moment of active love *out of* memory, fulfilling Laurel in an openness to the present world. In a poignant final scene, she waves farewell to the children on the school playground, giving us our last imagistic memory of Laurel at novel's end. She does not at last carry the desecrated breadboard with her, but she does carry its deepest nature as alive in memory. She knows it has been made in an act of love by Phil, an act which will last beyond any battering of the thing itself by any Fays who hold legal possession of it as a property.

Art in this local place, though an action of making consonant with memory's feeding, in an enlarging confluence with this present experience: That is the action proper to love, as Welty would have it. And *confluence* proves the summary word in her gathered memory of her beginnings as writer. In the light of what we have said, we might anticipate such a term, and anticipate as well Welty's borrowing from *The Optimist's Daughter* in concluding her lectures. She quotes a long passage in which Laurel remembers an epiphany out of confluence, the occasion of her seeing the actual joining of rivers from a train window as she and Phil, her new husband, head south from Chicago to that small, seemingly closed world of place, Mount Salus, Mississippi. (From a Chicago perspective, it may well appear a provincial town.) *Confluence*, says Welty, is "a wonderful word ... which of itself exists as a reality and a symbol in one." It is "the only kind of symbol that for me as a writer has any weight, testifying to the pattern, one of the chief patterns of human existence." It has a fullness such as the child discovered in a simpler manifestation in the word *moon*. And the "greatest confluence of all," she says, "is that which makes up the human memory—the individual human memory. My own is the treasure most dearly regarded to me, in my life and in my work as a writer." For the "memory is a living thing," she adds, always "in transit." One's daring in that action called "life," as a *person* or as a *writer*, lies in turning always to the present, bearing into the present moment *being* as ingathered: the memory of past experiences of encounter with existence as both holy and mysterious. That point we add to our writer's concluding words to her Harvard audience. We see the lecture's closing words concluding the novel as well.

In the novel's last page, just before the "last thing Laurel saw" in Mount Salus on her way to the airport, there begins her long delayed reconciliation to memory as a living thing. In that beginning of her understanding, she embraces as well the children's "twinkling of ... hands, the many small and unknown hands, wishing her goodbye." Now she sees that "Memory lived not in the initial possession but in the freed hands, pardoned and freed." That was her thought as she surrendered the breadboard to Fay in the empty kitchen of the old McKelva house. Fay had expected Laurel to strike her with the breadboard, only to find herself left holding a piece of wood, a dead inherited property only. For now Laurel is beginning to see that memory lives "in the heart that can empty but fill again, in the patterns restored by dreams." The restoration is through art lovingly undertaken, through patterns restored by anticipation. Dreams are therefore not nightmares, as they have been to her in the past as she falsely remembered them. That is what they seemed, until the frantic swift loosed her into a new unnamed terror, the anticipation of life's "meaning" as always in this present moment. Dreams prove a turning of desire toward hope. And such turning may be an opening of graves through love, beyond and arresting the entombing possession by memory as it dies in the darkened house of consciousness. Thus one may recover memory alive. Indeed, we may, in this light, be the more moved by the pathos enveloping Fay in our last view of her, in the empty kitchen looking at the battered breadboard which Laurel has laid "on the table where it belonged."

5

The purpose of the study of philosophy is not to learn what others have thought, but to learn how the truth of things stands.
                                             —St. Thomas Aquinas

We can ... say here: "It is not in St. Thomas or Aristotle, but in things, that the true realist sees everything he sees." So he will not hesitate to make use of these masters, whom he regards solely as guides towards reality itself.
                                             —Etienne Gilson, *Methodical Realism*

Let us say that one comes to an accommodation of consciousness with memory through desire, in a hope that does not submit to the terror of the present moment as inevitably a darkening of memory and of all its trophies. In our tradition it is the Romantic poet who struggles and fails in this accommodation, no more poignantly put than by John Keats in his "Ode on Melancholy." Caught up in a "melancholy fit" in which memory feeds upon itself in an arrest, the poet declares that Melancholy "dwells with Beauty ... and Joy," both of them now in the past. The most proximate place and time of reencounter is "the green hill in an April shroud," where one gnaws cankering death. Having thus stalked Melancholy at the expense of present life, one's soul tastes "the sadness of her might" finding himself hung "among her cloudy trophies." But Eudora Welty is no Romantic such as Keats, though she shares with him that special gift as poet, a gift of imagistic immediacy to her art through what Keats calls "negative capability," which we here prefer to call an intuitive openness of love to the immediacy of existence itself. It is a gift common to human nature, though differing in degree from person to person.

In *The Optimist's Daughter*, Laurel is initially Keatsean, reflectively susceptible to melancholy through her engagement with the mystery of memory. Fay, we have implied, is also endangered, but by a prospect of memory as an arresting entrapment which she resists in ways quite other than reflective melancholy. Fay's protection is her reaction in the present moment by a willful destruction of memory's intrusion with its prospective anticipations of death. Thus her violent attempt to raise Judge McKelva from his deathbed, an act of confused love whose spectacle can only appear to the reflective Laurel as self-centered. Fay responds more instinctively than intuitively, or so it must appear, in her reactions to the closing inevitability of death for Judge McKelva. For Fay would hold life regardlessly, the only seeming escape of the shadow. She forces the present, as if thereby making it exempt from both the dead past and a blind future. Hence, Fay denies her past to the extent that she denies having any family at all, till they show up to celebrate the Judge's death. Laurel, to the contrary, dwells upon a ghost of life, as a somnambulist of memory, appearing strangely to her bridesmaids as if she were walking in her sleep, though they attribute the strangeness to her grief and try to cheer her up. As we know (being privy to her reflections) she drifts tremulously among the detritus of memory, the cloudy trophies of her past experiences of the world which she now begins to encounter as dead bones of that past: her father's letters, her mother's old school papers and cookbooks in desks and cupboards and drawers. We see her holding to such artifacts, reflecting on them as evidence of her obligations to the past. She is arrested by these past deaths to which she is as yet unreconciled: recently her father's, and her mother's before that; but most especially, the death of her beloved husband Phil in a far-off *kamikaze* attack in the Pacific.

Now in the light of these reflections on the mystery of memory, we discover Eudora Welty's artistic center. In doing so, we may speak of her as a traditionalist who opposes desecrations of memory, whether like Fay's or Laurel's. Laurel, one might venture, is the more culpable, since she has reflective gifts beyond Fay's, knows herself called as artist. As for Welty, in this respect akin to her Laurel: She has a high concern for a reconciliation of desire through memory, the concern dramatized with such a labor by Eliot in his early poetry, up to the "mixing" of "memory and desire" in that Keatsean cruel April at the opening of the *Waste Land*. By this allusion, however, we are reminded that in Welty's art, the local appears more deceptively simple than Eliot's use of England and its history. She makes her "incarnational" art out of such ordinary local givens that a careless reader may be beguiled as if tourist in a provincial place, thus overlooking in her uses the presence of a comedy (in Dante's sense) beyond humor or satire or slapstick or the like, though one finds these in her work also. Hers is a comedy which, like Dante's, reaches well beyond her uses of myth as a technical means of ordering our response to the world's confusions through art. (That, incidentally, has been Eliot's first explanation of the poet's uses of myth in modern poetry—for art's sake—though he quickly discovered himself as person assumed beyond his attempt to merely *use* myth. His confident, and somewhat arrogant, pronouncement of myth as a suitable instrument (in his review of Joyce's *Ulysses*), stands in an ironic presence of the early Eliot to the later, who at last becomes overwhelmed by reality larger than his willed autonomy in such uses of myth.)[6]

For Eudora Welty, the local provides apt imagery in service to high matters of mind. She holds in her own memory simple experiences of birds and plants and people, local particularities of things from her actual experience in a Mississippi whose center for her is Jackson, and from which center she discovers increasingly a commonality of the local, wherever and whenever encountered by human consciousness. As such a traditionalist, she proves a member of the larger community of intellectual souls. She is made member through her discovery that mankind is obligated to an openness of love toward fulfillment of personhood, an openness possible only in response to local contingencies. That fulfillment is of the gifts peculiar to herself as discrete person. And given our own prospect of membership in that larger community, it is suitable to drawn to our concern companionable members of that community in love, bound as community through love of existence itself. Some of those companions may at first seem improbable, unless we take seriously what St. Thomas and Gilson say in the epigraphs used above.

I have in mind here Thomas Aquinas especially, who as philosopher makes two arguments that show us Welty's relation as maker, first to the things she makes, her stories, and then to us, her readers. St. Thomas insists that by our common nature as humans—as *persons*—we are each a unified, discrete creature. Each of us is singular, though we are also members as well within a common community of personhood by virtue of our nature as *incarnate intellectual souls*. And here Thomas anticipates a modern aberration which our imaginative writers and philosophers have had difficulty coming to terms with since Descartes and Immanuel Kant—the first bequeathing us consciousness declared alienated from existence, the other justifying this alienation of consciousness from creation through abstract "universals" removed from nature itself. Such is this recent modification of an older tradition which leaves John Keats responding to creation in such an agony of soul in his great odes. The Cartesean and Kantian modifications of traditional vision can have as their only spiritual issue a pathos in response to the mystery of memory. In our art, indeed, pathos has replaced both tragedy and the mystery of comedy as possible to the artist as recently as Dante.

Thomas maintains that as *person*, each of us is a singular, unified *one*. And as person, each is called to perfect his inherent potency: to bring to fulfillment the unique potentiality of this *specific* and discrete one, this *self*. The circumstance impinging upon this moral responsibility is at once a glorious gift and a gift as burden. Our inherent nature calls for fulfillment pursued by limited intellect. By our nature, that fulfillment lies in knowing the truth of things. But intellect as gift is limited in that it must act toward truth discursively. We are not, in Thomas's distinction, angelic intellects who know with an immediacy obviating the labor of discursiveness. But though discursiveness is a primary necessity of nature and therefore a limit to action as incarnate intellectual soul, we nevertheless share in the intuitive, the angelic mode, to lesser or greater degrees of gift. Some persons, we know from experience, are blessed more than others with intuitive capacity. So general is our recognition of this capacity that we tend to associate it beyond a particular manifestation in a particular person. We generalize. Thus we incline to credit the poet's gift as an enlargement of capacity for intuitive knowing. We may even associate that mode of knowing with sexual distinction: Women are significantly intuitive we say, though it is a risky argument at this juncture. It is as if the intuitive were taken as a species of intellectual action—as if the intuitive differs in kind rather than by degree in a distinction of the intuitive from the rational intellect. One effect of this confusion has been a residual myth about the poet given added currency by Freudianism: If *he* is a poet, he must be feminine. (A counter myth, popular at the close of the 20th century, is that if *she* is a poet, she is distorted male—a Sappho or Gertrude Stein or Emily Dickinson, as this assumption is turned upon the unknown.) St. Thomas argues against this confusion. By our very nature as created intellectual soul *embodied*, he says, each *person* shares a common nature though a discrete and unified intellect, despite Albigensian argument to the contrary. Persons differ only in degrees of intuitive-rational modes of response to the good, according to one's *specific* gift as person. The *rational* intellect is also to be seen as a mode of extension of the intuitive, each complementary to the other in our seeing the truth of things—as one's left and right eyes are complementary to a unified physical vision of things.

This is to touch, though only in passing, upon epistemology as of an increasing concern to the poet since Descartes, though seldom addressed by the poet in the philosopher's mode, and especially since the advent of Freud and Jung.[7] (Again, Eliot is a signal exception.) We need not pursue the problem in detail, though it is relevant to our concern for our present poet, Eudora Welty. We need only observe that some recent engagements of her presence among us have attempted a modernist address to her singularity as person out of Freudean-Jungean "science," with an intent of distracting us from her *personhood* by exaggerating her as feminist.[8] For our part, let us turn rather to what is common to our natures as intellectual *persons* whose sexual modes as incarnate creatures may differ. That we share the burden of discursiveness is witnessed by our dependence upon signs—signs as markers of our movement in quest of the truth of things, whether we are woman or man. Those signs stand more or less firmly as dependable markers, as witness to our existence, in varying degrees of accuracy measuring our relation to the reality of existence itself. If we were purely angelic, we should of course need no signs at all, knowing the truth of things with an immediacy of rest. (Neither would we—or so John Milton suspects—enjoy the limits of incarnation, being neither man nor woman. The question leads Milton to an addition to traditional angelology: food and sex no longer denied angelic natures.)

In Thomas's perspective, then, we are (as incarnate souls) unavoidably discursive, and discursive (primarily) as *rational* intellect, the rational mode guiding us as *homo viator* within the created world. Thus we order our signs in the quest for truth, and we do so under the auspices of what we *know* from actual experiences as our becoming: out of our present being which is also a present becoming supported by memory. In this present moment we *are*, in a degree relative to potentiality. And without this condition to our becoming, we would not only *not become*: We would not even *be*. In that recognition, made through reasoned use of sign as supported in memory, we make a way in the world—*becoming* as we *make*. For *making* is the proper habit of our being according to our given natures. In our callings, though discrete one from another, we are all makers, and that is the common ground in which we discover kinship in our various callings. Thus the poet and philosopher and scientist are discovered to be makers. Each makes through signs as intellect's active witness to the truth of things.

As we move according to this common nature as persons, we bear with us in memory known things, most especially the residual truths of our *beginnings* whereby we are the person we *are*. If this argument seems heavily scholastic, it is with a deliberate intent that it should. For we emphasize, in Thomas's defining phrase, that the poet's concern for the good of the thing he makes is through *reason in making*. That is the principle which Eudora Welty engages very centrally in *The Optimist's Daughter*. Thus we observe that Laurel's central problem is that she revolves around trophies, made things littering the empty house, arrested in memory, caught in their orbit out of her own becoming. She seems unable to move beyond her willing circling in memory within her childhood home. Between her willed entrapment and the arresting pull of experiences past, she is like that June bug (Figeater) a boy ties with sewing thread and holds it circling endlessly—till the tied leg breaks off. After which the freed, if maimed, creature whirs away. Or, in the actual figure Welty summons from her own experience as a householder, as if her trapped consciousness were a chimney swift flitting with growing panic in an empty house—that is, a house empty of life, though not of artifacts from life past. For so full of things is that McKelva house that it might well prove an attractive hotel, as Fay is urged to make of it by her random mother suddenly on the scene.

We come to know Laurel, the artist, to be circumscribed by things in her memory that seem empty of life. She is unable to move: suspended between staying in Mount Salus or returning to Chicago. But most of all, she is confused as to the nature of her obligation to remembered things. The spectacle of this seeming arrest is given comic presence through Laurel's "bridesmaids." They are no longer maids, but on Laurel's return to Mount Salus they assume their youth, which they think recovered out of their memories of her and of her happy marriage years ago. As persons these bridesmaids seem themselves to have ceased long since in their own becoming. They rather only grow older in body, drawn toward the emptiness of death. And sensing as much, they cling the more firmly to arrested memories of their own youth. In this confusing matrix of persons pretending to be a viable community, Laurel becomes the focusing center. It is an uncomfortable role, adding to her growing confusion. The little world of her own consciousness seems closing upon itself, becomes endangered by her temptation to an intellectual arrest of memory in dead ceremonial recollections of the past that so delights the bridesmaids.

In this thematic aspect of *The Optimist's Daughter*, we may see parallels emerging between Thomas Aquinas's view of human nature and Eudora Welty's own understanding of our gifts as persons, without the necessity of arguing intellectual influence. For one becomes member in such a community initially (by initiation) through seeing things in themselves, as Gilson reminds us. By that seeing, a person finds companionable presences, a diversity of members one of another, among whom may well be Plato and St. Thomas and St. Augustine and Dante and Keats and Eliot, and so on. The credential to membership is a common intent through a right will to the truth of things, not an "enclubment" as "Scholastic" or "Traditionalist" or "Romantic" or whatever club name is popular in the intellectual moment. There is, therefore, a considerable advantage in speculative associations of gifted philosophers or poets who share that common desire and who leave witness to that desire in signs; "what others have thought," as Thomas puts it.

That Eudora Welty, "sheltered," as she recalls, in the safety of home in Jackson, nevertheless witnesses truths about human nature paralleled by the witness of such seemingly remote persons as St. Augustine or St. Thomas Aquinas might disturb out content with any mere exercise of literary explication of her fiction. Nor can we be made comfortable at last through a reduction of this likeness in vision in unlike persons by intellectual games of philosophy whereby we pursue analogue through signs, contented with patterns of signs. We may thereby enjoy a sense of having established parallels in the signs used, patterns of correspondence to which are appended sufficient qualifications of disparities—such labor as yields the temporary pleasures akin to those of the scientist in his discernment of order in data. But to rest in this sense of intellectual accomplishment is an attempt to rest in abstraction, neglecting the end proper to such labors which are honorable in themselves but not a proper end of such labor. Such undertaking is out of a desire to both know and understand the truth of things, insofar as such parallels tend outward toward truth beyond mere intellectual abstractionism.

Intellectual analysis, popularly called "scholarship," is important of course, but only important at last in respect to proper ends, which are never sufficiently mere formulation. The signs of our knowing encourage us forward to satisfy the desire to understand more deeply than sign alone allows. To rest in signs is to fail in a recovery of awe and wonder in a present encounter with the truth of things. And to fail thus is to risk summoning despair out of the intellectual arrest, the dead letter of "life," dead sign. What our poet Welty and our philosopher Thomas pursue to the contrary, each responding to a peculiar calling as person, are fundamental truths about the nature of existence—about *beings*: truths discovered as sustaining the orders of nature including human nature itself. Both share that pursuit through awe and wonder that *any* thing at all exists. And both come at last to declare in a witness of signs the fundamental obligation to our nature as intellectual creature: a receptive but discriminating opening of the person to existence which both of them call *love*. The ordering of self toward perfection of gifts unique to the self: the action of *becoming* through a participatory submission called love.[9] That is their common calling.

The point is important in relation to memory as the deepest mystery to consciousness, since our age's usual response to the desire for order assumes that order is sustained by intellect's imposing order out of the authority of intellect as autonomous. That is the action whereby we declare that "knowledge is power." Thereby we imply that power over things is our ultimate end. It is a power gained through definition or controlled analogy in philosophy in its recent Nominalistic mode. Or it may be a power gained by that lesser but more pervasive mode in the popular mind, the imitation of nature in art or science to appetitive ends. Indeed, a willful misunderstanding here largely accounts for the antipathy of poet to philosopher, or of either to the scientist. Such antipathy has been an erosive presence in the intellectual community for several hundred years now and seems to be reaching a climactic impasse of oppositions at the beginning of another century. Out of supposition of power through signs, our philosophers and poets and critics (most of them) would supersede those older philosophers and poets and critics who address questions of truth directly out of awe and wonder that anything at all exists. And the notorious complaints of youth against the intellectual community in the last century, I suggest—whatever the labels under which they protest—are made less because of the seeming indifference of intellectual signs to life itself as reflected in specialized categories of signs than because the person of the specialist disappears behind the signs. He fails to witness awe and wonder beyond signs as ends to power. Thus specialization dislodges awe and wonder. Those confused spectacles of confrontation, leading to the anarchy of the 1960s (so I believe) support this judgment.

By a diminishing address to existence through specialized reductions of existence, in the interest of power over being rather than in the interest of a perfection as persons, we have largely become conditioned to live on the surface of the mystery of existence, oblivious to what Welty calls the "holiness of life." We lose love's obligation to the truth of things in themselves, upon which truth our speculations about order must properly be founded. We distract ourselves from the truth of things by the tacit or expressed supposition that order in nature is demonstrably an effect of finite intellectual actions upon nature, by intellect safely removed from any "other" than the self. The accelerating sophistication of technology, we suppose, proves the point. Our inherited disjunction of consciousness from nature through Descartes, strengthened by Kant's universalism, has effectively empowered science in particular in its impositions of order through *knowledge* freed of the obligations of *understanding*. That is the new condition to intellectual community in this "specialized" age. But it is a condition Thomas anticipated and resisted in treatise after treatise. And it is the condition Eudora Welty recognized and opposed by the exercise of her art in telling stories about persons in nature and community.

Welty speaks to the charge we make here against Modernist intellectual actions that are contrary to the truth of things, though she does not speak in scholastic terms such as we are using. Thus she will say that, as a living person, she is most thankful for her native curiosity, which from as long ago as she can remember has sustained *anticipation* in her. She is hardly of the Modernist persuasion, though she does not oppose that dominant ideology in the speculative manner of the philosopher. Rather, she keeps a close eye upon this immediate world, at this immediate moment to her. By that closeness she accepts a limited perspective: "a line of vision, the frame of vision" proper to art, whereby there is a "set distance" proper to the artistic vision of the truth of things at hand. She has never stopped "listening" and "seeing," in her quest for her own "voice"—to echo the titles of her Harvard lectures. Her unwavering intention is to *make*, through the voice of her art, her own celebration of the truth of things, and most especially of the complex truth she discovers as human nature.

As artist, she nevertheless always recognizes her perspective as partial, her perceptions as limited. For even with such considerable gifts as hers to the ordering of her songs in praise of life, she is acutely aware that her songs—her stories—are only partial responses to that larger inclusive mystery of existence itself that seems to center in consciousness, allowing the confusion whereby consciousness supposes itself the cause of existence. (It is another recognition she shares with St. Thomas.) And so she puts it, in remarking her perspective as artist: "Greater than scene ... is situation. Great than situation is implication. Greater than all of these is a single, entire human being, who will never be confined in any frame [by art or science]." Again, she sees her fictions "not as fiction ... [but], perhaps, as even greater mysteries than I knew. Writing fiction has developed in me an abiding respect for the unknown in a human lifetime and a sense of where to look for threads." She never supposes that the threads constitute a whole cloth of truth about human life in time and nature. She is not, that is, tempted to the heresy of *angelism* typical of the Modernist intellect, whether exhibited by the poet or philosopher or scientist.[10]

We come gradually through argument to a second point out of Thomas Aquinas pertinent to our partial song in celebration of Eudora Welty as person and storyteller. Thomas observes, as if once more in anticipation of distortions by Cartesean and Kantian Idealism that will dog our thoughts in the manger of memory, that we *know* before we know that we know. From the moment of self-awareness to consciousness, the self finds itself already possessed of memory, no matter how far back we go in our quest for *first* experience of some *other* than the self which might account for self-awareness. Jung builds a psychological metaphysics of memory on this worrisome task to intellect, his speculative psychology feeding a considerable portion of modern literature ravenous for metaphysics with his concept of the "Collective Unconscious." The poet discovers himself disfranchised of myth, especially that older orientation of Western poetry to worldly events in a First Fall in an Old Garden. And so Jung proves promising, his "Collective Unconscious" a substitute for a community transcendent of tribe or garden. Of course, Plato is famous for his own engagement of this worrisome problem with memory, a problem bequeathed to St. Augustine which the latter engages in rejecting Platonism.

A recognition of, but not an alarmed pursuit of, a now lost first memory is a central thread in Eudora Welty's Harvard lectures, *One Writer's Beginnings*. It is important to notice in the title the plural *beginnings*, in relation to Thomas's concern for *beginnings* as larger and more ancient than himself, as they are larger than Jung's tribal collective consciousness. Still, the locus of this self-discovery for Welty is, as with Thomas, a person's peculiar memory, whereby the discrete self—a little world included in a larger—engages the including matrix of existence that challenges its limited being, the effect of which on the self is awe and wonder before existence. When we bring the philosopher's argument or the poet's art to bear upon this mystery of memory, we discover that indeed we already *know* ourselves *now* to have experienced liveness *then*, before the burden of this present knowing. As a limited little world, though tempted to autonomy, we each have already responded intuitively to an *other than* the self, in accordance with the necessity to our nature as limited, finite, discursive self. Thus our experiences as finite creatures, within limited nature and through that limited nature, have in some mysterious manner preceded our present reason's discoveries about this most puzzling reality: our own consciousness in which resides knowledge of old experiences. The experience of existing at all, of *being*, is revealed in what must be granted as *becomings*—a confluence of *beginnings*—always known as a presence to this moment of consciousness as precisely *this* confluence of becomings, older in time than consciousness existing in this present moment. Our philosophical poet William Wordsworth speaks this epiphany: "The Child is father of the Man." And out of that recognition his prayer for a confluence of Child and Man, the inner self: "I could wish my days to be/ Bound each to each by natural piety."

That mark, that sign out of memory in this present whereby we celebrate epiphany, is signal of a new beginning. And so puzzle is added to puzzle, threatening to confound us in our own finitude, against which confusion reason struggles as best it may. Still, there is one certainty, as St. Augustine encourages us to recognize: We know in this moment ourself to have already been. We know that we now *are*. And with that recognition, through memory coming alive, we may venture at last in hope through reason. Life is always such a present act of *being* in motion—a becoming—so that we can never say with a confident finality, justified by reason: *here* is *the* point of my departure into a continuum of becomings—of experiences by myself in the world that join this present moment out of what is at once an engulfing and a melding memory. That is why the facile but popular assertion of pure beginning is so destructive. How false that hope declaring that "today is the first day of the rest of my life." How inevitably corrosive of beginnings. Eudora Welty insists to the contrary, concerning this confluence of an always present of life as inseparable from the self's continuum, that "memory is a living thing—it too is in transit." That is a vision which restores her faith in the artist's sign as a marker of our journeyings as *homo viator*, a vision maintained in a gravity of response to complex worlds by the mystery of this living memory in the self.

Now, gravity here is used in the physicist's sense, albeit metaphorically, not in the sense associated with solemnity as a deportment practiced against creation in what is sometimes called a "Puritan" manner, as if existence itself were irreparably hazardous to spiritual and intellectual health. Nevertheless, the artist's signs, anchored in creation by a gravity proper to the sensual dimension of creation, are always limited in themselves and are always used in limited perspective. Signs never effect a full revelation of truth of anything engaged by consciousness. If the art of the poet in his story can never "prove" anything (as Flannery O'Connor reminds us) the science of the scientist as maker never fully proves the truth of a thing, even such an economically precise formulation as $E=MC^2$. For not only the formula, but Einstein himself, is enveloped at last by mystery. That is why Welty affirms that the "single, entire human being" may never be "confined in any frame" of signs.

Yet signs rightly taken, in recognition of limited perspective, are appropriate to, as they are necessary to, the celebration of the holiness of existence. If never sufficient absolutely (though sometimes presumed to be so by autonomous intellect), the sign may yet point toward that larger holiness, despite the false presumption of poets and philosophers that, by their authority over signs, that holiness is commanded by the power of their signs. Welty's friend Walker Percy, much concerned with this mystery of sign in relation to man as *homo viator*, aptly speaks of his art in such phrases as "signposts in a strange land," a phrase used as title to his posthumous collection of essays. If St. Augustine or St. Thomas were to speak the point, each would insist (as would Percy) that "grace" is beyond the command of intellectual sign. Eudora Welty doesn't put it this way, but there is in her own signs a tacit recognition of the point.

There is also a recognition of the point in her deportment as person, a deportment which the saints would give the sign *humility*.

6

> I will pass beyond this power of my nature [my sensations], and ascending my steps to him who made me, I come into the fields and spacious palaces of memory, where are treasures of countless images of things of every manner, brought there from objects perceived by sense.... There too I encounter myself and recall myself, and what, and when, and where I did some deed, and how I was affected when I did it.... Without being actually joyful, I remember myself to have been joyful; without being actually sad, I recall my past sorrow. Without fear, I recollect that I was at one time fearful; and without desire, I am mindful of previous desire. Contrariwise, at times I remember with joy my bygone sorrow, and with sorrow I remember past joy.... When I say that there are four passions of the mind, I bring forth from memory desire, joy, sadness, and fear.
>
> —St. Augustine, *The Confessions*

In our concern to understand Eudora Welty's pursuit of her own voice through her listening and learning to see, it is more than a comparative literary device to introduce St. Augustine's *Confessions* to our concern, or St. Thomas Aquinas's address to the nature of the artist and art. In the light of our century's increasingly desperate concern for consciousness as alienated from all save itself, and its increasing desperation in its own company as its outer limit, it is not fancy that suggests, for instance, that the *Confessions* is a "modern novel." Intellectual cleverness, centering upon *ennui* as virtue, was a spiritual condition to St. Augustine long before it was made popular in the West by Baudelaire. A sophisticated Manichaean solution to the rescue of the self proved insufficient to St. Augustine, despite the flattering position to intellectual power thus allowed. And so, rejecting the arrest in self-satisfaction, which would become known as a spiritual state of *ennui* in the 19th and 20th centuries, St. Augustine risked the intellectual desert of his day, striking off toward Carthage, almost self-consumed in his burning desire whose object seemed yet to elude him. That is the turning, witnessed in his *Confessions*, which Eliot recognizes as his own necessity, though he disguises it with artful masking of voice in his *Waste Land*. In Section III ("The Fire Sermin") it is not Buddha who effects a turning from worldly disorientations through the senses, but Augustine, turning the poem and its voice to a death by water, which once past will be recognized not as death but as a restoration of life called Baptism: "To Carthage then I came/ Burning burning burning burning."[11]

What St. Augustine comes to in this risk, and what Thomas Aquinas accounts for in an orderly attempt to employ reason in the making of philosophical and theological arguments, is the validity of intellect's intuitive dependence upon memory for its rescue in the desert—its reconciliation within the tensional matrix of reality. Such is the circumstantial condition to consciousness described by Eric Voegelin as the condition to consciousness's existence, the *metaxy*. (Voegelin pursues this concern in his own speculations about memory, *Anamnesis* [1978].) Descartes recognized a necessity to distinguish some point of intersection of consciousness as discretely existing at a conjunction with the complexity of the *metaxy*, the nexus of experience. Influenced by an emerging empirical science, though himself an Idealist through his thought's alienation from the *metaxy*, he attempted to locate the point of intersection in the pineal gland dangling from the physical brain. That is, Descartes turned our attention to consciousness from a metaphysical to a physical perspective, and empirical science in its rapid development of sophisticated attention through techniques suited to the physical dimension of existence estranged intellect from the transcendent, while Cartesean and Kantian idealism in philosophy estranged intellect from nature itself. There developed such an exclusion of intellect from both the transcendent *and* the immanent that the haunting conditions to consciousness called "alienation" overwhelmed intellect in the 20th century. This was not without a certain advantage to intellect in its will to autonomy, however, since only by that double estrangement could it maintain the illusion of its own "transcendence" as autonomous.

The poet, it would appear, attempts accommodation more directly than scientist or philosopher, a difference that sets him at odds with them. Through his signs accepted on faith as anchored in the truth of reality and not by means of Nominalistic instruments as they appear to the new scientist or the new philosopher—to an empiricist or to an idealist such as Descartes—such is the poet's attempt.[12] And so long as that faith remains, the poets remain in that tradition in which, as with St. Thomas Aquinas, a metaphysical vision holds intellect as substantial in relation to the substantialities of that Platonic-Voegelenian *metaxy*. Thus reality is believed actual, independent of that intellectual intentionality which gradually becomes enslaved to Nominalistic presumption in the illusion of gaining thereby its absolute freedom. (To speak of *substantial reality* is to speak more largely of reality than to speak of the merely *material reality*, a distinction Thomistic metaphysics insists upon.) The sense of our being suspended in the *metaxy* and at once baffled by and disturbed by our seeming arrest in that suspension, requiring of us an intellectual movement, very probably accounts for the preponderance of the autobiographical in our century's art, and especially in our fiction and poetry.

What seems a hauntingly common aspect of verbal art in this century is its chirping lament for the isolation of consciousness, as if intellect were a random cricket in a desert. The dominant mood of this music is that of pathos, as distinct from tragedy or comedy. The pathos is out of the chirping voice's response to echoes of itself out of the void, as it longs for an answering chirping and not an echo. We have variously celebrated and reviled Eliot's *The Waste Land* as the signal literary work in this century, according to whether we see it in submission to or rejection of arrested helplessness. Conspicuously, Eliot's poem affected the intellectual community of the 1920s, letting loose a critical flood only now beginning to abate. This poem, sounding the intellectual void, came at a point when the intellectual community found itself committed to a science which was confident in its reductions of reality to summary abstraction and increasingly forced to conclude that intellect itself was but an effect of biological mechanism, man himself contained within a product of a larger mechanism, a closed universe.

To propose the universe infinitely expanding is not to escape that principle as a closed rather than an open one, since it sets aside all questions of ultimate ends by resting faith in an unexpected and unaccounted-for immanence as a species of Kantian universalisms which is only seemingly "brought down to earth," so to speak. And so the philosophers in our era, suspended between man as material chirp and the void of infinite space, in some desperation resort to a formulaic accounting of intellect itself. They become obsessed with phenomenalism, attempting an eventual self-rescue through an arrogant Existentialism which itself was also dependent upon Nominalistic signs to deny its own cricket-hood. That arrogant direction was somewhat softened, to the relief of some poets, by Henri Bergson's suggestions of a residual holiness in the closed universe, his famous *elan vital*. But Bergson could not, as Sartre could not, rescue the philosopher, who resorted increasingly to analysis of chirps, to a science of signs, as the ultimate reach possible to philosophy.

In this intellectual climate, the poet found himself at an impasse with sign, and his voiced signs became increasingly strident. Symbolism had seemed for a brief moment a promise of rescue, especially as advanced in the climate of Existentialism sprung out of phenomenology. In that development an increasing dominance of will became the only acceptable Creator, independent of biological and astronomical infinities in its pseudo-transcendence. So French Symbolism had seemed to Eliot, who was himself first a philosopher engaging the riddle of consciousness as speculatively advanced in tangled treatises from Descartes and Leibnitz and their successors down to Bradley. Then he discovered his principal calling to be that of the poet, in response to which this philosophical poet turned critic, highly influential upon his peers. Eliot was subsequently credited, then, as the intellectual mediator of French Symbolism into English and American poetry, supported in his advocacy by many of his contemporary poets, as diversely represented as by Ezra Pound and Wallace Stevens. To their common growing disappointment, however, Eliot found himself only further arrested after his initial fascination with French Symbolism, putting himself in the position of traitor to the cause as some of his peers saw it, including Pound and Stevens.

As for his difficulty, Eliot began to see that the self as imaged to itself in image, that subjectivist aspect of the new Symbolism, left consciousness burdened to the point of despair, in reaction not only to bald spots in the middle of one's hair as with Prufrock but to bald spots in the middle of consciousness itself. Symbolism's uses of the sign proved inadequate to an intrinsic desire of consciousness unsatisfied by self-echo. Voiced signs might for a moment please the ear or the imaginative interior eye, but proved finally and at best only a murky mirror, reflecting isolated consciousness most ambiguously. Sign (symbol) thus used proves opaque—as Eric Voegelin subsequently argues to have happened in 19th-century philosophy. And being opaque, such sign was capable only of reflecting back the assumed mask of the self in its pretenses to voice. The suspicion began to stir in Eliot that the fault lay not in sign but in the self, its cause a self-closure by the poet upon his fearful chirpings in the desert. Thus in his "Preludes" (contemporary to "Prufrock") the "he" developed in the city setting of Section IV is a "soul stretched tight across the skies," its experience that of being "trampled by insistent feet."

It is the soul dissipated through such images as "fingers stuffing pipes" and "newspapers"—images as detritus, unresolved by realities attendant upon consciousness. That soul is therefore routed by the "consciousness of a blackened street/ Impatient to assume the world," consuming thereby the consciousness struggling for its recovery through imagery, through signs, made truly *significant* in relation to reality. It is a desperate moment, at which the poem's maker voice suddenly bursts into the made thing, no longer a "he" but an "I." "I am moved," a present passive voice, whose agent is "fancies" within consciousness itself out of its desperation. The response to that desperation is that the "I" recognizes its own fancies at best as only "curled" around images, clinging to them, the images dissociated from nature. It is an action of a "notion" which is incapable of rising to the efficacy of hope, though what this consciousness has a "notion" of is "some infinitely gentle/ Infinitely suffering thing." Almost an epiphany. Almost an action called love, but not quite. Eliot (this is about 1910) out of fear still proves to have one eye fearfully upon the empty self, the senses feeding consciousness at such a primitive level that consciousness must be concluded at last to be only imagery's garbage dump, the source of image most uncertain. Unnoticed by the philosopher Eliot, his very disquiet with the effect of that prospect upon memory was already turning the garbage dump of decaying imagery into a compost heap in consciousness, making possible an unsuspected revival of image, through the sense's dependences in reality, such as we see underway in "Ash-Wednesday" and in the *Four Quartets*.

Meanwhile, French Symbolism as initially embraced by Eliot could at most mirror sensual responses to a most uncertain reality, leaving consciousness suspended. Those sensual responses were not out of love as proper deportment but led to a closing reaction of desperation by consciousness. Thus the conclusion seemed to be the sensual as ultimate end, doomed by the alien body's decay, a strange byproduct of which seemed to be image isolated in consciousness. That is the lament of "Gerontion" (1920), for instance, the portrait of consciousness as a "little old man" declining to vacuity, images as tenants of its "house" (the body) reduced to the thoughts of "a dry brain in a dry season."

We pursue Eliot here, in relation to Welty's concern for memory, as an economical way of presenting the impasse to which consciousness had come early in this century through the developments in philosophy and science in the Post-Renaissance West. And we note that by the time of "Ash-Wednesday" (1930) Eliot himself is capable of dramatizing that recovery of the life in memory which Miss Welty proposes by her drama of Laurel as a similar consciousness. In "Ash-Wednesday" Eliot's "little old man" has discovered himself an "aged eagle" knowing now that "time is always time" and "place ... always and only place." Those are the conditions to that "history" which was Gerontion's adversary because of all its "cunning passages, contrived corridors" and "issues" that entrap consciousness by its "vanities."

Before that recovery, it appeared to Eliot himself (consciousness as philosopher-turning-poet) that the senses were the most immediate memory. How inevitable, then, the temptation to Manichaean rejections of creation such as were disturbingly spoken of to the self through its inescapable sensual attachments that seemed so deadly. (Eliot had not yet escaped his New England Puritan forebears.) We see reflected in his poetry his somewhat timid withdrawal from the sensual dimension of his own nature, reflected in the imagery of his early poetry. It is especially evident in his portrait of Prufrock and in his "Portrait of Lady" (1917). But in the world beyond Eliot, there had begun an excess of sensualism, a surrender of consciousness to the appetitive which was dictated to human existence as ultimate end by the deterministic sciences. That conclusion emerges in Sartrean Existentialism, a dictation of *being* by Nominalistic command of the sensual enslaved, if will itself is to be established as the only Creator. The lingering effects of this strategy are now everywhere evident in our art and politics, crying out in headlines and newsbreaks in the daily media: Reports of sensual violence, whose promised escape now is said to be that of a "Virtual Reality," whereby we can have our violence at a most private level of self-isolation. For Virtual Reality is the ultimate Manichaean reaction to a closed universe.

In either response, whether toward will's dominance culminating in a rejection of reality by "virtual reality" or in ascetic withdrawal from reality by abrogation of sensual nature, our signs reflect the emptiness of the self in its attempts to give itself to itself. The illusional pretense to self-recovery increasingly exacerbates the panic of disorder of the self in the destructions of reality, loudly lamented as the disintegration of community of selves.

In that moment of intellectual and spiritual crisis at the turn of the 20th century, French Symbolism had seemed a promising strategy of self-rescue. But consciousness as a repository of experiences—imagery from which floats in "memory"—found itself inadequate to the present moment of crisis. Thus a "thousand sordid images" in consciousness, images of which the "soul is constituted" says the voice of "Preludes," at most flicker on the ceiling of a rented room in a dilapidating tenement house, where embodied consciousness stirs fitfully on a rented bed. Such is the proximate desert, indifferent to consciousness. Whatever "vision" it has of the outside street in this moment of its arrest does not fit any reality of that street, since the "street hardly understands" the vision now projected as images on the ceiling, a video projection of consciousness against white void. (The term *vision* in Eliot's poem is clearly ironic, the projecting consciousness recognizing *illusion* only.) Thus a strategy of imagery by the poet, the maker, in exploring the alienation of consciousness from nature, in which strategy memory itself becomes the operative concept.

But memory as thus taken, we see in "Rhapsody on a Windy Night," is capable only of throwing up "high and dry" that "crowd of twisted things." Remembering Welty's fascination, as a child, with *moon* both as word and when voiced a present thing in the mouth, we find Eliot's voice declaring that the "moon" has "lost her memory." And yet! And yet, somehow that concept memory is the only possible rescue. The trapped voice cries out, "Memory! You have the key...." It is only in risking a desert journey beyond such arrest of memory, a risk through a sensual re-engagement of reality in the desert, that any rescue becomes possible, and in *The Waste Land* it is evident that St. Augustine's *Confessions* prove witness of the presence to Eliot of that saint, a reassuring presence certifying memory's role to spiritual recovery. In memory lies at least the possibility of recovering hope of surviving in the wind-blown Modernist desert.

It appears increasingly to Eliot that the poet's helpful office is as steward to language, not as arbiter of social or political order as Shelley had insisted. Beyond merely recording the despair of isolation is the responsibility to "purify the dialect of the tribe." That purification lies in making, not in pronouncements about signs as if lecturing community. That is, the responsibility of the poet is the dramatizing of a recovery of signs as a recovery of consciousness from the Modernist desert, in which commitment the body of Eliot's poetry as a whole, from "Prufrock" to *Little Gidding*, unfolds *homo viator*. And the dramatic tension along the way is the voice in the signs, a reflection of consciousness in *anticipation*—a concept important to Welty in her address to memory in this present place. Insofar as a poet may rescue order and proportion to consciousness through his own voice in the desert as mediator of reality by anticipation, the illusion of echoes may not confound that voice at last. It is not easy for consciousness to recover order and proportion within the limits of its own nature, especially as it finds itself enveloped by illusional presumptions fostered and promulgated by Modernism's insistence on consciousness as autonomous. For what it must distinguish is its self-echo from a viable chorus, and so perverse is the illusion of chorus in the manipulations of musical signs by Modernism that only with great labor may the individual consciousness make its way back to a membership in that traditional chorus singing the goodness of existence. Manichaean distortions, supported by science, are an obstacle in Modernism's presumptions which must be overcome.

Our philosophical and theological and literary concerns are much beleaguered by the concept of *tradition*, so that to use such a phrase as "traditional chorus" may no doubt be alarming. Especially in literary concerns the problem arises, usually focusing upon the poet's concern for his own "originality" as threatened by literary tradition. In fear of joining a chorus, so to speak, he may well flee to the defense of self-echo as evidence of originality, and Eliot in an early essay, "Tradition and the Individual Talent," moves somewhat in this direction, concerned with his own voice's "originality." But a decade later, in *After Strange Gods*, he comes to reject originality as a treacherous concern to the poet, and to modify his earlier understanding of tradition, turning from it as too limited when viewed in relation to orthodoxy. In orthodoxy, the chorus in the desert—unrestricted by the desert's geography or temporal extension—sings the good, even of the desert itself, but not thereby in denigration of the person as an "individual talent."[13]

By such excursions into the nature of the continuing chorus as discovered by Eliot, we have been also concerned with Eudora Welty as member in that chorus. In her fiction and in her essays, she engages the relation of tradition to the individual talent in her quest for her own voice—not as an original voice through a separation of the self unto the self, but original in the possible harmony of adding its own gifts of singing to a chorus of praise—the tradition of art as ordered by the truth of things. It is in this respect that we call her a traditionalist—a member of a continuing community of voices in chorus (not without some cacophony, of course). She is so because she is in pursuit of the truth of things. In varying degrees of presence and harmony, we have introduced Plato and St. Augustine and St. Thomas Aquinas, and Dante and Keats and Eliot into a considerable membership in that tradition. In our concern, we have been particularly mindful of St. Augustine and St. Thomas, since they prove helpful in considering that mystery of memory which is central to Eudora Welty's concern for her own gifts of voice in relation to the reality of the existential world, which she affirms as "holy." Augustine and Aquinas engage the relation of "individual talent" and "tradition" philosophically and theologically, their concerns complementary to the poet's within a community of consciousness made variedly manifest through signs, beyond any seeming gulf of centuries or wide geography.

What we attempt to sort out in this concern is a valid tradition as adequately witnessed through signs. The governing principle is not the superficial one of "influence" of one consciousness or another, for "originality" is not at issue, but the validity of common recognitions—the validity measured by this present person's actual experiences understood. That is why St. Thomas's words are so important to sustain us along the way, words in which his "study of philosophy" is an inclusive concern to reflective intellect according to wide callings other than those of the philosopher: "The purpose of the study of philosophy," he says, "is not to learn what others have thought [that being a proper beginning], but to learn how the truth of things stands [here and now]." Even so self-sufficient a poet as Robert Frost will say very much the same of his own responsibility as poet. For the poet, he says, writes a poem "in the light of all the other poems that have been written." Out of the "light of," not mere imitation of, other poetry.

The Thomistic admonition, then, is common wisdom to us as persons, in that we share as persons a common nature; we are incarnate intellectual creatures and so exist proximately in creation, *here* in place, and *now* in the present. It is in this spirit of voice discontented with its isolation in a present desert that we turn to St. Thomas once more, recalling his argument that we are by nature makers, our signs bearing witness to our actual presence to contingent circumstances commonly shared. Though never shared in common degree, the circumstances are yet common in our personhood. For we differ in gift and in circumstance, though the difference is not in *essence* but by accidents of the peculiar self emergent from our actual, unique essence.

From St. Thomas's perspective, we declare that the artist is not creator but maker. This distinction emphasizes the artist's dependences, his uncertainties about contingent existence and about the power of his sheer (i.e., limited) knowledge to arrest and control or order nature through the science of his art. Of especial uncertainty is his own dependence in human nature, and in the potentialities of his own peculiar gifts as *this* person. Because of such dependency, a careless anticipation is likely to leave him disappointed in the perfections of those gifts. The danger can but be exacerbated by a human tendency to an absolute authority in determining the ends of his own intentionality, whereby he would transcend nature itself. Reason in support of intuition is his possible rescue, recalling him as person to conditions precedent to intentional acts in *making*. A person already *is* before an intentional act, and he is in a matrix of conditional circumstances that preexist his actual existence. Thus the person discovers himself at large among a confluence of the accidents of things, which we tend to summarize as "nature." It is out of this recognition that Eudora Welty explores the pattern revealed by retrospection— by memory—out of her own becomings.

"My instinct—the dramatic instinct—was to lead me, eventually on the right track for a storyteller," she says. and here we emphasize a distinction between *intuition* and *instinct*, which distinction I am confident that Welty would grant. *Intuition* suggests an intellectual action, as opposed to *instinct*, which suggests an animal action. She does say nevertheless that "Children, like animals, use all their senses to discover the world," adding that then "artists come along and discover it the same way, all over again." What she says corresponds to Aquinas's explication of the unified, simple intellect as both intuitive and rational in its actions. He insists that those actions are occasioned through sense actions, the aspect of persons that is "like animals." For whatever is in intellect is first in the senses.

And so she recovers an epiphany from memory. "Held in my mouth the moon became a word. It had the roundness of a Concord grape Grandpa took off his vine and gave me to such out of its skin and swallow whole, in Ohio." From Jackson to Ohio and back again, and then the podium at Harvard: a confluence of experiences of existence perceived beyond the limits of the mechanistic determinisms bequeathed us by 19th-century sciences. She speaks a freedom of the maker, despite limits to his making that are prescribed by his dependences in nature, includ-

ing his own dependence in the mystery of the *giveness* called his own existence. That freedom when properly oriented is the action of love, as she
will say again and again—directly in *One Writer's Beginnings*, and by
implication in story after story. Love is born out of the confluence of
experiences presently alive, and sacred because alive to the self in memory. *Confluence*: the drawing together into a present, heightening our
anticipation of existing in the present drawing moment. That proves to
be the perspective which our storywriter maintains by an unfolding of
scenes ripe with implications tested by our experiences. The "scenes" in
her fictions prove "full of hints, pointers, suggestions, and promises of
things to find out and know about human beings. ... I had to grow up
and learn to listen for the unspoken as well as the spoken." Thus she
becomes the "hidden observer," enabled to speak from a detachment
suited to the art of story making. But thereby she is enabled as well to
speak from a certain transcendence beyond the limits of nature itself, a
transcendence of natural limit which she calls love. Her detachment must
seek its own "voice," the voice of love. As she exercises her art, out of
her beginnings recovered alive in memory, she knows that hers are "the
turns of mind, the nature of temperament, of a privileged observer."
And "owing to the way I became so, it turned out that I became the loving kind." That *way* (we are saying) is her openness of love in her intellectual actions as maker.

What such a maker as Eudora Welty comes to understand is that—
as a person making—her self is always embedded in the limits of her own
discrete being, without which limits, indeed, she would not "be" at all.
In that recognition, she is prepared to engage enveloping limits of that
self, and the contingent circumstances to her being a person, whether
she finds herself in Ohio or on a mountain in West Virginia or in Jackson, Mississippi—or at a lectern before a Harvard audience. It is both
from within limits and because of such limits that our writer discovers
responsibility to her gifts. It is the responsibility called stewardship, exercised for the good of the thing she makes. That is the first responsibility, lest the writer become egocentric and consumed by self-love.

It is only through memory of actions within circumstantial existence
that a person as maker will come upon a paradox about his own existence as maker: He will discover that all along the deepest responsibility
of all has been that to his own existence, a knowledge of self-responsi-
bility intuitively known. A person comes upon this paradox by retrospection, by a recovering of memory. For the action of self-fulfillment
lies partially hidden from the self when the self concentrates upon the
good of the thing being made, whatever the person's calling. Thus a person discovers that to properly love the thing being made is, by a coordi-
nate effect out of that love, a proper loving of the self as well. And thus

he comes upon the sustaining virtue of prudence with deepened understanding.

7

> Of course the greatest confluence of all is that which makes up human memory—the individual human memory. My own is the treasure most dearly regarded by me, in my life and in my work as writer.
> —Eudora Welty, *One Writer's Beginnings*

The writer, if such a writer as Eudora Welty, discovers herself standing in creation in an attitude to creation called piety. Without that deportment a person cannot fully surrender to the good of the things beheld as existing, let alone to the good of the thing he would make in celebration of existence. As we have already suggested, however, the term *piety* has too solemn and bland a feel to it on our tongue. Our teeth are already set on edge in response to our Puritan fathers' abuses of piety. We recover from that confusion of taste in relation to existence somewhat, as Welty does to such a considerable degree, if we observe the child responding to creation through the senses. That is a late recovery of understanding to the adult, which Eliot remarks in "Ash-Wednesday" when the "smell renews" once more in response to the "salt savor of the sandy earth." Recovering, we respond to "the bent golden-rod" and to the "cry of quail and whirling plover." It is a moment of memory in us summoned by desire, out of our own past experiences, in which we recognize as not only actual but as common to adult and child a suitable deportment to existence. The child, person becoming, we discover, *anticipates*, with a restless presence to that child of awe and wonder. Never mind that the adult may by such recognition be tempted to sentimentality, may attempt to arrest a child out of the risks of anticipation in a Romantic self-pity over lost childhood. The recognition is of a valid response, to be recovered through sentiment ordered against the reductionism of sentimentality.

Curiosity, wonder, awe are prelude to St. Augustine's *desire, joy, sadness, fear*. However mixed we are in our recognitions of the child's setting forth as *homo viator*, however complicated the incipiency of the child's own address to the world (ah, the futility of "child psychology"), we may understand beyond mere knowing that such responses are out of the ground of experience, aspects in us of a piety toward that proper ground. Instead we turn solemn, as if joy were inappropriate as a response to the good itself. Eudora Welty recognizes this spiritual resonance of piety in its complex ambiguity of deportment among persons in nature and society. We may see that recognition in the dramatic use she makes of the child Wendell at the solemn occasion of Judge McKelva's wake. It is a recognition that requires no romanticizing of the child—though that is the popular public manner whose economic advantage is revealed at school—opening time or at Christmas or Easter—if we but look with skeptical eye at the media advertisements for such moments, and especially if we juxtapose these ads and the accompanying news of the latest neighborhood juvenile violence. Indeed, we might in doing so discover the erosive effect of nostalgia over our lost "selves," a nostalgia which the traditionalist must exorcise as he contends with the popular current slogan advocating substitution of illusion for reality: "Today is the first day of the rest of my life." Instant innocence as if instant coffee, achieved by the magic of a "sound-bite" glossing the mystery of reality itself. Through sign abused, "feeling" is elevated over thought itself.

And so, how apt to the actions of Laurel's own antagonists in *The Optimist's Daughter* is such a presence as the child Wendell, preparing the way for Laurel's recognition of herself as bent away from reality in a retreat into memory. Wendell responds cautiously through awe and wonder, but is already suspicious of this chaotic gathering of adults who would govern his responses to creation.[14] He suddenly appears with the Chisom clan out of Texas, as if they were a backward flow of empire (we still sing about the old Chisholm trail in a Western song). Wendell is a throwback almost as upsetting to his own family as to Mount Salus society, which sees itself as civilized. His child-like deportment is not simply childish through the absence of corporal discipline, as it must appear to such presences as the bridesmaids, in whom manners have become means of convenience to social encounter. The Chisom clan are decidedly primitive from that point of view, and Wendell is a clear evidence of the primitive. (From the perspective of a member of the First Baptist Church of Mount Salus, one would even suspect them of being Primitive Baptists at best.) Certainly their primitive social behavior seems out of a mere pretext of comforting one of their own, Fay, in her bereavement. Their curiosity about Fay's good fortune in marriage overcomes any pretense to sorrow over the Judge's death.

And so young Wendell proves disruptive of the social concerns at the wake, oriented to the body lying in state. His intrusiveness, counterpointed by Tish and by Fay's mother all the way to the uncertain grave, finds echo in Laurel's growing sense that she, too, is an outsider. The encounter of clans has reached a climax for Laurel in the spectacle of Fay's loud wailing over the body, her passionate embrace of the dead Judge after she enters the room dressed in glistening black satin. But such spectacle seems less a violation to Laurel (though she may only reach this conclusion in retrospect) than the flow of hypocritical words spoken by the Judge's long-time friends, their lies spoken as if absolute truth about the Judge's life in a dignified pretentiousness that brings Laurel almost to the point of an eruption which Wendell would be pleased by—or rather, fascinated by. Meanwhile, the comic intensity of Wendell's actions and words is disruptive of pretentious manners among the collectively incongruent adults, underlining for us the chaos beneath their empty rituals of grief. Wendell in action is as counterpoint to Laurel's interior anarchy. This correspondence suggests what Welty means in saying that a writer must recover "all over again" the child's spontaneous curiosity and wonder and awe and anticipation about things and situations, however unsettling that recovery may prove to the easy tenor of ways in decay in the immediate community.

The writer recovers proper human responses to remembered and present experiences, and it is in this range of recovery (not yet fully recognized and accomplished by Laurel) that we locate her tensional suspension. It is forced upon her, with an added presence of the comic to the reader which Laurel can hardly appreciate, in Wendell's seemingly irreverent behavior. A way is made for Laurel's recovery, we might say, by grace seemingly incongruous to the surface spectacle, though in the moment she finds herself almost overcome by despair. But hers, we contend, is a recovery always possible against despair, a recovery of hope through love such as is so endlessly variable in our poets' voices that the celebration of love against despair is a continuing one, beyond time and place though anchored always in time and place—in the local; art's inescapable necessity since the artist is not only intellectual soul, but such a soul *incarnate*.

That recovery, then, may be as gently effected as in a person's remembering a word sensually held—seeing and saying and tasting the *moon* from a Mississippi front yard, mouthing the word like an Ohio grape. To make that recovery, and especially to celebrate the recovery through the making of a story, requires always a subtle distinction of intent on the writer's part, about which once more Thomas Aquinas is helpful. Art, he says, is not an imitation of *nature*: It is rather an imitation of the *action* of nature. It is action called the *possible* or *probable*, rather than mirror reflection of the actual—of "history." The imitation of the actual has an art proper to it, we say, but that is a limited art called history. But art is concerned with anticipation, with a recovery of contingency to hope in a present moment. Again and again, the historian of course resorts to a use of hope, as if art and history were the same. That is, he turns prophetic, prescribing the actual future from past actualities.

Fay's imitation of nature's action is not that of artist but rather an attempt to determine her own "history" on false grounds. And so her actions violate both history and art, in which confusion she gains a purchase of sympathy as a pathetic creature. Though so far removed by her simplicity from those sophisticated disorientations possible to Laurel, she nevertheless may be said to represent a "trickle-down" effect of sophisticated distortions of consciousness's proper relation to reality. For nature has been turned into diverse boarding houses since the rise of historicism in the 18th century, within which ideology have proliferated utopian programs promising fulfillment of dreams through an intentional dictation of history. The disintegration of community to mere *collective* concern for *individual* conveniences is the principal burden to our world. Given historicism's tendency to mimic empirical science's reduction of nature to mechanistic laws as managed by will (though going in the robes of art), that command of history serves only reductionism, leaving the self alienated from both history as living memory and from this present moment of the self's existence. The alarmed cry raised at the close of the 19th century that those ignorant of history are destined to repeat it proves already burdened by *history* understood as something outside the self, a something which must be controlled by the self's will in order to determine history rather than be determined by it. The cry summons intellect to false grounds, which false grounds assure a deterministic victory in those grounds. (At last we seem to recognize this error in Hegel and Marx, but oppose it most usually by species of the same error.)

Such is the corrosive effect of disoriented intellect upon community, whereby the Western intellectual community chose to support the self in its intentions to power over history and nature, rather than to maintain and recover that action of anticipation which is Welty's concern, the action of love. If we are more like Laurel than like Fay (sophisticated intellectuals) we may seek an escape from the present moment of discontent through memory turning from a responsibility called love toward a false stewardship, some species of "historical preservation,' whether exercised in saving a breadboard from a Fay or a house of cards from storms of nature that inevitably shake down terrifying presences such as swifts.

Out of those personal memories shared with us in *One Writer's Beginnings* and encouraged by the artistry of *The Optimist's Daughter*, we discover the conflicting tensions between Laurel and Fay to be speaking more largely than as a comedy of manners occasioned by family disputes. (*Losing Battles* is also rich in implications to our point.) Each of us exercises love in distorted ways, though out of an intuited knowing of love's necessity. If we extrapolate to suggest correspondences in the larger community of which we ourselves are member, we may wonder whether a piece of property historically determined to community use can rescue persons. On the one hand, for instance, might be a national will to public housing; on the other a local will to preserve historical places, or a particular collapsing house where someone famously dead once lived. Such intentions must at some point erupt in violence over place itself. In the actual dramas—in "history"—we may indeed anticipate that a Wendell, if he does not sustain his curiosity beyond the surface levels of place and its history come alive, is most likely destined for a housing project, to speak metaphorically, even as Laurel very nearly succumbs to becoming custodian of a private historical preserve of the McKelva clan, a family museum in which she would dwell as the last of the McKelvas.

Our superb craftsman of dramatic implications about reality itself, Eudora Welty, leads us to see with Laurel the "irony" of her unexpected kinship with Fay. Laurel has been reluctant to admit that the McKelva house is inescapably a house of cards (as indeed are housing projects, as we finally recognized with alarm and panic in the social and political arena at the close of the 20th century). She is being forced to recognize correspondences between the actual house and the things in it gathering history's dust, paralleled by a chimeric presence of these in the museum of arrested memory. Fay holds to her inheritance of mere property, the literal house devoid of memory save that of the very recent Judge to whom she still clings in panic, having rejected all else. Fay, insofar as she can empty herself, denies memory. Her attempt proves a forlorn one at last, made comically evident by the advent of the Chisom clan she has attempted to deny out of existence. But one cannot exorcise ghosts from memory by denial, as Fay discovers when that invasion out of Texas erupts upon Mount Salus.

But how does one properly engage those ghosts flitting about the empty house of consciousness? How reconcile oneself to the present moment's impinging necessities of action without violating the truth of things? Such questions are beyond Fay, if not beyond Laurel, though both are engaged in violations of memory. Laurel's is a violation which is often characterized as nostalgia, and it is this agent against which Fay reacts when she "couldn't care less" about the breadboard as Phil Hand's "labor of love." Nostalgia is, in its distorting effect on the spirit, a reduction of the present life of consciousness. Desire is reduced to an end which lies lost in the history of consciousness, so the memory becomes reduced to what Gabriel Marcel describes as its self-isolation, disengaged *from* event rather than enlivened in this present moment of consciousness from *within* event, both past and present.[15]

That is a recognition, as we have already seen, to which Eliot comes, through which his own desire is turned out of nostalgia clinging about the images residual in the present out of past event. Memory's deepest secret lies in its turning desire out of the self and its dreams of Eden, which prove always dreams of past event. The mixing of memory and desire in this immediate cruel April to intellect may recover desire to an openness, through anticipation—a recovery of awe and wonder through love beyond self-pity. The opening section of "Ash-Wednesday" is Eliot's dramatizing of the agony of this turning.

His philosophical exploration lies just ahead, in his distinguishing *tradition* from *orthodoxy*. It is in respect to this distinction that we may properly consider Eudora Welty to be like Eliot. And so we quote him here, from *After Strange Gods* (1933), remarking as well that he develops the distinction directly in response to the position taken by the Southern poets of *I'll Take My Stand* (1980). That recognition of those Twelve Southerners, to whom we should add Cleanth Brooks, is worth noting because Eudora Welty is very much a part of the climate of thought initiated in that symposium. Cleanth Brooks and Robert Penn Warren (one of the twelve) in particular were early champions of her work.

Eliot, after a careful preparation, says:

> A *tradition* is rather a way of feeling and acting which characterizes a group throughout generations; and that must largely be, or ... many of the elements in it must be, unconscious; whereas the maintenance of *orthodoxy* is a matter which calls for the exercise of all conscious intelligence. The two will therefore considerably complement each other.

Given the poet's responsibility as artist to use reason in making (that "orthodox" position being one out of Aquinas) Eliot discovers that his own art all along engages the frictional tensions between tradition and orthodoxy. Or, put in terms we are just discussing, in our signs we find the friction between *tradition* as history, as opposed to *orthodoxy* as the mode of rescuing history to the present from *within* event. Tradition may, as Eliot sees, become an escape *from event*, to recall Marcel to the point. (See note 15.)

The phenomenon of the Southern Renaissance in 20th-century literature becomes subject to considerable distortion through critical concerns with *history* and *place* in relation to that literature. Unfortunately, many of the critical attempts to understand it result in critical oppositions to it; it is easily caricatured. On the one hand, the Modernist critic will dismiss it as an attempt to "turn back the clock," while in opposing such simplistic response some traditionalists will resort to nostalgic sentiment. On either hand, as Allen Tate recognizes in his arresting "Ode to the Confederate Dead," the attempt is to set up a grave in the house of consciousness. For if the misguided traditionalist attempts to arrest history by nostalgia for the past, the Modernist attempts to deny the present by his own nostalgia for the future. Thus both violate memory, in contention with each other on a false ground. What we are concerned to suggest is that we see in Fay as antagonist to Laurel this same polarity, reduced to comic spectacle but with implication far from the merely comic. Fay "desecrates" family memory, from Laurel's perspective—and indeed she does—but she does so out of a romantic attempt to escape the present upon which the past is always impinging, however much one deny the *present* as affected by memory. The philosopher would explore this through metaphysics, as Eliot attempts to do. The poet dramatizes it as the tensional constrictions on consciousness struggling to accommodate itself to this insistent present.

The Mount Salus natives refuse the issue, thus violating the Judge with false memories of him, desecrating reality, as Laurel sees with a rising fury bound to erupt. That fury erupts not against them but against Fay; the bridesmaids escape unscathed. Laurel is almost ready to shout "Lucifer! Liars!" against these false comforters, who see their comforting manners as civilized in contrast to outlandish comfort to Fay from her strange family. The Mount Salus community, gathered in support of Laurel, are false comforters in that they deny a life to memory, while the complex and imperfect Judge (as Laurel increasingly recognizes of him) lies dressed in the perfection of death, tidied in their memories of him. What begins to stir in Laurel is desire recovering hope, the counter to death in its always tenuous presence. What she will eventually discover is that in the mystery of love's engagement of the ghosts of experiences past, persons though dead are recovered as continuingly active in her own present. It is a discovery which must reorder desire to life itself as here and now present in her. We might underline that discovery by summoning that recent philosopher concerned with the mystery of love, Gabriel Marcel, who says that "in the long run all that is not done through Love and for Love must invariably end up being done against Love."

The passion of desire is a hunger for a deportment of love toward existence in its ordinate nature, and its ordinate relation to that complex of consciousness which we call memory is crucial to our fully existing as person. It is significant that the relationship of memory and desire has become a central theme in the literature of the 20th century, in which century we seem to have discovered ourselves alienated by a Cartesean separation of consciousness from actual existence. How appropriate, then, as we observed, that Eliot in his great poem about modern alienations begins with a recognition that a present sensual encounter of an April moment by our September perceptions must move beyond what Keats experiences on his own April hillside. There Keats succumbs to despair in remembering having "burst Joy's grape" only to "taste the sadness of [Queen Melancholy's] might." Welty makes more of such a moment in her tasted moon, though perhaps enabled by that Keatsean sensibility concerned with the sensual dimension of the soul's estate. (It is Keats's "soul" that tastes joy embittered by melancholy, we notice.)

Eliot, in a growing recognition of Keatsean Romanticism in himself, feels despair descending. He sets out in an April of lilacs blooming out of winter's depths. It is a moment that mixes "memory with desire, stirring/ Dull roots with spring rain." We have already recalled, closer to home, the same recognition in Allen Tate's "Ode to the Confederate Dead," in which the speaking voice attempts to reconcile a present desire to ambiguous passions of joy and sorrow borne by the memory of Southern history, only to discover that it is not history in any literalness—any "letteredness" of events—that is at issue, but a necessity of recovery from a false spiritual deportment. Such memory will serve only to set up the grave in the house—St. Augustine's "spacious palaces" of the mind. For then memory itself is but a ravenous grave, furnished with the isolated detritus of past experiences, the thousand "sordid images" of which one's soul is constituted. Such is the lesson learned by Eudora Welty's reflective protagonist in *The Optimist's Daughter*. Laurel moves toward a hope of joy past gathering sorrow in her present moments spent revisiting *herself* as remembered in her own past encounters of the world. She comes to "see" her parents as she never could before.

Our gathering of discoveries by Eliot and Tate, in relation to St. Augustine's exploration of the nature of memory as fundamental in human nature, is not gratuitous. What we discover is that Welty's recovered memories in *One Writer's Beginnings* and her dramatization of those discoveries in her novel gain an authority as experiences on the authority of St. Augustine, clearly. But by the act of our own remembering—we see that both bear an authority to us in a common testimony. Welty is firm in her witness to truths discovered, principally the truth that through love we must come to terms with memory in an affirmation of our present loving response to existence. It is a present action justified out of memory but not determined by it. For the self in the present moves beyond that old self encountered through reflection in the palaces of memory. She responds to the gifts of memory, the passions of joy and sorrow, fear and desire, but she does not by that response set up the grave in the house of memory. Nor does she, as writer, respond to those gifts with a concentration upon them as if ends in themselves—as if art were the agency of salvation of the self, as Keats dreamed it might be or Yeats at times declared it to be. (Yeats, we remember, was an important discovery to Welty when, green from home as it were, she went off to Meridian to college.) For to choose art as ultimate rather than proximate good is to turn away from life and its continuous mysteries. It would be an act rejecting the responsibilities of wayfaring, the condition to fulfillment as person, as *homo viator*.

By such an address to life, out of awe and wonder that accompanies her all along, Welty reveals a classical deportment such as we are encouraged to maintain by the philosophers and theologians and artists from Plato and Homer into our own day, in their continuing witness of formal signs that we yet treasure as Western literature. She responds to her gift of life itself as an intellectual soul experiencing the presence of holiness and mystery here and now—in this moment and in this place. The point we are emphasizing is that, unlike many writers of our century, Welty does not find her primary justification as person certified by her gifts as storyteller, though those gifts are both arrestingly impressive and contributive. That is why we find her so comfortable with a variety of persons who differ widely in their peculiar gifts. Even so, we may suspect she was more comfortable with the generality of her neighbors in Jackson, Mississippi, than with the gatherings of writers at literary conferences, though she was generous-spirited enough to venture often among such folk.

Not, of course, that Welty does not know the range of imperfections in human nature, most especially in near neighbors. Nevertheless, she takes great care to avoid a *judgmental* detachment as she imitates actions possible out of such imperfections of persons. Her first apprenticeship, she remembers, was that of listener. Looking back, she concludes that following the opening of the world to her through listening to her parents talk from a room away she became attuned to the "unspoken as well as the spoken—and to know a truth, I also had to recognize a lie." Thus she remembers her father as optimist, her mother as pessimist: "He the optimist was the one who prepared for the worst, and she the pessimist was the daredevil...." (Changes on this observation from childhood are played out in the novel.) Such was her preparation through listening, unrecognized then as an apprenticeship to her later calling as storyteller. What she learned thereby was to avoid judging her neighbor. At the same time, she must neither submit to the easy surface of things as optimist, denying the existence of evil by romanticizing the true reality of how things stand in truth, nor succumb to a severe pessimism as an opposite that finds reality evil, which response tempts to despair, to abandoning the deepest call of all: the call to love the true while not blinking the false.

Like the dead Phil Hand of *The Optimist's Daughter*, who in his own wise deportment to life is a surrogate presence for our storyteller, Welty is intent on perfection, but she does not suppose that the thing she would make perfect is therefore immortal. That is a present witness by Phil to his widow at novel's end, recovered by her in the breadboard he had made. Only at the end does Laurel understand: Phil had made houses "to stand, to last, to be lived in," while knowing all along that houses are "built of cards," in the light of inexorable nature. Phil, the remembered lover, comes to Laurel out of her memory to witness the delicate balance between caring too much and not caring enough. As Welty would have it, one builds solidly—whether a story or a breadboard—to the limit of one's gifts, knowing that the maker is limited from *creating* an eternal thing as if the poet were God. That has been a favorite role of the artist in the 20th century. Welty understands her calling to be that of maker, not creator, so she accepts her dependence as maker from existence itself. In the light of this understanding, art at last is seen as a thing at a secondary level of existence.[16]

That is why the fiction writer, imitating the action of human nature, knows (if he is Eudora Welty) that the person, "a single, entire human being ... will never be confined in any frame," however gifted the artist with this control of scene, situation, implication. That is the recognition necessary to avoid the confusion between *maker* and *creator*. For love's very freedom allows the temptation to an inordinate expectation of the effect of love upon the world. Laurel discovers as much through that dramatic rivalry into which she is drawn because of her surface understanding of her own father. In an attempt to maintain him by love, she distorts her own memory of him, leading to a bitter contest with the ravenous Fay, who would devour existence. Only late does Laurel see that through her disoriented love for her father she allows herself to mistake the issue. The contest is not "between the living and the dead [between the living Fay and her dead mother Becky], between the old wife and the new; it's between too much love and too little. There is no rivalry as bitter...."

Having said these things, we may add that in the scenes and situations deployed by the storyteller there are implications, echoing more resonantly than as simply a literary analogue, in words Eliot comes to at last in his "Ash-Wednesday." The resonance wakens memory of experiences in us of the difficult balance in love's response to existence. The voice in Eliot's poem, arrested between hope and despair, prays: "Teach us to care and not to care/ Teach us to sit still." That has been the balance Phil Hand maintained through his intent to a perfection in making (houses or breadboards), in the knowledge that whatever he makes as artist decays in time. It is the balance Laurel needs, a balance to be accomplished only through an ordinate love. She stumbles upon this truth at that point of suspense at novel's end when she confronts Fay in the kitchen and almost strikes her with the breadboard. The circumstances—Welty's "scene" and "situation" that concern her as maker of stories—is ripe with "implication" beyond the otherwise comically insignificant encounter. Fighting over a breadboard in an empty house? Fighting over a memento? At least Fay has found an active use for it, cracking walnuts on it with a hammer.

In *One Writer's Beginnings*, Welty observes that "What I do make my stories out of is the *whole* fund of my feelings, my real experiences of my own life, to the relationships that formed and changed it, that I have given most of myself to." And that "whole fund" of memory includes her experiences of the petty, the bizarre, the simple, the tender, the irritating feelings in response to experiences of the actual world that prove confluent out of memory into the present. She knows that although as a writer she "came from a sheltered life," even a sheltered life "can be a daring life as well. For all serious daring starts from within." Thus these final words in her remembering as artist. With such a perspective, there is a range of daring in her actions as artist, from "Why I Live at the P.O." to "Where Is the Voice Coming From?" If the voice as comic initiates the one and anger in response to social event the other, the artist is still required to find a balance between caring and not caring, lest as artist she presume authority to transform nature itself, either by the ironic ridicule by condescension to the world or judgmental intent of retribution in attempting to remake the world. Anger over the murder of Medgar Evers may have "lit the fuse," but, in a slow-burning stillness, she recovers herself as artist. For in her responsibility as fiction writer, she says, "I am minus an adversary." It became necessary that she "enter into the mind and inside the skin of a character who could hardly have been more alien or repugnant to me." and so, she concludes of that story, "I don't believe that my anger showed me anything about human character that my sympathy and rapport never had."

Given lively social issues such as that occasioning "Where Is the Voice Coming From?" we tend to be drawn to reflections of social context as current history as if primary to art's visionary stillpoint. To do so is to violate art, as Welty knows so well. If we find a character such as the murderous protagonist repugnant on principle, we may overlook what is at issue for Welty as artist, who is concerned beyond the moment's social issue as it bears political repercussions. She witnesses to the mystery of human nature in its permutations, and the possible or probable action upon which that witness depends is "the whole fund of ... feelings," the "responses to the real experiences [of the artist's] life." That is what Goethe is talking about when he remarks that as artist he imagines himself capable of doing whatever any person may. That is the complexity of "sympathy and rapport" which Welty has "about human character" which leads her to remind us that, however sheltered her circumstances as a person, there is "a serious daring" that starts from within even the most sheltered writer in the risk of imitating the actions out of human nature. What is possible or probable as action of human nature is in some sense surely possible or probable out of *me*, in that I share in human nature. If I am the artist, and concerned for the good of the thing

I would make as it depends from human nature, I must learn my way toward a "dramatic counterpart" out of the "*whole* fund of my feelings," out of the confluence of experiences remembered. I must, as artist, both care and not care. As artist I must be stilled before the daring necessity to me in making out of my own heart and mind, if I am to make a thing—a story—good in itself.

Teach me to sit still, Eliot's voice says in "Ash-Wednesday." As artist, Eudora Welty achieves that stillness, content to open her gifts to the world from that little house on Pinehurst in Jackson from which local place she has touched a world beyond geography. If we are to appreciate her daring in doing so, we too must sit still, observing the mystery of confluence, summoning out of her memory much in tribute to her as person, as a non-judgmental but never naïve witness to human nature as we know it in ourselves. And along the way, we are not arbitrarily confusing out concern if we summon St. Augustine in his *Confessions* to *One Writer's Beginnings*.

Or, nearer our own time, and even place, and for sharp contrast between the openness of this artist Eudora Welty to the mystery and holiness of existence and a closing against that mystery reflected in the art of another of her contemporaries, in whom the understanding of his calling differs widely from hers. That disparity is reflected very immediately by a comparison of Ernest Hemingway's *A Moveable Feast: Sketches of the Author's Life* (in Paris in the twenties) to Welty's *One Writer's Beginnings*. One observes as common to them an indebtedness of craft to Chekhov and Flaubert and Henry James, clearly. But beyond craft we must be struck by Hemingway's niggardly limits of sympathy and rapport with the human condition and understanding of human nature. Hemingway appears content with the pathos of self-pity, from which as person he seems never to have escaped. Hemingway, so defiantly concerned with "courage" as a human attribute, lacks the courage of love's openness. His gifts with signs as artist are most remarkable, but I suspect we must conclude at last that they are deployed in a limited, even stingy, response to existence, whose effect is of a closing upon the self in denial of the world—a world in which he could never come to terms with place, with the local, though always quivering on the cusp of that necessity. He is in revolt against a world he never made. Perhaps that is why he seems always a character in his own fictions, not having learned—out of all his experiences in St. Louis or Chicago or Paris or Spain or Africa—his way toward a dramatic counterpart of his making, a simulacrum of himself as a possible or probable person in art suggestive of his own recovery in reality itself through love transformed beyond the appetitive self.

8

What shall we say who have knowledge
Carried to the heart? Shall we take the act
To the grave? Shall we, more hopeful, set up the grave
In the house? The ravenous grave?
        —Allen Tate, "Ode to the Confederate Dead"

Considering the prominence of the theme of memory in Eudora Welty's *The Optimist's Daughter* and her dwelling on memory in her lectures, *One Writer's Beginnings*, one wonders whether she, as T.S. Eliot came to be, was well acquainted with St. Augustine's "Philosophy of Memory" in his *Confessions*. Again, a "literary" influence is not our concern here, but rather correspondences between St. Augustine's and Eliot's and Welty's actual experiences of existing as persons, correspondences certified common to persons by signs. As persons they undoubtedly differ essentially one from another. But in the witness of signs, whether those of such an open philosopher as St. Augustine or so gifted a poet as Eudora Welty, we discover correspondences witnessing the self as it discovers out of self-consciousness a mysterious gift to that self, namely memory. Now Descartes (we have remarked along the way) long ago was concerned with consciousness as proof of existence, though it was difficult for him to break beyond the separation of thought from any *other* in a communion of consciousness and creation. He argued that the pineal gland was the locus of the intersection of thought with whatever existed separate from thought. Since then science has pursued consciousness almost relentlessly, but it centers more and more on consciousness as a sort of spume rising out of biological processes more diffusely intersecting in nerve synapses than in as simple a place as the pineal gland.

Just how far these researches and speculations about consciousness have advanced since Descartes is in doubt, I think, though there is an impressive library of research aiding our collective memory on the question. Meanwhile, St. Augustine's philosophical and theological address to the mystery of memory proves still a viable one. He accepted memory as a gift of capacity to consciousness itself, but in its nature hardly reducible to formulae, though metaphor might somewhat serve consciousness in reaching accommocation with its memory of itself. Metaphor, qualified, may prove visionary, but used as formulae it becomes reductive in the attempt to deny mystery as a fundamental condition to existing at all. Thus we might say that memory is a holding *place* in one's continuous life, though it is no place such as the pineal gland. Limited to my consciousness, my memory is seemingly infinite in its holding capacity. It is an expandable container with no delineated margins, holding the self as continuously alive, unless that self attempt to freeze-dry consciousness by thought's action of arresting its own active continuity in this always continuous present moment.

Rather certainly, something like this is St. Augustine's view, though the terms of our playful metaphor are not his. And rather certainly Eudora Welty sees memory in this perspective. This seeing is crucial, she says, to her making of stories. Hers is a "seeing" which comes early and very comfortably to her as she discovers her calling as poet—as storymaker—in contrast to Eliot for instance, for whom an accommodation was most difficult—until he read St. Augustine. For though early he cries out "Memory!/ You have the key," he has not used that key to open a door upon the mystery of existence in his present moment. Consequently at that point his memory can only throw up "high and dry/ a crowd of twisted things" into consciousness. Welty, however, attunes herself early to memory as continuous presence of past experiences, signifying by such presence that intellect is alive—however much memory may pulse in consciousness, now bright, now dim. Thus our past and our present are inescapably entangled, requiring that we address both our past as we may now know it and the contingent present that confronts us always here and now—in this place and at this moment.

What Welty says of memory, deploying her concern for memory in an enveloping thematic order in her novel, sometimes raises striking echoes of what St. Augustine says of that mystery in Book X of his *Confessions*. In a dramatic parallel, St. Augustine addresses the nature of memory in a present moment as he is remembering his mother, St. Monica, only recently dead. The parallel is, of course, to Laurel McKelva Hand, come home to attend her father, Judge McKelva, who dies soon after that return, leaving her burdened with the mystery of memory. St. Augustine argues that it is through memory that we make fundamental recognitions concerning the truth of our own existence. By memory, we know that we possess knowledge, consequent perhaps upon an unremembered, initiating openness to existence itself, which reason concludes precedent to self-awareness. There follows a gathering "in memory" of knowledge—knowledge which impinges upon this present action of *knowing* that we *know*. Thus out of a relation of our own past to our own present, we respond to the world immediately contingent to our senses in this present moment. We do so out of a *past* which is *present* in a peculiar way, affecting our response to this contingent, immediate "real" world—this "existential reality" in which we find ourselves existing always in a present moment.

To put the point contingently: We either respond in a present moment by an opening of consciousness out of itself; or consciousness withers through will's refusal, through a closing of the self. The openness is possible through a paradoxical presentness of the past held in memory. The closing is a locking of consciousness against its present outward life. That is what Laurel slowly begins to recognize as her failure. Her initial address to memory, summoned by the present circumstances of grief over her father's death, is to freeze this present—misunderstanding her obligation to the past, her obligation to the "memory" of her father. Her mother, Becky, at the point of her own death, proved just such an embittered, closed person as Laurel threatens to become, and so she dies, as Laurel is prepared now to say, in "exile ad humiliation." There has also been this same turning from life present in her father, Judge McKelva, on his death bed. Dying, he clings to the second hand of his watch as it ticks him down to his own exile in death. (Suggestively, in relation to the titles of Miss Welty's Harvard lectures, ("Listening," "Learning to See," "Finding a Voice"), both Becky and Judge McKelva descend into death through an encroaching physical blindness.)

There is a property in this Augustinian knowing of the self—as a consciousness continuously alive through grace—which would emphasized that our knowing is certified by memory, so that we *now* know that our *now* is also a new beginning, a *re-newed* beginning. We describe this property to our knowing, in its present emotional effects upon us as we respond to existing: We are moved by *awe, wonder, curiosity, anticipation.* Such a stirring in us is possible only because we both exist and know that we exist. And out of these emotional effects, there rises in consciousness *joy* or *sorrow* or *fear* or *desire.* Such are the complex conditions to a present intellectual life to which Welty speaks in her Harvard lectures, as she remembers her own beginnings as writer. And to her Harvard audience she names as a continuing effect in her of these beginnings her open deportment to existence as a state of "anticipation." But anticipation of what?

In that first lecture, "Listening," she remembers herself as a child to have been "shy physically." She never rushed into things, "including relationships, headlong." Already by her nature, she is intent upon being "not effaced, but invisible," despite her "wild curiosity" about the world. In the security of her family she becomes comfortable as a "hidden observer," a "privileged observer," and so at last she becomes "the loving kind" of observer. Her circumstances are suited to her nature as she begins to write stories, and so she also begins to draw nearer to people, though slowly, "noting and guessing, apprehending, hoping." And she discovers of herself that her "wild curiosity was in the large part suspense." The suspense of anticipation, but not simply an anticipation of consequences of her actions in their surface spectacle, their presence to us as historical event that may be recorded and certified as mere history.

It is as if Welty knew by intuition from very early in life that if we confuse spectacle with action, we shall end by reacting to spectacle only, as Laurel does at first in her response to Fay's spectacular presence in *The Optimist's Daughter*. Thus to the simple-minded nurse and the confused Laurel, Fay can only be seen as abusing Judge McKelva, when she intends instead to force him by her physical rudeness into holding on to life against the terror in his ticking watch. Certainly there is a self-centeredness in Fay, but if that were all, she would have easily surrendered her old husband to death so that she might be freed to a life at the simplistic level of spectacle which she seems possessed by in Laurel's imagination. So convinced is Laurel that Fay in effect kills her father, thus confusing spectacle with depths of action out of human nature, that Laurel engages that conclusion with some fury. This occurs at that moment of terror as Laurel contends with the random chimney swift blown down into the empty McKelva house. As she follows the disoriented bird from room to room of her childhood home, she puts her charge against Fay legalistically: "Why, it would stand up in court! Laurel thought, as she heard the bird against the door, and felt the house itself shake in the rainy wind." Here lies a mastery of art, a metaphysical conceit as it were, whereby Welty implies inner weathers of the mind in the outer spectacle to that mind: Laurel is experiencing an afternoon thunderstorm, by herself in the empty house, engaging the panicked swift which has been blown down out of the chimney. The implied correspondences are to her confused consciousness, her house of memories buffeted by present weathers such as her father's death. She is unable to reconcile her terror in either haunted house at this present moment of loss.

As readers, we too find Fay's manner startling when she attempts to force Judge McKelva to hold on to life, to rise from his deathbed and walk into the carnival of the Mardi Gras outside the hospital room. Fay acts out of a dark movement toward despair, for hers is also a response to the always closing shadow of death, hovering in her more profoundly if more secretly than in Laurel, though she lacks sophistication sufficient to confront her terror. Fay is unequal to an understanding of her own actions, and her disorder is emphasized by her speech and dress and the actions that so disturb Mount Salus society from beginning to end. But so too is Laurel unequal to ambiguous terror in pursuit of the random swift, lacking an understanding sufficient to prevent terror's growing residue in her, namely, despair.

In this unfolding drama about memory, we are given a chorus of slowly aging "bridesmaids," who provide ironic counterpoint to the profound implications in the current trivial events that are awaiting Laurel's recognition as if significant in their implication. For more is at risk than surface spectacle. The chorus puts Laurel off the mark at first because she does not realize this. They tempt her to a growing anger against Fay, whom they see as simply vulgar in manner and dress. She is not a person such as each bridesmaid supposes herself to be. They remark in Fay a wild and random natural "life," in the most popular sense of "natural," as if she were limited to the merely biological plane of existence. The spectacle of Fay's presence to them suggests only that. But Fay, by her seeming dissonance to the settled Mount Salus society, plays against and so emphasizes to us the dying, almost dead nature of that closed society. From the dying center closing about the bridesmaids, such is the implicit reading they make of Fay's threatening presence that they find she will not put on the fig leaves of a deportment according to local customs. Human nature may indeed allow private titillations, but not such vulgar public display of emotions as Fay's. Of course, this chorus of bridesmaids is not averse to being titillated, so long as natural excesses, and pleasure in those excesses, are sufficiently clothed in a reserve of indirect language speaking "good taste."

Fay's dress and speech and public deportment demonstrate to the bridesmaids, as they say to Laurel in a variety of ways, just how right they are in maintaining their own manners, exercised in accord with their memories of their mamas' manners. Laurel proves susceptible, given that her most challenging problem is that of memory. For she is increasingly confused over responsibilities of a filial piety as buffeted by what she knows as the reality of her parents' lives. She becomes especially disturbed when all are gathered in the McKelva house where the Judge lies in state as Major Bullock and the local ladies summon memories of the Judge and his late wife, which Laurel knows to be simply lies about them, though spoken in their praise. Laurel begins to see that her bridesmaids in their own dress and chatter are most shallow. Their memory of the truth of things past is barely alive in this present, except remotely in the rote exercise of what they assume is required of them in remembering their own past as touched by the dead man in the parlor. It is a species of the same deportment with which they respond to Fay, as if spectacle or memory of spectacle were substance itself. Their own present spectacle to Laurel begins to speak of dying and sterile manners, dependent upon their own dying memory. And so what Laurel must contend with is the spectacle of social history arrested in this present moment of her grief.

There is a counter-strain within the choral unity in the person of Adele, the most sympathetic presence to Laurel among her old friends. It is she whom Laurel sees at novel's end with her first-graders waving goodbye, though the self-established chorus leader, Tish, is allowed to speak in the novel's last dialogue. Tish assures Laurel that she will make her plane for the flight to Chicago: "You'll make it by the skin of your teeth." Again, shallow cliché, but with profoundly implicit "implications" to Laurel beyond Tish's power to hear even as she speaks. Laurel is beginning to make many connections out of her memory as it begins to come alive. Meanwhile, Tish continues in her response to life at the level of whether one may catch a flight to Chicago or be inconvenienced by missing it; or have tea and cookies and gossip with the other bridesmaids in Laurel's garden, as they have recently done.

No wonder, given their world built on and dependent upon memory as ghostly spectacle, as is the general tendency holding the bridesmaids together. No wonder, then, that Laurel will be shocked by Fay. Still, the bridesmaids appear to Laurel as growing old before her eyes with the ticking down of the social clock, a recognition promising her some rescue by the insight itself. And the outlander Fay insists with a passion shocking to Laurel that she was "trying to scare [the Judge] into living!" That was the intent of her violent actions in the hospital room. This, in response to Laurel's own passion and confusion, out of which she charges Fay with having "desecrated" the McKelva house. Fay *knows*, at least intuitively, that life is good and to be held on to, though she cannot *understand* what she knows.

Life for a person is larger than its reductions to animal nature, despite the spectacles to the contrary surrounding our age's culture, to which Fay has proved susceptible. Even so, bad taste in dress and speech and manners may still be underlain by a nature more fundamental than appetitive limits, a recognition toward which Laurel herself is moving. Judged by appearances, Fay's response to existence seems shallow. But Laurel begins to see in herself a shallowness as well, that recognition beginning to surface out of the embattled tastes of the bridesmaids and Fay's family. Increasingly, Laurel is hard-pressed to choose between them, becoming more stand-offish from the two social worlds buffeting her in her moment of grief. The Chisom clan's breaches of manners (as measured from Mount Salus) raise questions about the roots of manners feeding the continuum of persons, whatever the moment's clannish community. Laurel is caught in a disturbing confluence of manners, of the Chisom clan with the Mount Salus vestals of local propriety, whose authority requires some ironic detachment. They are to be accepted with a grain if not a mountain of salt.

It would be our mistake to miss Fay's confusion in the midst of outrageous spectacle at the Judge's wake. Her actions, spectacularly gauche (as in her passionate embrace of the Judge's corpse) may well speak of a desire in her we must value. For it may be that her deportment is out of a love for the Judge which Laurel has not recognized, mixed as it is in the spectacle of Fay's inevitably awkward attempt to fulfill what she supposes to be the proper gestures out of her grief. At this point, at the wake, Laurel senses but does not yet see this possibility. She is further confused from the open gesture of love by Fay's grandfather, who brings her the shelled pecans. And there is the additional implication in the wild curiosity of the outlaw child, Wendell. And indeed there is more than stage-acting when Fay, glistening in black satin, wails over the body, as there is more than a simplistic gesture in the grandfather handing Laurel his love-offering, pecans he has shelled on a park bench on his difficult journey to pay his respects and witness to grief. Meanwhile Laurel, sensing but not recognizing such confusing aspects of the circus spectacle at her father's wake, is inclined to deliver a curse upon both the houses now so awkwardly gathered under what was once her roof but is now Fay's.

Fay may prove to have been moved to desperation, out of which stirs something of hope for her, though it be only a forlorn hope. It is with something of this recognition that Laurel parts from Fay at novel's end. Laurel's impassioned encounter with Fay over ownership of the breadboard modulates into Laurel's gentle withdrawal, as if she begins to understand at last that Fay in her grief is a pathetic creature, no less besieged by the Chisoms and by Mount Salus society than she. One of the anticipations with which we are left at the end is that Laurel will grow in understanding. What begins to stir in her in that fierceness over the seemingly trivial is *love*. She is already opening toward Fay. Tish would be horrified, of course. But we might thereby recover some hope of humanity as larger than random feral nature, even in a Fay. Even, we may add, in a Tish.

In thus dramatizing a disparity of recognition, a disparity of awkward attempts to recover the openness called love in such unlike creatures as Fay and Laurel, Welty reveals to us through her protagonist the beginnings of the maturity necessary to the artist. This occurs in a convergence between Laurel and her maker, Welty, who already occupies that wise understanding as maker—as the poet Dante does in contrast to the pilgrim Dante as met in the opening lines of the *Divine Comedy*.

We are here exploring a surrogation of Eudora Welty's own experiences of life as she has lived it, not in respect to any strict biographical detail, though *The Optimist's Daughter* as a history of the McKelva family carries a multitude of Welty biographical details adapted to the fiction. We need only compare extracted details from the novel to details from *One Writer's Beginnings*. What is at issue in both memoir and novel is not history, but a recovery of our personhood as common and to be valued beyond the limits of history. One instance of art adjusting history to that end, a fictional strategy using parallels between the two families, is the play in both these works with the two terms *optimist* and *pessimist*.

In remembering her own parents, Miss Welty remarks that "The optimist [her father] was the one who was prepared for the worst, and she the pessimist [her mother] was the daredevil." The modification of these parallels we see in Laurel's gradual recognition of both her parents' limited responses to life: "He, who had been declared optimist, had not once expressed hope." He "scowlingly called" himself optimist, but Laurel must now acknowledge his deportment was transparent to her mother as it becomes to Laurel in her remembering. It leads to Laurel's frustrations at the wake when she must endure in a mannerly deportment the false eulogies pronounced by the Judge's townsfolk, friends who now tell lies in honoring the dead, lest they violate memory itself in telling the truth. Their radical violations of *her* memory are almost more than Laurel can bear, drawing her toward an anarchy of honesty in that unmanageable child Wendell, to whom she is sympathetic.

Laurel can now value her mother's angry passion for the truth as she lay on her own deathbed, the Judge attempting to soothe her with lies. For the Judge's "optimistic" deportment was a hoax out of his profound helplessness in the face of death. He promises Laurel's mother Becky on her deathbed that he will carry her back for a visit to her childhood West Virginia, the memory of which she clings to through her Mississippi exile, in her own species of arrest despite her daredevil spectacles of action. But dying, Becky McKelva responds in fury to the Judge's promise: "Lucifer! ... Liar!" And so she dies, as Laurel can now see, "in exile and humiliation," exile not only from West Virginia but from her husband as well and from the falseness of Mount Salus as community, the response of which is now her final humiliation. Here is a counterpoint to Laurel's slowly emerging reunion with her husband Phil, who is alive to her at the end as never before.

What Laurel unfolds for us in her discoveries about memory is her own late opening to the holiness of existence, which Eudora Welty very early became attuned to through *love*. And Laurel's opening toward the world out of love at novel's end is in accord with the necessities of good making, whether one be interior decorator or storyteller. In the novel, our storyteller controls and modulates this opening toward an inclusive epiphany, wherein Laurel recognizes a confluence of past and present, bringing her dead husband and his love into an active presence through memory rightly taken.

For Laurel, memory comes alive in her present. Welty herself seems to have been born knowing this and accepts the obligation of understanding it as artist. She needs no shocking recognition of "desecrations" of memory, either by the Fays or bridesmaids of our world seen for a first time or by her own mother or father. And so as storyteller she can respond to the spectrum of persons with an equanimity suited to art. It has always been a lively pleasure to her to view this most various world with an anticipation hardly susceptible to shock, though on occasion she might be tempted by anger.

In addressing *anticipation* as we find it to be the rising action in Laurel, we may call anticipation a present hope in relation to a present desire. That hope is sustained by memory when memory is alive, as it so clearly was in Welty herself. We discover anew through her art not only that hope and desire are companionable, but that we have known them to be so, intuitively, all along. And that is the point at which we accept reason as a necessary complement to what we know intuitively, toward our understanding the contingent—the possible or probable to our anticipations, whether we speak of life or of art. Whatever degree of reason we possess, short of pathological disorder, we find it sufficient to the ordering of hope and desire in relation to circumstantial reality impinging upon consciousness. Even with a pathological complication, hope and desire seem manifest, a recognition we encounter again and again in so-called "Southern" fiction, as in Faulkner's Benjy in *The Sound and the Fury* or Flannery O'Connor's Bishop in *The Violent Bear It Away*.

Such is the nature of anticipation to be dealt with, whether as Laurel's dead husband, Phil Hand, dealt with it or, in less wise ways, as Laurel at first attempts to do. Phil would make perfect houses, himself conditioned in that making by guidance of his reason, recognizing through reason that the perfect houses he would build are nevertheless houses of cards. He is not a victim of a betrayal by himself through false optimism, as seems the unfortunate case in Judge McKelva's decline into death. The Judge's optimism has proved only a disguise of his terror before the specter of death, making him (as Becky cries out) a liar in denying death. At his own death, he seems almost destroyed by despair.

Reason, then, is an anticipation of understanding beyond a mere knowing. Reason thus sustains and values the *intuitively known*. By such anticipation of understanding our hope and desire may be reconciled, lest despair overcome us in the last moment of our exile and humiliation, at whatever place or time we find ourselves in the world when our death comes. If Fay lacks a refined intuitive knowing such as Becky's, she yet recognizes in Judge McKelva very much what Becky recognized, and so attempts to shock him into life, as Becky attempted to shock him with the epithets *Lucifer* and *liar*. (One of the papers Laurel burns in purging her own memory is her mother's schoolgirl paper on Milton's *Paradise Lost*.)

These are high matters at issue in Welty's fiction, despite the often comic spectacle attaching to character or situation in the novel. They are matters which a poet may engage in a high manner, as does T.S. Eliot—especially in his *Four Quartets*. In those poems Eliot dramatizes the movements of a sophisticated intellect within a sophisticated context of literary, philosophical, and theological traditions. Eudora Welty's response to the virtues of a living memory engages the same high matters as Eliot's, in a quite different context.

Her own childhood adventures in West Virginia, her responses to birds, flowers, and folk songs, the comedy of family love, differ from Eliot's in respect to the spectacle of events which each has remembered from childhood. But in their differing responses, they prove to hold the same vision of *homo viator* (pilgrim man). In his late poetry, Eliot attempts to recover memory alive to his philosophical and theological inheritances from Plato and St. Augustine down to Dante and Aquinas. What both Welty and Eliot come to know in common is that these high concerns about human nature are always to be engaged in the immediacy of place, in this present moment, according to peculiar circumstances. Consciousness must enjoin the *human* nature of the self here and now, and most fundamentally. That is the concern of Eliot's *Little Gidding*, which concludes insistently on this point that "The end of all our exploring/ Will be to arrive where we started/ And know the place for the first time." That is a summary of Laurel's actions in Miss Welty's novel.

That is why we must inevitably discover, in consequence of a common vision independently earned, even in such seemingly disparate poets as Welty and Eliot, correspondences between them of a high theme, however dissimilar the enveloping imagery which informs the art of such theme. Nor should we be surprised to discover correspondences between their common theme and that of their kinsmen, remote in time and place but bearing a present common vision, whether that kinsman be St. Augustine or St. Thomas Aquinas. Eliot's art and essays carry deliberate and explicit acknowledgments of recognized kinship through literary allusions, as in his *Waste Land* and in "Ash-Wednesday." But we may anticipate as well discovering parallels between Welty's understanding of nature and art and the understanding held by so unlikely a kinsman to her as Thomas Aquinas, in respect to which kinship ours is (once more) not a concern for historical influences. For both the philosopher and our poet (Welty) are joined in a common deportment to truth, a piety toward the holiness of creation. Theirs is a common devotion to the truth of things, however differing their modes or manners in paying homage to that holiness.

St. Thomas says of art, as Phil Hand might well say, that it requires reason in making. What we know intuitively about our own nature as person is that we are called to a perfection through our devotion to reasoned making, however various the modes of making as differentiated in discrete and peculiar gifts to each person. Reason devoted to making engages the known, in anticipation of understanding; and understanding is a condition of our individual nature fulfilled according to the degree of love in our actions in response to creation. Or so both Aquinas and Welty believe. Through understanding, we accept as maker that we are responsible to the good of the thing we make. That is what Phil Hand in Welty's novel understood most clearly. He would make perfect the thing, whether a house or a breadboard. But collaterally, by his act of making in which there is the intent to the good of the thing he makes, he fulfills his own nature, a nature made more or less perfect when in accord with the limits of his gifts as maker.

Within the limits of gift: That is the paradoxical witness Phil Hand bears in his makings, though Laurel comes late to see it. Thus, alone in her family's empty house in Mount Salus, she remembers Phil's hands at work. They were "double-jointed where they left the palms, nearly at right angles; their long, blunt tips curved strongly back. When she watched his right hand go about its work, it looked like the Hand of his name." Laurel's is a recognition of convergence of person and world, more complex in its fictional correspondences than Welty's earlier childhood experience of the word *moon* in her mouth like an Ohio grape, but essentially a like epiphany, made singular in remembrance. In such devices, we recognize an artistic wit at work as she explores in a fiction the mystery of making in relation to memory. The perfect house, Phil Hand argues, is made to a proximate but not eternal end. A house is a thing made in a place for people to live in, temporarily. Its perfection in proximate nature must be understood as a limit to any good that any hand makes through art. For in the light of eternity, as we used to say, any house can be understood only as a house of cards. That is the shocking recognition of the truth about worldly things to which Laurel comes, and in doing so she begins to approach the wisdom of our proper deportment in the world. And so as Eliot puts it, in the form of a prayer in "Ash-Wednesday," we must learn "to care and not to care." That is the recognition in Phil, when he at once perfects the house he would make, but knows it to be a house of cards nevertheless.

What is to be gained through understanding this paradox, whose proper virtue is piety, is a balance toward creation whereby a person at once cares for the proximate as its obligated steward, but does not care for it with such a growing obsession as transmutes stewardship into sheer ownership, as if by that ownership we are transmuted into creators of the thing possessed. Our artists make that point to us repeatedly in their abandoning the made thing, the poem or painting, to the world, in turning to a new making. We tend to make too much of history's irony in this sort of event. There is a public auction of a painting in London, perhaps. It is acquired for several million dollars, but our main recollection about it is that it fetched its maker only a few francs when he was finished with it. Such a confusion about *making* no doubt exacerbates our concerns as a society for our poets and painters, as often as not with the effect of our corrupting them through a patronage divorced from a vision of art proper to patron no less than to artist. The vision of the artist, in his devotion to the good of the thing he makes, is always the central necessity to a spiritual state of the artist—the maker—whether a Phil Hand or Laurel McKelva Hand, or Eudora Welty or T.S. Eliot. And properly speaking, so it must be to any intruding patron.

Even Judge McKelva as an old man, having lost Becky, responds intuitively to this truth, consequent to Becky's scathing anathema delivered upon him from her deathbed. He does so, though he lacks an understanding sufficient to the truth. And so he ends at last in a fixation upon the second hand of his watch as it mechanically measures him down to his death. But he had made a right move toward recovery. He attempted to recover memory alive, pruning Becky's rose bush, brought long ago from West Virginia by Becky the pessimist into her exile, a gesture prompted by love larger than her love of her new husband. In the Judge's attempt at recovery, or so in her anger Fay argues, he hurt his eyes, initiating the decline into death. Fay rejects such attempts to rescue memory alive. After all, here is a present proof of its danger, her dead husband. and yet Fay also responds to that necessity, awkwardly and with a display scandalizing her Mount Salus neighbors—her deportment at the wake. She attempts a ceremonial expiation of grief which, culturally speaking—as we are so fond of speaking these days—embarrasses those maintaining any dying local culture. Fay is nevertheless, however gauche, vaguely attempting a ceremonial accommodation of memory to the present moment. With a comic relief within the cultural chaos, we see Major Bullock, the proximate cause of the Chisom invasion, saved embarrassment himself, and any sense of guilt, by the grace of good Southern bourbon ceremonially imbibed. (Given the disparity of encounters in this scene, one might recall the more orderly chaos of traditional wakes, especially that record of intellectual and spiritual disintegration so monumentally undertaken by Joyce in *Finnegans Wake* in his ironic detachment as maker.)

Thomas Aquinas, attuned to the ceremonies of grief and joy as of a special concern to the artist, remarks the artist's primary responsibility to be to the good of the thing he makes and to that alone—as artist. The artist *as maker* has only a secondary concern for his own perfection through his making, however often artists mistake themselves as the primary end in their worldly conduct. The self-love of artists is notorious, especially in our century, in sharp contrast to such witness as Welty's. For her, the maker's special "calling" is to the good of the thing being made, in a self-sacrifice of gifts to the made thing. That is the proper stewardship of the artist's gifts, a moral responsibility to those gifts peculiar to this particular person. We are talking directly here of the making of stories, but the point is general and applies to pruning rose bushes, building houses, or decorating made houses. Thus Phil Hand bears witness to Welty's own vision, which she dramatizes through Laurel's actions in recovering his memory alive. (As surrogate witness to Welty's own position, there is a convenience in Phil Hand's being dead: She does not have to maintain him in a continuous perfection of this wise deportment, which might so easily make him a more unconvincing persona.)

Laurel's recovery of Phil out of memory coming alive completes the unfolding action in the novel. Phil thus succeeds in bringing reason into concert with Laurel's intuitive recognition of the limits of her calling. That is, Phil had understood, as Laurel at last does, that one anticipates, through love, the perfection of the thing made. He was thereby enabled to move beyond the danger of despair over recognizing perfection doomed, limited by time or eternity, whether a despair threatening him as a person or artist. And so the paradox: His is a surrender through love that enables him to make a "perfect" breadboard, even as he knows it vulnerable, given the nature of worldly, made things. As they are almost in physical combat over the breadboard, Fay demands of Laurel, "What do you see in that thing?" The question arrests the spectacle of action as Laurel is at last able to respond, "The whole story, Fay. The whole solid past." She draws nearer to her own earlier anticipation that "Phil could still tell her of her life," though long dead. "For her life, any life, she had to believe, was nothing but the continuity of its love."

If Laurel in this moment with the breadboard had immediate access to the tradition held by Eliot's speaker in *Little Gidding*, she might conclude her pilgrimage to Mount Salus by saying that "all shall be well, and all manner of thing shall be well," summoning Dame Julian of Norwich out of memory. Dame Julian, reaching Laurel's conclusion, holds a hazelnut on her open palm in a quiet moment and discovers in that lowly thing of nature, as Welty seems to discover in birds and flowers and even in people, the "continuity of love." Laurel, though her discovery is in a moment of spectacle when she is about to strike Fay with the breadboard, remembers at that point that Phil had made it out of love for her mother Becky. Hazelnut or breadboard? What we remark is that the *created* thing in nature or the thing *made* by art—hazelnut or breadboard—depends from the actual nature of creation and by existing at all is limited to the conditions of its nature, whereby it is the thing it is. For any existence is by limit.

This means that the made thing is especially limited by the actual and specific nature of the maker and by the material nature with which he must make. For he can in no wise create *ex nihilo*. One need not be surprised therefore should Fay as "maker," perhaps taking her mother's advice, turn the McKelva house into a boarding house, though that would prove a formidable undertaking given the opposition of the bridesmaids. A reader, responding to the bridesmaids in irritation, might even encourage Fay to make such a thing of the house, but out of malice and not love: It would serve them right! Whatever the present species of makings by a various community of persons, the thing made proves transient nevertheless, whether a boarding house or a breadboard. Or petitions for the possession of the breadboard before a small claims court, or a zoning petition to a city council in order to turn an empty house into a boarding house.

Laurel, we may as reader anticipate, returns to Chicago with a growing understanding of the mystery of confluent memory alive, yielding through her an active love in this always present moment. She, too, must cease in this world at last, as her mother and father have done and as Phil has done before them. The bridesmaids and Fay must as well. One need only remember the shifting nature of things as encountered in Mount Salus, Mississippi, to know this. Or one may note Welty's remembering of Jackson in *One Writer's Beginnings*. There, for instance, we find her lively memory of her own father's insurance building now radically changed on its Jackson ground. So, too, the McKelva house must come to be changed. What Laurel carries with her, then, as Eudora Welty has done for so long, is a growing recognition of love's rescue of the present moment, a rescue supported by memory when memory is rightly taken.

What Laurel rejects in doing so is her old dependence upon the shifting sands of memory growing sterile. By such a dependence, we may only be tempted to some variety of a program oriented to some species of "historical preservation," which if centering upon the Old McKelva house would no doubt be made a common cause to the chorus of Laurel's bridesmaids trying to prevent its being made into a neighborhood boarding house. Welty's own home on Pinehurst Street in Jackson likely has such a fate in store, though from what we know of her, we might suspect she would prefer a boarding house to a museum.

Though we share in a common nature as makers, if we confuse a sure arrest of memory in sterile sands with what Laurel calls memory as a "continuity of love" we shall prove false to our common nature. History so arrested is dead history. However artfully posted may be our historical house or district with maps and signs, we shall only certify memory dead if we do not discover how memory may recover us in our nature as makers, not as creators. That requires humility and piety in response to our very nature as limited, specifically in relation to our intrinsic limits as *this* particular person.

That is the necessary recognition to us as makers that Thomas Aquinas addressed in the last year of his life, just before he set his own pen aside and turned to silence, in his *Collationes Credo in Deum.* We have this work only in Latin, but Thomas spoke to an appreciative audience in his native vernacular, the Neapolitan dialect. (What he says comes down to us by translation into Medieval Latin.) He speaks with a directness to our point. He has come home at last. His dialect would have seemed no doubt quaint to his intellectual familiars at the University of Paris, as perhaps Eudora Welty's may have seemed to some of her Harvard audience. The truth in what he says may indeed seem quaint to some of us. Although human beings are not able to make anything without preexistent material, he says, that is because "they are makers of the particular and are not able to draw forth this form without material determined and presupposed from another. The reason is that their own virtuosity is limited to the form alone, and therefore can be the cause only of this form. ... To create differs from to make insofar as to create is to make something from nothing."

I myself have no doubt that Thomas Aquinas spoke to his hometown audience in a manner less formal and austere than his words seem to us at this remove, words that come to us out of the memory of his attendant, Reginald, who translated and so preserved these spoken things in formal Latin. In "school" Latin. Even so, I am equally confident that the truth borne so formally to us is one shared by Eudora Welty. Her openness of love toward creation, including the desperateness of humanity itself, bears witness to the correspondence between her and Thomas. It is in the joyful humility and piety toward existence which she evidences in her makings through art, in perfections of things made out of recognition of her own most considerable gifts in making, which nevertheless—as Phil Hand or Eliot would say—are in response to limits within which we must both care and not care, lest we forget that our own made things are always houses of cards. For we must care for perfection in making, but not care at last, knowing that the thing we make is in the light of slow-chapped time or the light of eternity already in decay. Even so, the truth living in such houses or stories for so short a time is a permanent thing, namely the truth that *love* is an open surrender to the good, a surrender made always, in this most present and local moment of making, whether the making of a memoir or a novel—or this present paper in celebration of those things Eudora Welty made through her lively love of creation.

PART II

Walker Percy's Quest for the Word Within the Word: A Preliminary

Still is the unspoken word, the Word unheard,
The Word without a word, the Word within
The world and for the world....
> T. S. Eliot, "Ash-Wednesday"

All you got to do is drive through the suburbs of New
Orleans and of Baton Rouge, and it looks like Los Angeles. There is a word for it. It is called: losangelization.
That's not good.... What I am trying to do is to figure
out how a man can come to himself, living in a place like
that.
> Walker Percy to Jan Nordby Gretlund,
> "Laying the Ghost of Marcus Aurelius?"

1

No one perceives himself to know except from the fact that he knows some object, because knowledge of some object is prior to knowledge of oneself in such a way that it immediately apprehends itself, but it arrives at knowledge of itself by the fact that it perceives other things.

— St. Thomas Aquinas,
Questiones disputate de veritate, 10, 8

We shall be talking of Walker Percy, the person recently among us and traveling just ahead of us. He has left us some remarkable signposts in what seems to some of us, as it often seemed to him, a desert necessary to our journeying. Such are his signposts as "objects" providing knowledge of our "self" that we pause here in a waystation of that journey, trying his signs with signs of our own. Our concern is that we not travel the desert in circles when we set out once more and so become lost. We value his signposts as promising not only Thomas's "knowledge of oneself," coordinates of the self in the desert, but a sense of his continuing fellowship, that fellowship of the living and the dead on a common journey.

I emphasize that term *fellowship* here, remembering signs left us by yet another recent traveler in this desert maze of conflicting signs, Jacques Maritain. Percy knew him as fellow traveler also, perhaps through Maritain's very early *Art and Scholasticism* (1930) as particularly helpful to any poet as traveler. But I am recalling Maritain's "Truth and Human Fellowship" (1957), in which he argues that there can be "no *toleration* between systems"—a system cannot *tolerate* another system, though "there can be *justice*, intellectual justice, between philosophical systems." Maritain's concern is that, under the banner of *tolerance*, we tend (lest offense be given through signs) to make truth itself the first victim. As *homo viator* (a term congenial to Percy, discovered in Gabriel Marcel), we travel in unavoidable company with each other, alternately drawn together and thrust apart through conflicting readings of signs along our way. But we are suggesting that when signs are reduced to absolute systems, though in the name of truth, truth itself seems likely to be reduced to imprisonment or cast toward outer darkness. That is the danger of systems which we speak of as *ideologies*.

Walker Percy as *homo viator* began to recognize this truth spoken by Maritain, himself initially firmly held in an intellectual system we shall have to engage at this present rest-stop speculation over inherited maps. We speak of *science* as distinct from *philosophy* or *poetry*. These are terms we shall be concerned to argue as justifying not systems, but perspectives,

93

recorded in moments of time afforded to man as sign-maker. Signs seem always to reveal a person's perspective, as affecting systems—maps—of the country of that consciousness Percy calls the "self." To make our attempt is perhaps to recover the message Maritain would bequeath us: that we are each pilgrim, blessed as such by intellect, however waveringly we may use intellect in our attempts to "cipher" signs to derive systems. As pilgrims, we are always haunted by the possibility of discovering in system itself our rescue. When all signs conform to system, we tend to suppose, those signs will resolve the unknown before us. Thus the abiding mystery of existence may be forced to yield to system.

That is the intellectual dilemma for Percy, which he addresses to us in Maritain's sense of *fellowship*. It is an address through which he proves a continuing presence to us in the signs he has left us—his essays and novels. Not *tolerance*, Maritain says, but *fellowship* is the better naming of our proper deportment as *homo viator*. It is so because that word "conjures up the image of travelling companions, who meet here below by chance and journey through life—however fundamental their differences may be—good humoredly, in cordial solidarity and human agreement, or better to say, friendly and cooperative disagreement." That seems an apt description of Walker Percy's manner of presence to our journey, witnessed in the signposts he leaves us. And this observation is to remind us that the prospect of our reaching a sense of fellowship with him is through the mediation of his signs engaged by our own, remembering that the words we use toward recovering fellowship are not only a necessity to us but also a hazardous mediation of that fellowship.

Words as necessary but hazardous to fellowship, given the undeniable "fundamental differences" of person from person as Maritain says: that was the challenge to Walker Percy, gradually waking from pursuit of a system which in his very waking was increasingly revealed as insufficient to his journey's end: *science*, a manner of deportment necessary but not ultimately sufficient to that inherent inclination in us to an end vested in a mystery beyond science's power. *Science*: needed by the journeyman under the auspices of reason—various *sciences*—but not to be taken as absolute, as justifying ideological systems excluding the continuing mystery of the desert and of the self lost in it. That is a dawning in Percy, out of which he discovers his calling as physician-poet, or in the title to his reflection in signs upon this mystery of himself as a Self—the "Physician as Novelist."

As such he approaches his making of signs as a diagnostician of the self in its Modernist deportment, lost in a desert which exacerbates the self in its suffering from a debilitating malady. His most proximate patient: his own self. As analyst, he will diagnose a spiritual sickness such as what one of his early fellow "physician" teachers, Kierkegaard, names a "Sickness unto Death." Percy's approach to this malady is to engage it in a surgical theater, as it were—that of his public essays and fictions. Through them we learn that his concern is not an autopsy of the dead self, but an exploratory analysis with promise of recovery of a very sick patient: himself the patient waking to life. He is at once good humored and cordial in sharing his procedure, and cautious about it as well. As for his caution, lest as physician he seem to promise inevitable recovery, he is a novelist of the possible, given to that indirection in his careful exposition of the malady.

If we somewhat labor metaphorical analogy here, we do so in part because Percy turns and returns to this analogy of himself as novelist. It is a difference between him and his contemporary fellow traveler who also recognizes the spiritual disease but from a different perspective. Not a physician-novelist, Flannery O'Connor will rather say that her perspective is that of the novelist as prophet, "a realist of distances." They differ in the naming of their offices and of the symptoms of the common patient waylaid on his journeying by a disease of the spirit. But both see the same condition in us as patient-pilgrim, as Modernist man.

Our present approach to an immediate intellectual concern for *homo viator's* spiritual state shares something of the perspective of both the physician-poet and the prophet-poet, though it is with the physician-poet and his perspective that we are most centrally concerned in this present venture. By word—sign—we must understand his word in relation to our actual experiences as pilgrims delayed briefly at this rest-stop, however impatient to resume the journey. Our concern is to recover health for the journey we must continue. How fortunate to have in fellowship with us at a new setting-out not only the prophet-poet O'Connor but the physician-poet Percy, a goodly fellowship of concern for our recovery. As for the *word* in relation to *experiences* we have known, we find both the word and the experience affected by each other, modifying our intellectual actions, our thoughts, in consequence of reflections at way-stations along our way. But we find both also affected by that larger complex of inclusive existence, creation, more comfortably spoken of by Modernist musing as cosmos, but a world in either case hiding the *way* and so a world seemingly a desert. The horizon recedes to misty outer limits, within which our experience and our sign-play occur in relation to each other, often confusingly, so that we fear that by our very sign-play we may become more and more lost. We find ourselves talking about *things* then, as best we may, whether we mean the term *thing* to signify our word or an outer star beyond our galaxy. It is thus that, as intellectual creatures, we find ourselves always in some degree lost in the cosmos.

And so I say we talk "about" things, to emphasize the limit of sign in recovering us from being lost. It is the limit of sign as instrument to the rescue of the soul that we must always acknowledge in our serious play with signs, lest we come to suppose that self-help through our signs is sufficient to our understanding of our dislocation in the cosmos, believing signs to be the unaided instruments to our rescue and our own creation. We lose recognition of things themselves as signs antecedent to our journeying. That is to say, none of our signs, through which we attempt to touch and certify the experiences we have of a reality bearing mystery, will ever by that touching *comprehend* (in a literal sense) any *thing touched upon* through our senses and named in a pride of signs. That is the price of our finitude. And the recognition of our continuing failure, we might say, is the continuing proof of our finite nature as intellectual creatures, a disquieting gift. Our recognition of limit as peculiar to created intellect sets us again and again to desire and pursue a metaphysics through which we may reach some peace of mind, after our repeated failures to reach such a peace of mind through mere science. Hence the unquiet journey Percy shares with us: the quest for the Word in the world itself.

The accommodation of desire to our intellectual finitude becomes the end we seek, deliberately or intuitively, through intellectual actions seeking accommodation of our word to the Word. So a continuing recognition of the limit of intellectual certitude, in relation to our anticipation of things as actual, might prevent intellectual despair. To recognize this point is to know in advance that we shall be unable to come to full *comprehension* of things through signs, or of any singular thing in the end, even (in a startling recognition) a full comprehension of our own well-ordered sign: a poem, a novel signed with our name. We will be able to say only so much *about* a thing or things, because we can know only so much *out* of things, limited as we are as maker, not Creator. That is why, first and last, our exploration promises no happy issue into full intellectual citizenship in an ultimate country of truth. That is a country we believe to exist out of our faith, whether we think ourselves nihilist or theist. For, whether intellectual nihilist or theist, we are burdened by our very nature with a desire to issue as a self beyond signs and their threatening entrapment of our self: We desire passport into a pure estate of intellect in a far country, a country for which we have no name that can bind us without fissure as an intellectual community here and now, requiring of us a fellowship larger than tolerance. What does bind us, in the end, is the necessity in us to move toward an uncertain country through hope, believing (if we are in fellowship with Percy) it to be the country of Love.

That journey of mind, as we cannot deny, is signaled by signs, the residue of which litter the sands of history: yesterday, today, tomorrow.

Walker Percy acutely appreciated the circumstance of sign to the necessity of his own desire, the mystery of that very desire which is so difficult to "sign." Fr. Patrick Samway gives Percy's posthumously collected essays a most apt title, then, out of Percy's own notes toward a projected novel "about the End of the World." The novelist finds himself setting forth "with a stranger in a strange land where the signposts are enigmatic but which he sets out to explore nevertheless." Not simply the novelist, let us say, but the novice—the person journeying intellectually (since that is his given mode as traveler to that far country) through the strange land called *existence* or *creation* or *universe* or *cosmos*—his intellectual gear always proving helpful but not decisively so. He discards his signs in waystations, for whatever help they may be to anyone stumbling after him, but at last knowing they are, *as signs*, inadequate in themselves alone to bring any traveler to that believed country of truth which lies beyond the necessity of signs.

2

In his analysis of what he calls "the age of the theorist-consumer," Walker Percy late in his life remarks the erosion of intellect by the theorist. He is characterizing our age in the interest of addressing, as best he can, the repeated question put to him, "Why Are You a Catholic?" (*Crisis*, September 1990). "Theory supersedes political antinomies like 'conservative' versus 'liberal,' Fascist versus Communist, right versus left." Those terms are in such decay as not to speak to the heart of any significant concept. But then, surprisingly, Percy at once begins to use the term *liberal* in a pejorative sense to describe an amalgam of the theorist and the consumer, by implication a Modernist creature—one of those "denizens of the present age" who is "intoxicated by the theories and the goods of the age." (One is reminded of Flannery O'Connor's remark that "the theories are worse than the furies.") Percy is engaging in a rhetorical strategy that concerns us.

We see what is afoot when he maintains that "America is probably the last and best hope of the world" because, "it preserves a certain innocence and freedom." Brave words, confronted by overwhelming reality, so that these words must be for Percy himself an expression of forlorn hope. For, though "Americans are the nicest, most generous, and sentimental people on earth," it is the Americans who "have killed more unborn children than any nation in history." How is one to reconcile such "niceness" with such destruction? Percy attempts to do so, though one is not convinced that he is himself convinced of the possibility of reconciling the poles of this inescapable contradiction in the national character. Anyone seriously interested in Percy as either essayist or novelist will have but perverted his work not to address as very real and crucial to his work this insurmountable contradiction to which he returns again and again. It is in the interest of persuading us to consider it in its manifestations in our social fabric, in order to recognize its entrenchment in the intellectual deportment of "Americans," that he practices the specific rhetorical strategy at hand.

What he effects by the strategy is to shift the inclusive term *American* to the vaguer term *liberal*, a term to which over the past two or three decades has accrued a heavy pejorative sense. He here uses it to represent a thoughtless amalgam of theorist-consumer, an intellectual failure through which there occurs the horror of the slaughter of innocents by abortion. And in remarking his shifting of terms, we must remember a cautionary note struck at the very beginning of his essay, as it is often struck by Percy in interviews and in essays. He puts it teasingly. Novelists, he says, "are a devious lot to begin with, disinclined to say anything straight out." That playful disclaimer softens for the theorist-consumer American the Jeremiad about to descend upon him. Though repeatedly insistent that he is neither philosopher nor prophet but a novelist, Percy's inescapable burden of words is an indictment of our age as one of failed theory, out of which rises its consequent unbridled appetite. The argument is "deviously" advanced by this particular novelist: That is, he advances it by indirection through wit and humor in a complex satiric indirection whose playfulness draws us into the deadly serious realities of our age, ourselves the most central object indicted. The novelist, he says here, comes at "things and people from the side so to speak, especially the blind side, the better to get at them."

The devious shift of term from *American* to *liberal*, then, makes more subtle the devastating point he is making as a central indictment of our age, a point carried throughout his fiction by indirection, though it emerges most directly in his *Thanatos Syndrome*, the last of his novels. *American* is the inclusive term, *liberal* a specific which allows us "Americans" a moment of suspense from the inclusive indictment underway. Thus, if antinomy of terms is not superseded by a general intellectual collapse preventing even the novelist his indirection—or rather, if the decay of terms is an effect of such a collapse more than a cause of it— it is a cautionary advantage to the novelist as prophet of that reality to be very careful with his *devil terms*, as Richard Weaver, that kindred rhetorical critic of "liberalism," put it.

Percy would no doubt take an amused interest in the recent attempt to justify the liberal mind he is here attacking, an attempt to recover the term from its "devil" dimension in the general pejorative sense of *liberal*.

There is current an almost whimsically satiric counter-offensive. One hears self-declared liberals speaking of the "L word" as if thereby defending an ideal, through a piety afraid to speak its name, though by typography rebuking the "conservative" hesitancy to use scatological signs. Indeed, that the name is dangerous to the self-declared liberal politician has proved adequately evidenced, as for instance in the 1992 primary elections in the fate of Iowa's Tom Harkin, who announced himself from the beginning as "proud" to be called a "liberal." One fares little better in rescuing the term by a recent frontal assault in defense of liberalism such as David Barash's *The L Word*, published by Morrow in 1991. Barash's subtitle speaks with an aggressive truculence as the only possible way to restore the politically discredited position: *An Unapologetic Thoroughly Biased Long Overdue Explication and Celebration of Liberalism*.

Our interest in the current battle over the "L" word is of some importance to our concern. For Percy as a "devious" novelist, the social and political wars between "liberals" and "conservatives" have been very much in evidence throughout his life as destructive of fellowship through signs. In his indirection, we shall find him describing himself as "liberal," and resisting the attempt to categorize him as "conservative" in light of his continuing opposition to abortion and euthanasia. We observe, then, as in the instance of Barash's book, a certain devious playfulness in the very theorist-consumer mind upon which Percy performs his exploratory surgery with signs, a pathological exploration from which Percy does not entirely exclude himself, perhaps making his exploration more persuasive thereby. Beware of terms, he insists, until the term is firmly related to the reality of existence itself, and especially in relation to our existence as social or political creatures, who have set aside our true nature named by such a sign as *intellectual soul incarnate*.

Now Barash, by his reductionist attack upon the "conservative" in defense of his idealized "liberal," intends to rob his opponent of a pejorative purchase in the term he would defend. But the attempt to rescue through satiric wit or explosive ridicule such as Barash's seems hardly effective. As abandoned signs in the political desert nevertheless remind us, Tom Harkin received 2 percent of the Georgia primary vote, in a meager voter turnout. In Colorado, which gave a majority to one Jerry Brown, Harkin also received 2 percent. Among neither liberals nor conservatives is it apparent that beneath the confusion of the political scene lies any viable grounding of an "American" position. As for Georgia, Percy remarks wryly, there is that "certain type of Southern Presbyterian lady," especially Georgian, who doesn't mince words about his Catholicism. After a devastating paraphrase of such a lady's objection to his betrayal of his family and tradition, by joining "them," the Catholics, he sums up, through a satiric indirect quotation, her objection as she might make it: "I mean there's a difference between a simple encounter with God in a plain place with one's own kind without all that business of red candles and beads and priest in a box—I mean, how could you?"

These Americans are, from Percy's perspective, whether Tom Harkin the Iowa "liberal" or the Georgia Presbyterian lady "conservative," primarily patrons of the theorist-consumer state of mind. Their own rhetorical maneuvers with terms are but a surface encounter of reality which their terms as shibboleths allow them in their setting themselves apart from each other. Of this general failure of "Americans" Percy is certain. From his position he sees their shallow certitude: Through *science* applied to *appetite*, in its broadest sense, Tom Harkin and the Georgia lady share a consensus position, oblivious of their kinships. Indeed, science as an instrument to justify appetite leads to a new doctrine, explicit or implicit, replacing the old doctrine called Original Sin. We might call it the Cholesterol Doctrine, if we recognize how generally applicable it is to the texture of our lives and not limited to a reading of our blood. It is a doctrine emphatically centered in life as merely biological. To apply Percy's words to justify our term Cholesterol Doctrine, "It is appropriate that actions be carried out as the applications of theory and the needs of consumption require." Those needs are on every hand given a social justification as a substitute for either philosophical or theological grounding to our "needs." It is applicable, then, within our political, environmental, social expectations, whether Tom Harkin's liberalism or the Georgia Presbyterian lady's concern for her Catholic kinsman (Percy) who declares himself to her embarrassment "one of *them*," meaning the hoi polloi of humanity in Covington, Louisiana: "Irish, Germans, Poles, Italians, Cajuns, Hispanics, Syrians, and God knows what else," as Percy summarizes his neighbors.

3

Such is our deracinated estate as Americans, whether as wandering liberals or settled conservatives. And that is why, though we might be properly shocked, we ought not to be surprised, providing only that we look with open honesty at the realities of "the American way." At the close of our century and the beginning a new one, we are confronted by strange contradictions in ourselves. That openness, from Percy's perspective, lies in being "open to signs." If one has eyes to see, ears to hear, certain realities of our disordered circumstances as community are inescapable. How could we fail to consider then that this "American"—this "liberal"—

way of social and political deportment favors abortion (in Percy's words) "just as the Nazis did years ago. The only difference is that the Nazis favored it for theoretical reasons (eugenics, racial purity), while present-day liberals favor it for consumer needs (unwanted, inconvenience)." There is no inconsistency here, says Percy. That is, there is no *logical* inconsistency, since both liberal and Nazi positions are founded in a common initiating principle established by the theorist and bequeathed as a residual "scientific" feeling about the meaning of life itself to the consumer. That feeling we embrace, as consumers, as if it were a religious principle. It is built into the supposition of the holiness of our "self" as established by our "need," which is better termed a convenience to our unexamined desire.

Hence, says Percy, "Liberals understandably see no contradiction" in their "favoring abortion and euthanasia on the one hand and the 'sacredness of the individual,' care for the poor, the homeless, the oppressed on the other." Consider the "liberal editor," he suggests. Such a Noman, assuming the authority of Everyman in this media age, may see and be disturbed by the poor and homeless "on his way to work," but once in that bastion of righteousness, his office, he reads "a medical statistic in his own paper about one million abortions" and it registers as only a statistic, far removed from the reality of the destruction of specific, individual persons. That persons are the victim of abortion is the reality from which the statistic is derived, and the horrible is sanitized by its reduction to mere statistic.

Percy relentlessly concludes that his liberal editor (a species of intellect repeatedly demonstrated by various studies as overwhelmingly dominant in the general media) and the Nazi are "both consistent in an age of theory and consumption."[1] Untouched by the continuing holocaust of abortion, little troubled by the growing justification of euthanasia, and increasingly advocating euthanasia as a legal social policy, it is little wonder that such a mind can see as only quaint a figure like Mother Teresa, with her warning: "If a mother can kill her unborn child, then I can kill you and you can kill me." How can Percy's "liberal" take Mother Teresa as anything but quaint? He may speak of her as "other-worldly," meaning unrelated to the realities of *this* world—in which his own survival and prospering are the central issue. That small figure of an aged nun "kill" *anyone*? Preposterous. And so one is relieved of thought through the spectacle of her person, her words seen as comic in relation to those supposed realities in the liberal perspective upon which she delivers her own devastating critique. Hers is "just a way of saying something, her opinion, with which I do not agree. Mine is a better opinion, certified as general by statistical evidence of popular acceptance and support." Or so Percy's "editor" might put his conclusion in signs.

In the light of such difficulty with our signs in relation to the realities we would have them signify, we have yet to *understand* our last century, though we *know* so much about it. And the most central failure of understanding lies in our failure of responsibility to signs. Our ways of saying things have succeeded in the 20th century, more than in any other, in destroying things by the acts of our mis-saying. That is Percy's continuous concern, from the time of his awakening to the problem when he read Kierkegaard and St. Thomas Aquinas at a crucial point in his own "liberal" life. After that point he could but react with increasing horror to the realities of our age, though his coming to terms with that horror, lest despair overwhelm him, was to take an incisive indirection through signs to recall us to reality. The sheer horror intrudes again and again, witnessed in such essays as "Why Are You a Catholic?" and also in his 1988 letter to the *New York Times* (see Note 1), a letter not only unpublished but unacknowledged. Given Percy's general presence among us, that refusal says much about the "liberal" editor and his statistics.

The perversion of sign in the interest of avoiding reality, to the comfort of the theorist-consumer: That is the pervasive disease Percy set himself to remedy as physician of sign, as novelist. To say that a mother's unborn child is not a child but a physical disease to be treated, as advocates of abortion have sometimes said, justifies the continuing hidden holocaust, in which as "Americans," as consumer "liberals" and "conservatives," we participate. Thus the abortionist calls himself a "health care provider" and his clinic "a health care facility." He or she is justified as serving in a high calling when pregnancy is defined and generally accepted as a disease. That such a definition not be taken as my own rhetorical excess: Dr. Elizabeth Connell, an associate director of the Rockefeller Foundation, who at the time was also President of Planned Parenthood Physicians, declared to an audience (in 1976) that "pregnancy is a kind of nasty communicable disease." Her speech at the particular conference of concerned abortionists had been prepared by an opening paper, written by employees of the United States Department of Health, Education, and Welfare at the Centers for Disease Control in Atlanta, Georgia—a paper entitled "Unwanted Pregnancy: A Sexually Transmitted Disease." What higher "official" authority is possible to the cause? Thus editors are reassured by "scientists" as superseding philosophers and theologians.

Thus stated, one is hard-pressed to distinguish pregnancy from either syphilis or AIDS. What gives the lie to these signs, of course, is the reality of the *thing* misnamed, a reality which intrudes at last upon our recognition through actual, immediate experience separate from any naming of the experience. Any parent knows this, holding his first newborn and suddenly engaged by the child's eyes for the first time. In that moment, the whole world is changed, for father or mother. Still, Nominalism as the science of public policy in our day continues its actively destructive role against reality. And we are required, by our possible rescue of the sign back to reality, to call things aright, to name things for what they are. Here then, let us say that abortion and euthanasia as understood and practiced at the close of the 20th century and in our bright prospect for convenience in the next are species of an inevitable spiritual cannibalism, once *person* is reduced from its sacredness. Meanwhile, the sophistications of biotechnology obscure from us that ours are acts of retrogression. Our acts are made to seem, through the spectacles of applied science—that is, of science applied to our hungers for "consumer needs"—awe-inspiring justifications of appetites. Under that climate of feeling, technical advances are "progressive." Little wonder that against this perverse destructiveness of the existential world through the manipulation of signs Percy sets himself so resolutely. That is at the heart of his unceasing concern for signs in relation to truth. He does not intend to mince words but at times will shout that truth—even to the editors of the *New York Times*: The nihilism pervasive in our theorist-consumer justifications of *needs* is in its reality a spiritual cannibalism whose principal victim proves ironically to be the theorist-consumer himself. How have we come to this pass? Percy as deracinated Southerner engages that question with growing recognitions that lead him to a more comfortable but more intense accommodation to that question, a paradox we must explore.

4

There are two signal events which one might use to bracket the intellectual arena within which Walker Percy emerges as philosophical novelist, both of them occurring in Tennessee. The first is the Scopes Trial at Dayton in 1925. The second, a few months after Percy's Jefferson Lecture and a few months before his death, was the 1989 divorce trial, at Maryville, of Mary Davis and Junior L. Davis. The first, sensationalized by H. L. Mencken, is deeply embedded in our memory. The second has largely escaped our notice, though its significance makes it a crucial moment in Western thought. One need not dwell too long on the Scopes Trial, a test case brought in consequence of the Tennessee legislature's "Anti-Evolution Bill" enacted in March of 1925. We may nevertheless suggest a broadening of our understanding of that event, given the popular reading of it as an indictment of the benighted South. We might remember, for instance, that there was also a prohibition by law of teaching of the Bible in the state-supported institutions of Tennessee at that time. As for the conduct of that trial, Richard Weaver presents an arresting critique in his "Dialectic and Rhetoric at Dayton, Tennessee," *The Ethics of Rhetoric* (1953).[2]

For our immediate purpose, we recall that this event was largely responsible for turning that group of young poets at Vanderbilt, the Fugitives, to their "Agrarian" phase, leading to *I'll Take My Stand* (1930). Those young minds, who had begun by declaring themselves fugitive from "the high-caste Brahmins of the Old South" in the interest of recovering viable roots in nature and tradition through their poetry, turned to polemics. That they were about something far deeper than a concern for a romantic relation with the soil is evident in their 1930 manifesto, when carefully read with the attention to sign learned of the New Criticism—in which those same young minds were active participants. Indeed, one might well return to the concerns in *I'll Take My Stand* with the advantages of hindsight as strengthened by the later work of Eric Voegelin, especially his *From Enlightenment to Revolution* (1975); or more directly to the point of the disquiet raised by the Scopes Trial, to Etienne Gilson's *From Aristotle to Darwin, and Back Again* (1971, 1984). To name these writers and their signs is to be reminded of the intellectual community within which Percy engages his own enigma: his "Southernness."

We remember the Fugitive-Agrarians as those of whom Walker Percy remarked that "I never fitted in with those fellows." But given their initiating perspective upon Modernism as it might be understood by hindsight, one might argue that he fitted rather better than he supposed. Certainly, their concern was precisely the one Percy himself comes to emphasize in his interview with *Crisis* on the occasion of his Jefferson Lecture: the destructive effect of the theorist-consumer ambiance permeating our age.[3] It is Percy's concern, given his understanding of *person* as more than abstract theory and certainly more than a designation of an infectious consumer of the world's body. For the Agrarian position has as its premise the spiritual nature of man as *person*, understanding that nature as the ground proper to the emergence of any viable community. Their concern is far more complex than a "back-to-the-soil" movement as it is frequently caricatured. It is that popular caricature, one suspects, which set Percy himself away from them—that, plus his initial skepticism as a detached Stoic at the time of his early encounter of them, under the early Virgil to his intellectual journeying, his "Uncle Will" Percy, remembered for *Lanterns on the Levee*.

What the Fugitive-Agrarians opposed initially, and what Percy comes to oppose in the end, is the *scientism* of the theorist. In their early attacks upon the scientism originating in Darwinian Evolution, they were rebuffed by the Chancellor of Vanderbilt: "We shall build more laboratories," said the Chancellor in response to them. That has been the increasing academic (theoretical) pressure upon community since the 1920s. But the irony of Chancellor Kirkland's prescription to cure the benighted position he saw in his young faculty is that it comes to fruition in our second event, the trial at Marysville on August 10, 1989. For *scientism*, the popular ambiance of thought binding theorist and consumer in a Modernist stance, is at last being called in to question by science itself.[4] The central issue in this later trial is science's discoveries about the emergence of *person* as uniquely particular in nature from inception.

Ignatius Press, in *The Concentration Can* (1992), has published an account of the expert testimony given by the late Jérôme Lejeune, M.D., Ph.D., professor of fundamental genetics at the René Descartes University of Paris (the name of that institution an added irony, Percy would note), at the 1989 trial in Tennessee mentioned above. Lejeune was a Fellow of the Pontifical Academy of Science (Rome) and of the American Academy of Arts and Sciences. He received the prestigious Kennedy Award for discovering the chromosomal basis of mongolism. His credentials run on and on. Included in *The Concentration Can* are the transcripts of Professor Lejeune's testimony and of the cross-examination, and the opinion delivered by Judge William Dale Young, along with other relevant material. There are especially the accompanying observations of Professor Lejeune in looking back upon his experience in a Tennessee courtroom. What one has in the volume, then, is a significant "case book" in which the testimony of science emerges in support of the argument of philosophers such as Jacques Maritain and Etienne Gilson, and of scholastics such as Thomas Aquinas, on *personhood* as unique and as existing from the point of biological conception.

The question at issue in the divorce trial at Maryville, Tennessee (the place name an added irony), is surrounded by a confusing context of Modernist thought. A civil divorce was underway, initiated by Mary Davis after nine years of marriage. Physically unable to bear children, she and her husband had earlier participated in an *in vitro* fertilization of her eggs, with the intent of implanting the embryos in Mary Davis's womb. (On the questionable issue of *in vitro* fertilization as a principle, one would do well to read Donald De Marco's *Biotechnology and the Assault on Parenthood*, 1991.) But the issue facing Judge Young was a *fait accompli*, the present existence of seven fertilized embryos maintained in liquid nitrogen. The question at issue between the Davises, in Professor Lejeune's formulation, was whether those presences were a property or persons; the husband argued that they were the former, the wife the latter. His own position is that they are undeniably persons, on the evidence of the science of genetics. They are persons suspended in a "concentration can," the tube of liquid nitrogen. And his argument brings to bear the accumulated knowledge of genetic science as of August 1989. The evidence he articulates clearly and directly, so that portions of the transcript, as spontaneously given on short notice, are most remarkable and arresting.

The immediate circumstances are worth reporting. Professor Lejeune was called by a representative of Mary Davis on Monday, August 7, and requested to fly from Paris to Tennessee to bear expert witness on the question on her behalf. Professor Lejeune, having heard report of Mary Davis's position (she "calls them her children" he was told) agreed to come at once, but he could not come before Thursday because of commitments to his patients. The final hearing, scheduled for that Wednesday, was delayed one day, and Professor Lejeune appeared on Thursday after his hurried trip. He came at considerable personal and financial expense because of Mary Davis's attitude toward her "children." But the convincing point was Professor Palmer's saying to Lejeune (Palmer an intermediary), "She even stated she would prefer to see them raised by another to whom they could be given rather than know that they were to be frozen forever." To that remark Professor Lejeune responded, "If the mother said that, the trial is already decided. The true mother is the one who wants the life of the child—Solomon decided that once and for all; who, therefore, would oppose it?"

The answer to that question, as Professor Lejeune knew all too well, is that the whole Modernist temper opposes it, since *person* has been progressively reduced to *property*, whether by the state as in Nazi Germany and the Soviet Union or by the consumer-theorist spirit in the West in the name of appetitive convenience. In short, by the reductionist philosophy underlying Modernism. What Professor Lejeune was confronting, specifically in his own words, was "a nominalist quarrel" with the "partisans of the nonhumanity" of the embryo, those who had long since coined and used the "meaningless neologism, the term pre-embryo." For there is "no pre-embryo, since by definition the embryo is the youngest form of a being." His task as witness, then, was to bring to the support of that definition his considerable knowledge of genetics. Mary Davis's "children," in the light of that evidence, were enslaved in a "concentration can" by liquid nitrogen so that without "reestablishing slavery there is no third term," no middle road between the human that the law protects and the rest, of which one disposes as he pleases, i.e., a disposal as mere "property."

His task, then, was to present the scientific evidence justifying his position that, from the moment of conception, an embryo is a unique person, the evidence biological and not theological. His testimony was that of the scientist, and not that of philosopher or theologian, which is why he proved discomfiting to the nominalist opposition, including his cross-examiner, Charles Clifford. Clifford pressed Professor Lejeune: "The zygote should be treated with the same respect as an adult human being?" The tone of incredulity in the question is more apparent in the context. Professor Lejeune's response: "I'm telling you, he is a human being" judged by scientific evidence. It is "the judge who will tell whether this human being has the same rights as the others." Whether or not Lejeune approves of *in vitro* fertilization is also quite beside the point, for the issue at hand is that the seven fertilized eggs exist in suspension within a "concentration can," and the question is whether they are to be understood as persons or as property, and if property, then destroyed.

The evidence introduced by this expert witness was not only technical, but complicated in the extreme, so that both Professor Lejeune's gift of analogy and his wit and good humor were needed to clarify the evidence for the court. At the heart of the evidence is the current understanding of geneticists, respected in the scientific community itself, regarding the nature of the chromosomes affecting a new creature at the point of encounter of sperm with egg at conception. The engagement of sperm and egg at fertilization "produces a personal constitution, entirely typical of this very one human being, which has never occurred before and will never occur again." In this uniqueness lies the evidential ground that the fertilized egg is from that moment no longer a property to be held, either separately or by joint custody, by the paternal and maternal contributors to its being.

The mystery of this incarnation of person lies in the "program" which is written in the DNA, Professor Lejeune testified, his immediate analogy related to the computer, but carefully distinguished from it. There are, he reminded the court, "twenty-three different pieces of program carried by the spermatozoa and there are twenty-three different homologous pieces carried by the ovum." The symmetry is misleading if one does not know the latest discoveries about the relation between the joined chromosomes, evidence which makes the argument for an *equal* participation in the new being by sperm and ovum a facile argument quite beside the mystery of this unique incarnation. But before this latest discovery about fertilization can be added to his argument, he must make further preparation.

The chromosome's nature is important: "A long thread of DNA in which information is written." In this respect it bears analogy "to a mini-cassette, in which a symphony is written." In the wedding of chromosomes at inception there is effected a "whole symphony," a symphony which "plays itself." That is, it is a new person, its life its peculiar music. As for that mini-cassette, now initiated into a playing of itself, it is *mini* indeed. Were we to imagine a physical gathering of chromosomes sufficient to generate the number of persons necessary to replace the entire population of the earth, one for one, it would be a gathering the size of "two aspirin tablets." And yet within the single chromosome the incipient language in its calling forth of a particular being is such that the information is beyond measure. One has initial DNA, one set from father and one from mother, each of which carries "bits of information" numbered at ten to the eleventh power. Adding the information about the "subscript" in a person now individuated by conception raises it to ten to the fifteenth power. "To give you an idea, just to print letter by letter all that is written in the DNA of a fertilized egg ... you would need five times the Encyclopedia Britannica.... But now you have also the care of all the molecules that are inside the cytoplasm which will recognize the message, which will send a message to the next cell," a matter of "some million times more bits of information." No computer is adequate to the complex, and if it were, Professor Lejeune added under cross-examination, the "machine would be a fertilized egg itself."

Now, just as in the reproduction of a statue in bronze, the producing of this new person is by *form* as the genius of DNA, as the sculpture is a *form* of the genius of the sculptor. And here lies a telling point for Professor Lejeune. For what is "printed" is not *matter* but the *information*, an inspiring to, an inspiriting of, matter. For "matter cannot live at all. What occurs is an animation of matter." We are here still speaking of the single zygote, the fertilized, undivided, initiating cell, about whose nature recent genetic knowledge is prophetically revealing. That first cell is not differentiated as later cells will be, developing the nervous system or fingers or brain. But it already contains the whole of the initiated being, in which respect this first cell "knows more and is more specialized ... than any cell which is later in our organism." It is, says Professor Lejeune, on the evidence of genetic science, the "very young human being."

In respect to this unfolding incarnation of this "young human being," through the division of the initiating cell, there follows a demonstrated event: It first splits into two cells and then one of these splits, constituting a three-cell stage to the becoming. After this stage, the division proceeds by multiples of two, a decided change in the relation of the cells to the evidence concerning a three-cell stage. There is then an intricate relation at this early stage, differentiating the three cells from the population of cells such as is represented in a tissue culture. The three cells together bear the "full imago, that is, the whole form" of this unique young person. What happens? The *understanding* of this mystery of person as *becoming* is incomplete, but the *evidence* of the reality is decisive for Prof. Lejeune. No other cell will ever have the fullness implicit in the initiated cell. "When it's split in two we know that exchange of information comes from one cell to the other one. When it's split in three it receives information: We are an individual."

But past this stage of becoming, the underlying system is progressively changed. Cells begin to differentiate, to become specialized in a manner subordinate to that unique summary of person carried by the initiating cell. Some develop nails or skin or brain, and so on. The mystery is that what is "written" in the first cell, the potential wholeness of a unique person, is not written in the individual cells past the three-cell stage. In the experimental manipulation of cells, specifically with mice, the experimenters discover that four cells will not work, nor will five. Only three, the experiment involving the disassembly of cells "inside the zona pellucida of a sixteen-cell embryo of a mouse." The three-cell stage following fertilization "knows" that "we are not a population of cells, we are bound to be an individual," an individual which "will build himself according to his own rule," that is, according to the information it knows of its own particularity. (One cannot, of course, escape metaphorical language in attempting to articulate the genetic discoveries. Nevertheless, Professor Lejeune speaks quite comfortably of the "knowledge" carried by the DNA as distinct from the mere "matter" that carries that knowledge as its form.)

As for this knowledge, Professor Lejeune likens it to the bar code familiar to us on products we buy in the grocery store, a code "read" by the cash register. It is now clearly established that this "bar code" of the discrete person is unique, he says, so that it is "not any longer a theory that each of us is unique." An additional advance in genetic knowledge is that one can detect in the single cell of an organism its originality, its relation to that whole organism made up of the differentiating cells from which the cell has been taken. But the most revolutionary discovery is that "some bases of DNA" carry "an extra little piece we call a methyl … which is just hooked on it and changes a little the form of one of the bars of this long scale which is the DNA molecule." The discovery, by M. A. Surani, reveals a characteristic of the DNA molecule which is "exactly comparable to what an intelligent reader does when he wants to underline with a pen, to highlight some passage or to scratch, delete another sentence." Thus a gene will be "put to silence, but if it is demethylated on the next division, on the next cell, then it will speak again." Such is "a kind of language telling the chromosome: You have to give this information, but for this other information, shut up, do not say this for the moment." For, in the light of the prodigious "knowledge" carried by the discrete chromosome, if it expressed everything it "knows" every time, "the energy spent in one cell would be much more than the energy of our whole body."

It develops out of this discovery that the DNA carried by the sperm "is not underlined or crossed by this methylation on the same place as the equivalent chromosomes carried by the ovum." Both sperm and ovum contribute a distinct speaking to the differentiated person, the fertilized ovum, but the messages differ, each message a discrete gift to the effected person, the young one-cell person. The difference is explored experimentally, when with mice there is made a pseudo-zygote, a pseudo fertilized cell. On the one hand there is the diploid cell, "containing only two sets of nuclei, both from the sperm," but "it fails to grow." The same experiment with two nuclei of maternal origin, which by earlier theory ought to grow, will not. But there is an interesting development nevertheless. Though they do not build a "full imago," a mouse, a whole form, they do specialize. The male nuclei will produce little cysts which "look like the membranes and placenta that the child normally builds around himself" in the womb. This "*androgenote*" develops from male nuclei. But the development out of two joined female nuclei makes "spare parts," "pieces of skin, ... teeth, ... a little nail, but all that in a full disorder." All this is experimental, with mice. What of humans?

There is the evidence of "*dermoid cysts*," the division of a non-fertilized egg inside the ovary of a virgin girl, medically established. "It will never give a little baby, but it makes the spare parts, teeth, nails, all ... mixed in incomprehensible disorder." Additionally, after normal fertilization there develops on occasion, cysts called *hydatidiformis moles*, an effect when the maternal pronuclei, for unknown reason, has died. In the light of these clinically established anomalies and from the experimental information from mice, one concludes that there is "a specialized" information carried by the sperm differing from the information carried by the ovum. At this "extra-ordinarily tiny level of information built into the chromosomes," says Professor Lejeune, what is being discovered is that "paternal duty was to build the shelter and to make the gathering of food; to build the hut and do the hunting. And the maternal trick was household and building of spare parts so that the individual can build itself."

Given our current confused climate of concern for the family, for the relation of paternal and maternal duties, these are surely fighting words to some. But they require a most careful consideration. And lest the blind battle of the sexes that presently divides community distort this intricate mystery of personhood, we must remember that we are speaking of *person* as uniquely originated, but only by the participation of both a paternal and maternal chromosomal engagement, in which new relationship from the evidence of science those easy shibboleths used in gender contentions are quite beside the reality of this new person. What is also clear is that the embodiment of this participation, the incarnation of a unique person as zygote by maternal-paternal gift, bears in it a continuing presence of both the paternal and maternal participation. If one were much given to mysticism, he might conclude that here lies a sign of the mystery of the Holy Trinity, in this single cell which Professor Lejeune speaks of as an "*imago*."

How richly appropriate, Professor Lejeune's exposition, to Walker Percy's concerns. For it is as scientist turned Catholic that Percy engages the theorist-consumer for whom abortion is a "right" centering in a conception of the person as but biological entity in an accidental cosmos. It can only be unsettling to such an ideological "self" as Percy's "liberal" to have to deal with such ambient mystery gathered about *person* by such "scientific" evidence of the nature of life itself. Indeed, Percy as scientist will discover himself to be also poet in his response to the mystery of life. And in Professor Lejeune's exposition lies a metaphor speaking to the mystery of life in this *imago*, this actual unique person who is so at the point of conception. If we reject the Nominalistic disjunction of signs from reality, whereby metaphor becomes arbitrary (as both Professor Lejeune and Percy explicitly reject Nominalism), we are drawn by metaphor closer to the mystery of life in such a coming-into-unique-being as this *imago*, remembering that old metaphor which declares the person created "in the image of god."

How welcome Professor Lejeune's scientific revelations about the mystery of life would be as well to Thomas Aquinas—and to a Thomistic realist. As such, one might explore that metaphor as suggestive of the nature of intellect potential in the incipient single cell—the *image* of a Creator Source as enabled by that Source *through* the mediation of paternal and maternal participation in becoming one by sexual union. A newly created person is joined most miraculously in this single cell. As unique intellect, this new person—from Thomas's epistemological perspective—will move out of its biological incarnation through the actions of intuitive and rational faculties of intellect. The one—dare one say it—is metaphorically "feminine"—the intuitive; the other "masculine"—the rational. They complement each other in ways whose analogy might lie in the fascinating genetic discovery of that complementary, but differing, specialization of information carried by sperm and ovum. Indeed, Thomas, were he actually with us, would probably pursue the analogy.

In the sexual act, then, a new word is spoken by conception. And slowly that new word, already spoken in the fertilized cell, reveals itself. At three weeks, for instance, one knows a fetus as Tom Thumb, Professor Lejeune suggests, a creature in detail already like the person yet to be "born," but just the "size of my thumb." He adds: "Each of us has been a Tom Thumb in the womb of his mother. Women have always known that there was a kind of underground country, a kind of vaulted shelter, with a kind of red light and curious noise, in which very tiny humans were having a very curious and marvelous life. That is the story of Tom Thumb."

What women have always "known" is not the Word spoken, but that they have in their keep a new word spoken under the mysterious aegis of the Word. And they know it under the Thomistic principle of proper proportionality. It is reflected in that early Mary's "Behold the handmaid of the Lord; be it unto me according to thy word." When we say *know* here, we do not mean "know in rational formulation." It has been most destructive of the community of family to deprecate intuitive knowledge, a distortion largely to the discredit of the rational, the "male," intellect. This "knowing" by immediacy is the grounding of rational knowledge, as St. Thomas recognizes. Thus by intuitive intellect one knows, without the necessity of sophistications of terminology, the distinction of *Word* from *word*. That is the central recognition which turns that once rationalist poet, T. S. Eliot, from a rational detachment from reality after his spiritual trauma witnessed by *The Waste Land*. Nor need one *know rationally* the complexity of *proper proportionality*, on which the whole of Thomism is built.[5]

Given our emotionally charged moment, it will continue to be possible to reject or disregard, without refuting, the evidence of genetic science as presented by Professor Lejeune: At conception a unique life exists.[6] But in the end the Tennessee Supreme Court reversed Judge Young's decision (on June 1, 1992), that court holding that the father of the embryos, Junior L. Davis, could not be required to consent to their survival. By such a judgment, that court rejected as if inconsequential the very probable reality of Professor Lejeune's testimony to the holiness in individual life itself. The high court thus holds the embryos to be property and not persons. It is an act whereby they reject reality through a gnostic *feeling*, rather than by the gnostic *thought* which one ordinarily attributes to the theorist, and in the interest of a convenience to the father in this instance. That *feeling* thus justifies an appetitive intention in the nay-sayer, to the satisfaction of a self-love, the intention which is most destructive of the self.

Walker Percy was deeply given to thought as the proper governor of feeling, and we know him more largely given to scientific than to philosophical thought, despite his acknowledged debt to Kierkegaard and St. Augustine and St. Thomas Aquinas. He is uncomfortable when addressed as a "philosophical" novelist, but becomes increasingly comfortable when engaging the aberrant Modernist spirit from the context of its own pretenses to empirical science. That is why, among other reasons, Dr. Lejeune's testimony on *person* as reduced to *property* in our theorist-consumer age is highly appropriate to an understanding of Percy's position. Both look at a Modernist inclination to death by reduction as an effect out of pseudo-empiricism parading as science, the new *scientism* which delivers such arresting products as *in vitro* conception. Lejeune's perspective is that of the practiced geneticist. Percy's is that of the experienced psychologist, a medical man who himself underwent three years of psychiatric therapy, slowly turning to the context of mind as larger than the science of psychology. He is so turned at first by reading a Danish philosopher and also an old scholastic. He comes at last to the larger embrace of philosophy and science and theology by Mother Church.

As for this address to the Modernist reduction of life to mechanistic death, we propose the poet's parable in support of these wiser empiricists, Percy and Lejeune, the parable bearing a certain "Southern" flavor that Percy might appreciate. It addresses, through a Percy-like indirection, pretensions to empirical certainties held doggedly by the theorist-consumer mind, a mind bound from nowhere to nowhere. Two truck drivers, the parable says, have come to an overpass across their road. The ten-foot clearance, clearly marked, won't let their twelve-foot trailer pass under. But one driver says to the other, after looking around carefully, "I don't see any cops. Let's make a run for it!"

5

Percy remarks at the close of "Why Are You a Catholic?" in *Crisis* magazine that "in the desert of theory and consumption, nothing of significance remains but signs. And only two signs are of significance in a world where all theoretical cats are gray. One is oneself and the other is the Jews." There is an ambiguity in his terms with which we must come to terms. But nevertheless we may at once agree with what we sense as intended in the argument, making a distinction of our own as we approach Percy's observations about the *sign*. Oneself *is*, i.e., exists, so that *oneself* is not itself a sign but an existential thing of which we are already self-aware. The Jews, too, *are*: They exist. This is to say that these two things (the Jews and the self) exist, in recognition of which we seek an understanding through signs. By our experience of them as actual we would certify realities by concept, and share that recognition as common to created intellectual souls through the mediation of signs. Percy—this demurrer aside for the moment—argues that these (our particular *self* as immediate to our consciousness and the *Jews* as a continuing body of selves in history) confront our intellectual complacency because neither can be reduced from their existential reality to mere theory. The point is valid, as evidenced by our separate, discrete experience of our *self* and of those continuing presences in history separate from that self, the Jews as a people—a continuing community despite the ravages of history.

Nevertheless, one wants to approach this mystery of the inescapable self, which Dr. Lejeune's genetic science establishes, and its relation to the *other*, as dramatized by Percy early and late, which he finds represented by the Jews as continuing witness. We may assert as self-evident to our experience (each of us as *this* person) that both the self and the Jews exist as realities beyond the inevitable reductionism of our signs, whether the signs of science or philosophy. For signs are never *comprehensive* of the thing itself. As intellectual creatures, we are burdened by the gift of signs as allowing a certain but limited purchase upon particularly existing things under their own finitudes within an inclusive, existential reality, the limitations of which we attempt to signify by *time* and *space*. The sign is a necessary instrument to intellect, according to its nature, and so it becomes the necessary instrument not only to Percy but as well to Percy's antithetic gnostic theorist who would control being. It seems probable, indeed, that the sign, while it may rescue intellect somewhat in the desert of existential reality, may also serve to lead intellect deeper into parching sands and away from any rescuing water. Destructiveness of the self through the sign, let us say, occurs precisely at that point at which *sign* is confused with *reality*, rather than being taken as a signal of a reality which the sign is incapable of reducing to an absolute comprehension by intellect. The dream of such a reduction by which intellect sees possible an absolute control of reality—if not today, then tomorrow—is the dream of the theorist whom Percy would oppose. For it is the theorist in his extremity of intent who supposes that sign may *literally* comprehend, thus certifying the theorist as not only omniscient but omnipotent in relation to existential reality. Such is his authority of the letter over the thing itself. Or so he dreams. Sign so used limits sign itself to Nominalistic enslavement to the will, but reduces the self to an enslavement to illusion.

That Percy understands this distinction emerges in his argument, although his own choice of terms somewhat obscures his point. The intent appears, for instance, in his version of an old argument of C. S. Lewis's against the presumptuous theorist. Lewis remarks that Freudianism can explain all, it would seem, except Sigmund Freud himself. Percy says, "You will look in vain in Darwin's *Origin of the Species* for an explanation of Darwin's behavior in writing *Origin of the Species*." And again, "The theorist is not encompassed by his theory. One's self is always a leftover from one's theory." Similarly, the Jews "are both a sign and a stumbling block" since they cannot be reduced to theory. (We might here remember a root sense of *scandal: stumbling block*.) May we not put the point more clearly if we say that, because the Jews are a continuing reality to our continuing experience, escaping theory, they are a stumbling block to the presumptions of the sign-maker theorist, who through sign intends a reduction of their reality as a people to the control of his sign? That is, they are a *presence*, as the *self* is a presence to that specific, unique consciousness which we designate "I." Both are undeniable realities, certified by our experience but not *comprehended* by any sign. The implication of experience as signified by intellect, as "signed forth" by intellect, is the crucial juncture for concern in our intellectually disintegrated age.

As for the *self* at the very center of this age of "dementia," as Percy also characterizes it, the very term is one of the most insistently abused. Because it is, that abuse affords Percy matter for his witty and devastating satire upon the theorists in his "Last Self-Help Book," *Lost in the Cosmos*. It is not that the *self* is not significant of an existential reality but that the term requires recovery to a clearer signification. For sign properly bears a truth in relation to the thing of which it is a sign, albeit a limited—not a comprehensive—truth. This haunting reality which we term the *self*, which cannot be subsumed by any theory using the instrumentality of signs, we must nevertheless attempt to *acknowledge* by sign. Let us say of it then that it is an immediate presence which its own intellect certifies as an experienced truth. There is an undeniable, self-evident knowledge of one's own actual existence, demonstrated to the self by its encounter with anything not the self. It is in recognition of this reality of consciousness that St. Augustine declares that even "If I am deceived, I exist." That is, despite intellectual error and though under the illusion of possessing truth, "I" must *be* if I am deluded. And so (in *The City of God*, XI, 26) he declares: "Without any delusive representation of images or phantasms, I am certain that I am, that I know, and that I delight in this. On none of these points do I fear the arguments of the skeptics of the Academy who say: What if you are deceived? For if I am deceived, I am."

Such is the fundamental, experiential certification of the self which refutes Cartesian Idealism even before it arises, over which Idealism so much rich ink has been spilt since Descartes. And we should observe that it is Cartesian Idealism which Percy finds a principal source of intellectual destruction in our Age of the Theorist-Consumer. That is his concern in his "The Fateful Rift: The San Andreas Fault in the Modern Mind." We suggest that the concept of the self, so troubling to the theorist, is *as concept* an effect in intellect consequent to a held truth: the held truth that oneself undeniably exists. What this means is that intellect possesses a certain knowledge which is precedent to its active reflection, whereby logic is deployed by reason in response to what is already known intellectually. Common sense, the common enemy of the gnostic theorist, recognizes that truth. It is this recognition by common sense which grounds a realism discomfiting to Cartesian Idealism. (The exposition of that realism is handily and incisively presented in refutation of Cartesian Idealism by Etienne Gilson in *Methodical Realism,* Christendom Press, 1990.)

We are engaged with an awkwardness of signification in the term *sign* as Percy intends his terms, but his concern for sign is a principal theme of his work early and late. Let us observe that he echoes T. S. Eliot's concern for language, but with a difference to be noted. Percy, like Eliot, is acutely aware always of (in Percy's words) "the infirmity of language itself." Words decay. As Eliot puts it, in *Burnt Norton,* words "Crack and sometimes break ... slip, slide, perish." They do so under the burden of our "imprecision of feeling," our very words assaulted by undisciplined "squads of emotion" (*East Coker*) as we struggle to establish a community between our awareness and existential reality, a community of which we are aware as an *other,* even as we are aware of our "self" as a part in it. But where Eliot would locate that decay which confuses in the word itself, the decay is rather in intellect, the proximate cause of the sign. Words are destroyed by intellectual neglect or abuse. Percy, however, would have it that "Language is a living organism and, as such, is subject to certain organic ailments." One might make the argument metaphorically, but it seems for Percy an argument carrying more literal burden than metaphorical, and as such contrasts to Eliot's. For Eliot, each venture of intellect is "a raid on the inarticulate" with signs, with "shabby equipment always deteriorating" (*East Coker*).

Percy's sense of the nature of language is closer to the argument made by Brice Parain, in *A Metaphysics of Language* (1971). Parain, too, finds language organic: "What is revealed to us ... in our moments of silence is that we are a kind of compost heap on which language germinates, grows, and flowers." In his little book, Parain is attempting to escape the entrapment of intellect by Cartesian Idealism. It is no accident that Parain is a favored philosopher of that pathos-ridden intellect similarly entrapped, Albert Camus, nor that Cartesian Idealism is a principal generator of that once-celebrated entrapment of the self, Existential philosophy, which figures prominently in Percy's own awakening. (Among those Percy recalls as important to his own thought are Camus and Sartre, but also Gabriel Marcel, somewhat superficially identified as a "Christian Existentialist" in surveys of recent philosophy.)

Insofar as it was through the Existentialists that Percy was alerted to the displacement of modern man by Cartesian Idealism, his tribute to these French philosophers is just. But one fears a lingering effect of Camus's and Sartre's thought on Percy's own conception of the *sign,* not healthful to his emerging vision of reality. It is an effect hinted at in his description of the nature of language as organic, a position which Marcel would hardly endorse. It is perhaps more evident in his understand-

ing of his responsibility, as novelist, to the mystery of sign. He says in
"Why Are You a Catholic?" that "One of the tasks of the saints is to renew
language, to sing a new song. The novelist, no saint, has a humbler task
… to deliver religion from the merely edifying." Eliot, after long engagement with the question of the poet's or novelist's responsibility to language, comes to a different conclusion from Percy's concern to rescue
religion. In the last of his major poems, *Little Gidding*, the poet declares
it his responsibility to "purify the dialect of the tribe."

What Eliot holds, by this point of his own wandering in the desert
as aided by uncertain signs, is that the responsibility of the poet is to his
"making," a recovery of intellect to existential reality through the sign.
It is for him an intellectual making which may prove fundamental to the
possibility of sainthood, for in the recovery of the sign to the truth of
things, to the sign's proper limited relation to existential reality, sainthood becomes a possibility. But that is not the poet's (the novelist's) primary responsibility as poet. The distinction here is one increasingly
evident to Percy (as it became for Eliot), as would have been made evident to them in Jacques Maritain's *Art and Scholasticism*. St. Thomas
argues against any primary intent of art to "edification," since the artist
has not as his first priority the moral rectitude of his fellows. His responsibility is to the good of the thing itself which he as poet *makes*, whether
he as artist makes a table or a garden or a poem or a novel.

6

What is to happen to language, to our words adjusted insofar as
active consciousness can adjust them to those realities in which consciousness is active participant? For language left to a recovery by the
saint will become the property of the scientist. That is, awaiting the recovery of community to that wisdom in it bespeaking the authority of the
saint, the specialized activities of consciousness through their pragmatic,
empirical activities will assume authority over language by default. Most
surely this will happen in a world so little given to sainthood. Such are
the intellectual circumstances to community with which Walker Percy
found himself confronted, and with which we still have to deal. When
Percy, with satiric wit, gives our age the epithet "The Age of the Theorist-Consumer," he is speaking to this failure in community itself. He
means by *theorist* the scientist intoxicated by science and thereby seduced
into *scientism* as the religion proper to autonomous intellect. By *consumer*,
he suggests that those members of community (*member* in St. Paul's
sense) become dismembered from the body of community, turning to

the promises of the scientists to satisfy each his own appetitive desires. The objects of desires are to be defined by the cell of the self which has ceased to be a member of a body called community, that office of detached autonomy assumed to be an absolute "right" of the "self."

It is in this distortion that science becomes the new godhead. How that comes about, seen in a retrospective accounting by some scientists themselves, we may consider in specific instances of their own accountancy of progress, arguments about human nature presumed limited to that of a biochemical entity, the human body as the ultimate arena of the self in an accidental universe. Percy would no doubt engage our example with incisive wit, subjecting our theorist here to such whimsical treatment as is possible from a scientist turned novelist. And, indeed, he does so in *Thanatos Syndrome*, unable to resist the humor of the whimsical grotesque in showing us his scientists as worshippers of their own scientism. There is that zoo scene when Dr. Tom More visits his colleague Dr. Van Dorn, one of those whom Father Smith speaks of as "The Louisiana Weimar psychiatrists," at Dr. Van Dorn's institute. They have been experimenting with a heavy-sodium additive to the community water. It will, they insist, have such Utopian effects as to reduce New Orleans crime by 87 percent, child abuse and teenage pregnancy by 85 percent. In the issue, Van Dorn, partaking of the magic potion himself, exhibits strange symptoms and is at last confined "to the State Forensic Hospital in Jackson" (Percy perhaps here tweaking his good friend Eudora Welty of Jackson). Tom More reports that, visiting Dr. Van Dorn in his confinement, he found the changed Doctor "would at first rattle the bars, roar, and thump his chest. Then, after the ruckus, he would knuckle over to the toilet and cower behind it." A victim of a devolution self-inflicted.

Against this backdrop from Percy's *Thanatos Syndrome*, we turn to a recent engagement, made with good intentions to rescue humanity, published the year before Percy's novel. The work reveals (from Percy's perspective in distinguishing *scientism* from *science*—scientism thus presuming philosophical authority) a dead end, though a less spectacular one than that of Dr. Van Dorn. It does so through inadequacies of a language used in pursuit of mystery but assuming the power of magic in the word as instrument. Thus language is used somewhat like Dr. Van Dorn's use of heavy sodium. What Percy suggests at last is that when technical language is used as potion to reconstitute nature, it prevents all visionary language. That is the nature of gnostic dislocations of intellect from reality such as those Eric Voegelin examines, Voegelin being one of Percy's admired thinkers, committed to the purification of the dialect of that tribe called philosophers. What Percy (and Voegelin) recognize is that when the scientist usurps authority over being through language, wrested from the keep of the rare saint among us (Mother Teresa recognized by Percy as such a saint), scientism would as well wrest authority over signs from the poet and the philosopher. Where then could we end as consciousnesses save at a dead end such as Percy gives us metaphorically in the figure of Dr. Van Dorn in that State Forensic Hospital at Jackson?

The work I have in mind as parable here deals with the sorts of questions Walker Percy found intriguing as prospects to his "fictions." What is the physiological dimension of consciousness? What hath science to say of what the philosopher or theologian calls *soul*? Science writers Judith Hooper and Dick Teresi published a little book under the title *The 3-Pound Universe* in 1986. But it is the subtitle that is most engaging: *Revolutionary Discoveries about the Brain—From the Chemistry of the Mind to the New Frontiers of the Soul* (Jeremy P. Tarcher, Inc., 1986). This is an account from science's perspective, as opposed to philosophy's or theology's, of the struggle to localize consciousness in relation to the physical brain. That is, the concern is to detail the *place* of thought. Etienne Gilson argues that thought, being immaterial though actual, has no "place." But Hooper remarks that the scientist's recent supposition has been that the relation of thought to brain is "merely an exquisitely complex bit of circuitry that could be understood (eventually) by dismantling it bit by bit, patiently labeling all the components and wires, until you got to whatever it was that controlled consciousness." (That prospect of discovery has even been encouraged by the political powers. President George Bush the Elder endorsed a Congressional fiat declaring the 1990s the "Decade of the Brain.")

In the new "Introduction" to a reissue of *The 3-Pound Universe* in 1991 (the year after Percy died), Hooper surveys the progress since the first publication in 1986. "[I]f anything, we seem to be even further from the consciousness atom.... [N]ow we cannot even be sure that consciousness is contained within the brain at all." In effect, we seem to have reached an end to that pursuit of consciousness set under way in the 18th century by the rationalist position that held all existing things, man included, to be mechanisms that yield to firm comprehension as mechanism. But comprehension *by what*? That is the snake in the mechanistic garden, of course. Meanwhile, a most curious development out of the pursuit: By 1991 the address to the relation of thought and mind to the body had approached closer and closer to St. Thomas Aquinas's definition of *person* as a *substantial* unity, soul and body indivisible. Not that this new approach is made from the position of philosophy and certainly not from theology, though science is increasingly, and in its various departments—from particle physics to astronomy—pressed toward the necessity of a metaphysics. From science's position of concern for consciousness in relation to the material brain, there now develops apace PNI—psychoneuroimmunology. The emerging discipline is much concerned with a unity of mind-brain, or mind-body, in pursuit of a rational explanation of consciousness. The elements diagnosed are the psycho-neuro-immunological relations of a mysterious unity: the discrete universe of the singular person. Hence the formidable scientific name of the discipline, lest it become confused with philosophy or theology: *psychoneuroimmunology*.

In *The 3-Pound Universe*, Candace Pert, a neuroscientist concerned with this mystery, asserts, "It's all one system.... Is consciousness in your head? No, it's in your whole body. I no longer believe in disease at all. Disease is a hundred percent mental. It's just your brain state being reflected in your body." The problem here with such a belief, leading Pert to her Mary Baker Eddy view of disease, is her residual commitment to "system" abstracted from mechanism, over which system intellect itself must nevertheless preside as autonomously detached. But how may intellect do so if not freed from the onus of an original sin, its existence as consequent to the body as itself a mere mechanism. Some species of angelism is necessary, but one derived from mindless mechanism, alas. That necessity escapes notice as contradictory in mind itself when mind is bent upon autonomous freedom, even from accident as its acknowledged first cause. There is a commendable desire to understand an *essential* unity of the *person*, but a desire hesitant to subscribe to a possible visionary perspective upon any unifying principle which speaks toward that gift of love: *soul*. We note with emphasis the progressive journey in *The 3-Pound Universe*'s subtitle, from *chemistry* to *mind* to "the New Frontiers of the Soul." Without a perspective aided by philosophy, this direction will evolve up to a point, though not into a "Christian Science." It is headed toward a vague "Pagan Science" such as is already widely abroad—as Walker Percy often remarks—made popular by new theologians of this science—and especially by such fundamentalist activists as a Shirley MacLaine, whom Percy singles out with satiric humor. If we correct the "mental" we shall thereby heal the "body," under the general auspices of the latest sciences of the body as caused mechanistically—specifically uncovered through genetic engineering revealing an effect of machinery called "life."

In this direction of a control of "disease" implicit in Constance Pert's statement, Hooper suggests that "Drugs that mimic brain chemicals may bolster an immune system debilitated by grief. A futuristic biofeedback apparatus linked to a blood analyzer might train a person to crank out more antibodies or to mobilize natural killer cells. Faith healing, a placebo effect, laying-on of hands, even voodoo, are coming out of the twilight zone and into the fine print of learned journals." In the light of such "futuristic" solutions to grief and cancer, let alone sin, the system of restructuring society which Percy addresses as the latest possibility to science out of chemistry, dramatized in his *Thanatos Syndrome*, is primitive indeed. But it is in this climate, breathed by all of us as intellectual creatures becoming lost in the cosmos, that Walker Percy engages with a continuing good humor the hope of recovery, as in that "Last Self-Help Book," *Lost in the Cosmos*. He maintains hope, believing that "the sacraments, especially the Eucharist ... whatever else they do, confer the highest significance upon the ordinary things of this world, bread, wine, water, touch, breath, words, talking, listening." For we move in a real world, however much obscured by delusive words in support of systems antagonistic to reality itself. It is "a real world of real things, a world which is a sacrament and a mystery." These words are very near the end of his life, in "The Holiness of the Ordinary," and they mark a point of his closest convergence in a visionary perspective with his fellow Southerner and Catholic, Flannery O'Connor.

Meanwhile, what of consciousness in this new climate of thought? Concerns for that mystery of our nature, which is the object of an intellectual action out of the magic of science such as here described, is a subject "still taboo" in most scientific circles, Judith Hooper says. She quotes Professor Pert: "It is not considered a suitable scientific topic." And Hooper adds by way of corroboration that a recent symposium of the American Association for the Advancement of Science was concerned with the subject of this new science. Well, enough. But, alas, "mentioning consciousness" at a meeting of the Society for Neuroscience "would be a bit like mentioning God or flying saucers; it belongs in the realm of things that are primitive and unscientific."

If Candace Pert reaches a point where she can declare that consciousness is "in your whole body," as opposed to Judith Hooper's pursuit of a "consciousness atom" that yet proves elusive to Positivistic science in its genetic mappings, both may be moving closer to St. Thomas's understanding of the intellectual soul as the *formal* principle of the person, though perhaps themselves yet somewhat "primitive and unscientific"—lacking that scientific openness distinguishing the thinker as *scientist* from entrapment by *scientism*. Thomas's is a recognition of the *possible* beyond science's measure. For Thomas, *this* intellectual soul incarnate is a simple unity existing in a mystery of person as transcendent of his own empirical measure by his finite instrumentalities of thought. Not that the scientist—become committed to scientism rather than holding science to be a discipline of intellect in relation to intellect's finitude—will make that leap required out of his cozy magic into the risks of mystery. Instead, the devotee of scientism maintains his particular species of Cartesian Idealism as justified by his own Positivistic authority—as if Positivism were scholastic philosophy to scientism as a religion. Thus a species of materialogy as religion is supported by a fundamentalism, which nevertheless finds itself at least required to depend heavily (and somewhat embarrassingly) upon the poet's metaphors to convert wayward intellects to its support, lest such minds discover Percy's recognition that creation itself is "a sacrament and a mystery." The argument, dependent upon metaphor derived from creation as both actual and a mystery unyielding to finite reason, must of necessity declare that such metaphor is a mere convenience out of fancy, a Nominalistic strategy of self-protection for the Positivistic scholastic. Otherwise, he might be forced to confess his inadequacy to an absolute comprehension of the world he would maintain as a materialistic accident, the doctrine to his faith necessary to scientism as a religion.

Perhaps it is with some relief, then, that after a failure to comprehend the "3-pound Universe" (the brain), there now appears a more mystical version of a possible rescue of scientism. Joseph Le Doux's *Synaptic Self* (2002) promises to reveal "how the brain, and particularly its synapses, creates and maintains personality," thus the celebration of the book to a public relief, since scientism's Utopian promises have been so long delayed. It is a work which challenges "the common view" that regards the self as a "process" in what we might term a Little Bang Theory. In the synapses of the nervous system is stored information which is mysteriously coordinated across the body's many systems. It is at this point, in the three-pound brain presumably, that a nervous impulse (its own cause inconsequential) passes from one neuron to another. The point of this magic event is the interstice. At a *vacuum* in earthly terms? Or a point of nothingness out of which the command: "Let there be personality" rises? Here the little explosion occurs, out of which emerges what we call "personality." It may seem a bang to scientism's ear, but only a whimper to the ear of the philosopher—or theologian. As a Little Bang, the book's promotional blurb signals a possible rescue of scientistic fundamentalism. It declares that "Ultimately, it is at the level of the synapse that psychology, culture, and even spirituality meet, where memory joins with genes to create the ineffable essence of personality." In our remembering (and by means of whatever synapses allowed us) we return to Walker Percy's *Love in the Ruins* and especially to his *Thanatos Syndrome*. In remembering his play with scientism in those novels, we know at once that such a confident explanation of "personality" would prove grist for Percy's mill, he no mean scientist, though skeptical of such confusions as these in the promotional blurb.

There we have it. Judith Hooper, taking us to the "New Frontiers of the Soul" to be discovered in this three-pound brain which can be held "in the palm of your hand," whereas a "computer with the same number of 'bits' would be a hundred stories tall and cover the state of Texas." Meanwhile, even for Hooper (one fears) the mystery of existence, of the essential unity of the "consciousness," is endangered by such "primitive and unscientific" concepts as *God*, which is a concept on the same level as *flying saucers*. The way in which she puts her concern for the seriousness of *consciousness* as an existential reality seems also to close off philosophy no less than theology from the concern. Just how science *as science* is to explain an immaterial presence beyond science's own intrinsic limits of knowing remains in doubt.

In such an address to the "3-pound Universe," we may have come to a new frontier of the soul; but in such an address to that unknown country lying just ahead, science seems doomed to arrest its journey, choosing an entrenchment against the "unknown" on that frontier—bogging down on the demarcation line between science and philosophy. And this is to speak nothing of that other line of demarcation between science and theology, the one where God continues to be seen as but a "primitive" superstition as viewed from the settled, entrenched certitude of this new science which pretends nevertheless to have brought us once more under the shadow of the "soul" in the wilderness frontier encroaching upon intellect itself. Not that this new science yet recognizes having moved this far.

In the recovered circumstance of the soul at large in creation, the person on his way—Percy's *homo viator*—we set aside the adolescent limits of scientism. We may then find ourselves more crucially concerned by the nature of and limit to sign along our way. It is the necessity to our recovery of true bearings in a strange world. This is the recognition governing Percy's use of signs, whether in his direct essays or by indirection in his fictions. It has also become, since Percy's death, the concern of some bold scientists such as those exploring with their science, recognized as a *limited* intellectual discipline not to be perverted into ideological scientism, the evidences of "Intelligent Design" in the cosmos. They contend, contrary to Hooper or Le Doux, that this mysterious "3-pound Universe" is a *given*, not a sheer accident become laboriously a machine over millennia through subsequent accidents, in which as machine "personality" is manufactured out of nothing, in interstices between nerve endings—without an initiating Cause or consequential End. Common sense, this is to say, seems to be a promising recovery from fantastic philosophy serving an ideological scientism calling itself science.

7

Percy is fascinated with the mystery of sign, and especially with semiotics as the science addressed to that mystery. It is to his "idea" of semiotics that we now turn, an idea with which he has a continuing lover's quarrel. He sees in it the weakness of assuming itself *comprehensive* as a science, preventing the scientist from seeing himself as servant to the truth of things but deluded by the growing belief that he is himself the cause of signs and therefore the cause of truth itself. Such is Percy's own gift with words that his fascination becomes infectious to us, particularly so since by his enthusiasm there is a refreshing delight such as he himself might find in the four-year-old waking to the mystery of the sign. In *Lost in the Cosmos,* Percy cites *The Gesell Institute's Child from One to Six* (Harper & Row, 1979). That work, in its summary of the four-year-old, says that the child "tends to be rather a joy. His enthusiasm, his exuberance, his willingness to go more than half way to meet others in a spirit of fun are all extremely refreshing," an apt description of many of us on meeting Percy in his *Lost in the Cosmos.* As dark as he paints our prospects there, he does so with a delight in recognizing the wide variations in our fallenness that leave an effect in us of hope when all is said.

Percy remarks in a footnote that "The four-year-old is a concelebrant of the world and even of his own peers." But for the "seven-year-old? Something has happened in the interval." This, in remarking within his text the consequences of a turning inward upon the "self" in self-consciousness: "From the moment the signifying sign-making self turned inward and became conscious of itself, trouble began as the sparks flew up." It is a change inexplicable perhaps, except "through the wisdom (or folly) of religion and myth." From the openness of joy in the four-year-old as described in the Gesell Institute volume, the seven-year-old withdraws into the "self," a self-protecting retreat, since the seven-year-old is "unwilling to expose knowledge, for fear of being laughed at or criticized." But so concerned, he comes "to expect too much of self." Fearing a vulnerability in openness, he becomes niggardly with his signs. By analogy, as Percy would be aware, such is an apt description of Percy himself initially as he turns toward play with signs as novelist, as if having been awakened from his intellectual "seven-year-oldness" by the traumatic effect of that arrest by tuberculosis in the midst of his intended career as physician. "Science" itself up to that point had seemed sufficiently protective as if exhibiting a "seven-year-old" syndrome such as described by the Gesell work. Our delight in Percy's mode, as both essayist and as novelist (after we get beyond that rather sober exploration of sign in *The Message in the Bottle*), is in his recovered intentional pur-

suit of the four-year-old's joy in creation. He pursues an un-self-reflect-
ing openness by reflection, concentrating attention upon the sign. That
is the delight we participate in as we read, say, his *Lost in the Cosmos* perhaps. It is a work which invites us to recover a "spirit of fun" despite our
circumstances as a self in what is the undeniably very dark age shadow-
ing consciousness itself.

What Percy is immediately interested in here, in this description by
the Gesell Institute, is the four-year-old's fascination with names, stirring in him his own insatiable hunger for the names of things. That is a
hunger which when fed by signs, Percy considers, evidences the child's
breaking through a "dyadic" system of organisms in creation, in the cosmos, beyond his "organic" limit. *Dyadic* is a term he borrows from
Charles S. Peirce, upon whom he depends heavily in his explications of
the nature of *sign*. This breakthrough from the dyadic, he declares, issues
into a realm of intellect which Peirce proposed as a "triadic" event in
consciousness, whereby the "self" as Percy would have it comes to be
the self. And the medium of this leap in being, the effecting cause, is the
sign.

In relation to the four-year-old's appetite for names as evidencing
an awakening of the self to itself (in the Percy-Peirce view of the event,
transforming a dyadic state of consciousness into a triadic state), let us
recall a remark of G. K. Chesterton in his *Orthodoxy* (1908), a work contemporary to Peirce. In "The Ethics of Elfland," Chesterton remarks that
"A child of seven is excited by being told that Tommy opened a door
and saw a dragon. But a child of three is excited by being told that
Tommy opened a door." The difference in excitement is less of magnitude than of distance—in the proximity of intellect to the immediacy of
an existing thing, let us say. Even a *Tommy* and a *door* are exciting to
intellect merely as perceptible through signs, as existing in that waking
moment to the mystery of things known with unreflective immediacy.
Dragons are another challenge, requiring an imaginative act of making.
The Gesell Institute, incidentally, had issued a book earlier than its child
"from one to six," a book called *The Child from Five to Ten* (1946) from
which Percy quotes in pursuing his seven-year-old: The seven-year-old
is more "aware of and withdrawn into self.... Seems to be in 'another
world.' ... Self-conscious about own body..." That is a retreat into an
interior country where most various dragons prove fascinating, as we
may discover perhaps in Descartes. By our bringing Chesterton to witness, perhaps we have gained some further recognition of what Percy is
about in his adapting the novelist's wily indirection in a teasing offering
of his "self-help" book. His concern, which is not very deeply hidden
though playfully deployed, is for the relation of things known—not to
fancy's myth but in quest of the wisdom of religion. What is necessary

to a recovery from Cartesian dislocations from reality, from a self-centeredness "scientifically" suggested in the actions of the seven-year-old's withdrawal, is something of a "four-year-old's" delight in the present reality of actual things to our senses. That is a recovery from the self-love dramatized at its extremity by Dostoevsky in his *Notes from Underground*, and by Eliot in his "Love Song of J. Alfred Prufrock," portraits of highly sophisticated "seven-year-olds."

What is common to the interest of Chesterton and Walker Percy is the perceptive observation that the child is given to signs as he grows in personhood. Involved is an intellectual journey into "elf-land" along that way, but perhaps the prospect as well of a turning outward from the temptations to an arrest in that interior country of self-consciousness. Chesterton suggests something lost requiring compensation in that movement from sheer wonder—the joy in the actuality of things experienced—to the journeying toward recovery of that "original" state of joy in the existence of objects in themselves. It is a journey from the wonder of *doors* and of another *person*—of sunlight on trees, a cat, the sound of a dog barking—to imaginative remembrances of that prime moment in the journey. There begins an intellectual journey into elf-land, which we are suggesting is dangerous to undertake in that it is a turning into the "self." At an extreme of that journey occurs that imagined illusion of autonomy in restoring an original moment, the certainties of *scientism* which establish the strangest of all "elf-lands"—that of the theorist-consumer in a new Eden.

It is against this distortion that Chesterton writes an account of his own escape from being lost in the cosmos, his *Orthodoxy* (1908), in which escape "The Ethics of Elfland" prove centrally important. Indeed, Chesterton's *Orthodoxy* is a "self-help" book still valid as such, and complementary to the one Percy gives us. Concerning Chesterton's "child of three" in relation to the "child of seven" (his categories), it is the child of seven who requires nursery tales against becoming lost. For, Chesterton says, "nursery tales only echo an almost pre-natal leap of interest and amazement. These tales say that apples were golden only to refresh the forgotten moment when we found that they were green. They make rivers run with wine only to make us remember, for one wild moment, that they run with water."

St. Thomas Aquinas, in his concern for that relation of wine to water, of wine to blood, explores this dangerous journey Chesterton presents with whimsy and wit in quest of the truth of human nature. St. Thomas makes an observation revealing of the joy of the three- or four-year-old responding to *Tommy* or a *door*, to apples *green* and rivers of *running water*. "None," he says, "perceives himself to know except from the fact that he knows some object, because knowledge of some object is prior to knowledge of oneself in such a way that it immediately apprehends itself, but it arrives at knowledge of itself by the fact that it perceives other things." (This, from *Questiones disputate de veritate.*) If Thomas speaks a truth about our action of knowing (as a moment's reflection suggests he does), then he is speaking of an intellectual movement in a consciousness before that consciousness deals with the necessity of signs. That it is a truth witnessing our actual experiences of things (apples, water) is underlined by the act of thinking, of reflecting, for in that act—in an intellectual movement toward concept and then toward a sign for concept—we discover that we make a beginning, but only as a response to something *already known*, already held in intellect—a consequent effect in the "self" of having experienced some *object*, St. Thomas says. By that experience antecedent to concept or sign we know the self as actual. St. Augustine has insisted on this point against the "skeptics" of the Academy: Even if I am deceived in the act of knowing I must exist before being so deceived.

But illusion accepted as reality by the confident self may effect self-elevation of the self by the actual experience of knowing the self. So begins the losing of the way, a wandering in the actual woods no longer seen—Thomas's objects—with few signposts to recover the "way" back. It may become for the journeyman a most agitated arrest of the self in a dark wood, in a state Eliot suggests in "Ash-Wednesday": "Against the Word the unstilled world still whirled/ About the center of the silent Word." A moment of retrospection, hinting a gradual recognition of the "Word" as still and silent but at the center of the unstilled and whirling self. Indeed, that is a moment of a new beginning such as that of St. Augustine, which follows his account in Book 9 of *The Confessions* of a recovery of the Word in things. After that recovery, he turns to signs marking the *discovered* as always present, that Word waiting even in him as a created thing. In Book 10 there follows a development of the recognition set in signs which he calls a "Philosophy of Memory," through which he adumbrates in sign that intellectual action of discovery: God dwells always in his memory. "I find you there when I call you to mind." There follows that painful cry of contrition: "Too late have I loved you, O Beauty so ancient and so new."

The recovery is of a knowledge of that enveloping and intrinsic Presence whereby any thing *is*. It is a Presence without which there would be no Tommy opening a door, no four-year-old openness to things in a participation within ineffable beauty of apples, green or golden, since all depends upon that Augustinian Beauty. It is the discovery testified to by Eliot as well in *Little Gidding* and by Walker Percy in his "Holiness of the Ordinary." To echo Eliot's closing of his last important poem once more, the child in us at last may return to that country of his first joy, which paradoxically lies always ahead of us and not behind us in a lost childhood. In a progress of return we may "for the first time" see things with a new understanding. It is an understanding that sets "Elfland" aright in our knowing, lest Chesterton's Elfland be confused with Eden Lost. In pursuit of Eden Lost, through the illusion of self-autonomy through angelism, we would will that existence be other than it is, an act of self-denigration.

In such mystery, ripe with paradox, we may awaken to the reality of existence itself—things in themselves, as they *are*—in this present moment. Such is that recognition leading Percy to affirm that ours is "a real world of real things, a world which is a sacrament and a mystery." But as Percy knows, and warns us against, out of this initial awakening to the mystery of existence itself (apples as green), there follows a shying away into the self—a seven-year-old's retreat. It is a movement in the self requiring a turning and returning to the point of departure, to the real world as a sacrament sustaining the self in ways always escaping in some degree of not-knowing our signs marking that place. The life recovered continues a mystery. (That is the moment incidentally for the old grandmother in Flannery O'Connor's "A Good Man Is Hard to Find," in which, for that moment of recovery, by an act of love she is a "good" woman. The Misfit's response at the story's conclusion speaks toward the point we attempt to make concerning four-year-olds and seven-year-olds: She would have remained a good woman, he says, "if it had been somebody there to shoot her every minute of her life.")

To echo Eliot, then, the child in us struggles to return to that country of first joy to see yet again "for the first time," see it with a new understanding through grace. Just what is one to make of this journey which, in its end, seems destined to a return to its beginning? Such a return seems strange in its necessities to the person engaging intellectually the *intellectual* dimension of this journey, but it proves inescapable for Percy no less than for Eliot. Especially, what is one to make of that journey's relation to sign as related to that ever-circling journeying? For it is a journey in which the person attempts a coordination at every point through signs, lest the journey be but back-tracking or circling and not a progress. It is in relation to this fear that we pause: Between the observations of the child awakening to the journey as remarked by Chesterton on the one hand and by Gesell and Percy on the other, there appears a subtle but important difference.

Percy, as diagnostician of Modernist man, is concerned with the environment of that intellectual creature in which it has breathed in a Cartesian air of self-isolation, since the seventeenth century Percy says. He observes, in "Diagnosing the Modern Malaise" (1985), that there has occurred a "radical transformation of the very consciousness of Western man in an entirely unexpected way by the scientific and technological worldview," an observation which nevertheless does not turn him against science itself, though he is incisively critical of the uses of science as a reductionist "scientism." What is to be remembered is a commonplace to valid scientific thinking: "The scientist, in practicing the scientific method, cannot utter a single word about an individual thing or creature insofar as it is an individual but only insofar as it resembles other individuals." That science, if become scientism, effects a disease of mind, a malady widely evident to Percy. And it suggests the immediate source to be that plague of Cartesian Idealism as appropriated to the authority of intellect itself so that it may order creation as separate from the self. He credits his recognition as discovered, not through science as he had pursued it, but through reading Kierkegaard and Dostoevsky. They "convinced me that *only* the writer, the existentialist philosopher, or the novelist can explore this gap [in the scientific view of the world] with all the passion and seriousness and expectation of discovery of, say, an Einstein who had discovered that Newtonian physics no longer works."

So convinced, Percy understands himself as diagnostician, his subject becoming the self and the most proximate patient to be diagnosed himself as affected by this "Modern Malaise." How appropriate, the metaphorical approach he takes, he having been struck down by tuberculosis—an act of grace, he will conclude. In that malady there is such a labor of breathing in the long and slow recovery ahead of him that it took him from New York to the Southwest and at last to Covington over a long period of time. By an indirection as novelist, he then undertakes his diagnosis, concerned with the "self" as victim of the contamination accrued gradually out of the intellectual air we breathe. He will observe that "self," which used to be called the *soul* perhaps, in its attempt at a self-rescue, turning from the contaminated world but increasingly turning into itself. Slowly he comes to his own "self," finding it to have been lost in a dark wood, "lost in the cosmos," isolated the more by that turning inward. Its recuperation, he begins to argue, is possible through science's recovery of an epistemology suited to the intellectual breathing of that self in a world common to selves.

The long recovery: to be made through epistemology scientifically arrived at, a system as a filter for intellectual action of a self. Such is his theory. The system must be devised analytically, with a point of departure out of Charles Peirce—the American philosopher who posits a *dyadic* and *triadic* process of intellectual action in a philosophy used as if it were a "science" of epistemology. Near the end of his life, in his "The Fateful Rift: The San Andreas Fault in the Modern Mind" (1989), Percy still finds Peirce a "rigorous scientific realist" who "reserved the truth, as he saw it, of philosophical realism from Aristotle to the seventeenth century," that is from Aristotle down to Descartes. If Percy's contemporary Southern Catholic writer Flannery O'Connor found her antidote to the Modernist contamination to lie in Thomas Aquinas (who was as well of some, more limited, rescue to Percy's self), if her recent intellectual fathers were Gilson and Maritain, it is Peirce's adaptations of Duns Scotus as philosopher (Scotus a somewhat distant father of Existentialism) that Percy concentrates upon. He follows Peirce's "Dyadic" speculations in relation to Heidegger (whom O'Connor also read). And that leads him to a special concern for the French Existentialists, not only for Camus and Sartre fortunately, but for Gabriel Marcel as "Christian Existentialist" as well. Of special importance and lasting effect to Percy were Marcel's essays collected as *Homo Viator: Introduction to a Metaphysic of Hope* (1951).

Here we once more remark Percy's response to his calling as writer as understood by him metaphorically to be that of the "physician" called to diagnose the human intellectual condition. O'Connor takes her calling as rather that of the poet seeking a moral, more than a scientific, accommodation to the disease of Modernism which had so radically transformed the consciousness of Western man. She sees symptomatic evidences as does Percy in the transmuted "scientific and technological worldview" of the intellectual within the climate of Modernist ideologies. Thus she will say (in a letter to her friend "A," January 13, 1956) that "the moral basis of poetry is the accurate naming of the things of God," an intent shared by Percy, but with a concern as scientist more than as poet or theologian. For her, the accuracy lies not in science's promises of a recovered epistemology, analytically naming its truths as science may assume in an empirical logic. Hers is more immediate in response to the actualities of experience as metaphysically explained by Thomistic philosophy. That both Percy and O'Connor intend the same end is evident, but their understanding of epistemological realities—the realities of intellectual action in response to things actual in themselves—differ considerably. She would be more cautious of Charles Peirce as an intellectual Virgil than is Percy.

We observe that what holds them toward a common end is a recognition of a mystery, Revelation. The one as "scientific" in his analysis of intellect's Modernist malignity, the other as "poet" in response to it, share but in differing modes in that crucial phrase from O'Connor, "the accurate naming of *the things of God.*" Modernist man denies things as "of God," so that there occurs that rift characterized by Percy in his concluding sentence of the essay celebrating the possibility of a healing through Peirce's "scientific realism" as philosopher. If Heidegger's version of the "self" as *Dasin* is of one "suffering a *Verfallen,*" Percy says, the Heideggerian *fallenness* requires of man a recovery as *homo viator,* as pilgrim. Though Heidegger (and after him, Camus and Sartre) is hardly committed to that recovery on the authority of Revelation, Gabriel Marcel as a "Christian existentialist" is more persuasive (for Percy) as he explores the openness necessary to the self in "Judeo-Christian notions" of man as having fallen "prey to the worldliness of the world."

In contrast, Modernist man in consequence of his submission to worldliness, attempts his salvation as if an intellectual creature were sufficient to its own rescue, through a reason governed by the disciplines proper to science as the decisive authority over truth itself. Thus Percy's conclusion, having at the beginning of this essay defined *science* "in the root sense of the word." It is "the discovery and knowing of something which can be demonstrated and verified within a community." But whether that something so demonstrated and verified is done by scientist or by poet may prove problematic. It was problematic for Flannery O'Connor, for what of those real experiences she would call *epiphanies*, a seeing of truth in a new dimension, allowed by grace to the seeing in response to circumstances to a "self" at a moment in this world? Epiphanies sustain hope. But an *epiphany* proves unyielding to *demonstration* and *verification* within community as that community might be persuaded its water is contaminated or its apples blighted. In response to that difficulty, the poet resorts to metaphor, finding it suggestive of the reality experienced as a mystery beyond science's measure. Beyond even the assurances of metaphor, the poet must acknowledge, though it may be that the poet carries community closer to the threshold of such mystery through metaphor yielding analogy of Truth to truth, of Beauty to beauty. (That is the argument Chesterton makes, the source of ethics derived from the mystery of elfland.)

In his little book called *Chaucer* (1932) G. K. Chesterton says: "A certain break or sharp change in history can hardly be sketched more sharply than by saying that up to a certain time life was conceived as a Dance, and after that time life was conceived as a Race." It is the dance which Dante celebrates in the elaborate life revealed to him in the Multifoliate Rose, his imagistic vision of Paradise at the closing of the *Divine Comedy*. But the dance becomes a race of intellect in pursuit of autonomous authority over being—whether we take a point of departure with Occam's Nominalism or Bacon's Empiricism or Descartes' confusion out of the centripetal collapse of the self into self-isolation—that philosophy of the "seven-year-old." As the dance becomes a race, we come to borrow metaphor from scientism itself: Life becomes a Rat Race. Chesterton's observation, then, may leave us somewhat uncertain about semiotics as theory's system promising a recovery of the dance such as that made as semionic theory built by Percy in his *Lost in the Cosmos*. Before and after that delightful tour de force, in his essays he attempts to recover the way out of the maze by a science of sign. He seeks *home* in rescue from the maze, within which maze occurs a losangelization of the suburbs, making a precise street address difficult. It is a home to be recovered, if we but find keys to the locks of closed doors within the maze. The keys? Signs rightly read. But first, given the maze so littered by signs, selectively read as pointing out the Modernist Maze, how are signs to be read aright?

How challenging those signs to Percy, especially since he encounters them so far from home. There is roused in him by those very signs a sense—an intimation—that home lies yet before him, though whenever recovered for a moment, home seems only a way station for *homo viator*. Does it prove to be the place from which he first set out, or only a place from which he must set out yet again? How apt to our concern here is the passage from Percy's "Notes for a Novel about the End of the World." From those notes Patrick Samway chooses his title for the posthumous collection of Percy's essays: "Instead of constructing a plot and creating a cast of characters from a world familiar to everybody," Percy says, the novelist "is more apt to set forth with a stranger in a strange land where the signposts are enigmatic but which he sets out to explore nevertheless." The novelist here is, of course, Percy himself as *homo viator*, though he recognizes himself as differing from his fellow Southern writers with whom he feels a close affinity, Eudora Welty and Flannery O'Connor. Eudora Welty seems early arrived at home—to have discovered herself steadily at the place from which she set out as she begins her writing. So too Flannery O'Connor, but with a difference. That is, unlike Welty, O'Connor's engagement of home is from a deeply held Thomistic understanding of her circumstances, she having also arrived home early in her writing career. She did so earlier than Percy, though in like circumstances to his longer wandering. She is arrested by lupus, as her father had been, and recognizes it as a death sentence. O'Connor's is a recovery of joy in consequence, but it was already precipitated in her before she left Georgia: Hers is a strong faith long held making her at home at Andalusia in ways differing from Welty's being at home in Jackson. Both no doubt puzzling—at first—to the restless Walker Percy.

O'Connor, too, is concerned for signs, though not with the *science* of signs that so fascinates Percy early and late. To that point, an anecdote from a conversation she engaged in, far from home—up East among non–Southerners in a gathering of intellectuals examining signs. The conversation comes to center on the Eucharist, and the contention is made that it is a sign, a symbol, the implication being that the "real presence" is only symbolic. Her response, approximately: "Well, if it is just a symbol, I say to Hell with it." Hers then is the position Percy will at last affirm in saying at his life's end that Modernist man in his predicament finds himself "on the move in a real world of real things, a world which is a sacrament and a mystery" even though a reality not yet recognized by a pilgrim. How is that "self"—man in his predicament of isolation from that real world—to find recovery? How is he "to get back into a body, live in a place, at a street address"? This is Percy's final sentence of declaration of necessity to the writer in celebration of "Eudora Welty in Jackson": "Eudora Welty will be a valuable clue" to that necessary return to concrete things as actual, out of Cartesian wanderings in the interior maze of the "self."

Perhaps it is this clue discovered in Eudora Welty quietly at home in Jackson that leads to Percy's playfully satiric postmortem of the self, after his having survived as himself an "ex-suicide." In his infectious book *Lost in the Cosmos*, Percy gives his reader warning about the central portion of the book: "A Semiotic Primer of the Self" (pages 86–126). Those pages are not "technical" but rather "theoretical—i.e., [they attempt] an elementary semiotic grounding of the theory of the self taken for granted" in the rest of the book. For that reason, we are advised, we might well skip that whole section. We note at once Percy's presence as himself a "theorist," having seen his devastating indictment of theorists in relation to the office of the theorist in multiplying consumers. The advice to skip the section, however, is not intended to rescue us from Percy the Theorist. It is rather calculated, with Percy's typical indirection, to draw us into the section. By indirection he slips up on our blind side, as he admits is the novelist's manner with a reader. What is at issue in this section is "not texts and other coded sign utterances but the self which produces texts or hears sign utterances." The "subject of inquiry," then, is the dominant subject of all Percy's work, the mystery of the *self*, which is to be approached by him as a sign of equal importance with that other sign in the desert, the *Jew*. In drawing his late essay "Why Are You a Catholic?" to its close, he says that "In this desert, that of theory and consumption," there remains only one sign other than that of the *self*, "the Jews. By 'the Jews' I mean not only Israel, the exclusive people of God, but the worldwide *ecclesia* instituted by one of them, God-become-man, a Jew."

He published a few years earlier than this essay, with an audacity of playfulness, his *Lost in the Cosmos* with its general epigraph from Nietzsche that begins "We are unknown, we knowers, to ourselves." As we risk entry into the pages of "A Semiotic Primer of the Self" which we have been cautioned to skip—with its charts and figures and esoteric references—we do so through a playful preamble as subtitle: "A Short History of the Cosmos with Emphasis on the Nature and Origin of the Self, plus a Semiotic Model for Computing Impoverishment in the Midst of

Plenty, or Why it is Possible to Feel Bad in a Good Environment and Good in a Bad Environment"—a subtle mimicking of the typography of 17th-century descriptive titles of sometimes abstruse arguments. But if a playful preamble, what we discover at once on entering the text itself is a very serious engagement of his concern. The serious tonal quality of the pages in this section is made immediately evident in an initial long footnote discussion of the title's term, *semiotic*. There are additional lengthy notes bearing the same serious concern, one of which we have already cited, the note dealing with the four-year-old in relation to the seven-year-old child.

What we remark initially is Percy's serious insistence that the *self* as a reality is not only justified by the sign; it is by virtue of the sign that the self exists. That this is a steady concern for Percy is dramatized much earlier in Binx Bolling's struggle to "insert" himself into the cosmos. A form of Binx's attempt is his fascination with watching people watch other people. It is a stage toward a self-recognition by Binx as a brilliant "seven-year-old." We might say that it echoes metaphorically perhaps Adam in the Garden before the advent of Eve. It shows Binx's attempt to recover joy. That is, in Binx's anticipation there is a restlessness speaking Adam's incompleteness. It is an incompleteness we may respond to most variously, in Binx his sense of being suspended within the actual world, against which world ironic wit tending to the sardonic becomes a defense. He is at risk of a descent into despair as a "self," leading Percy to his careful epigraph from Kierkegaard's *Sickness Unto Death*: "…the specific character of despair is precisely this: it is unaware of being despair." Binx's quest, let us say, is for signs allowing a rescue from suspension, the sign most needed perhaps a naming of himself beyond what seems his more or less accidental name as it appears.

How apt that circumstance to *homo viator*, with Percy's Binx Bolling a fictional figure of that entity, the "self" in quest of name, of sign. It is from that paragraph of Chesterton's concerned with the three-year-old and seven-year-old—concerned with a *Tommy* and a *door* and a *dragon*—that we intrude an epigraph for Percy's concern as diagnostic novelist of the self. "We have all read," Chesterton says, "in scientific books, and, indeed, in all romances, the story of the man who has forgotten his name. This man walks about the streets and can see and appreciate everything; only he cannot remember who he is. Well, every man is that man in the story. Every man has forgotten who he is. One may understand the cosmos but never the ego; the self is more distant than any star. Thou shalt love the Lord thy God; but thou shalt not know thyself. We are all under the same mental calamity; we have all forgotten our name." How apt a passage to Binx's wanderings "about the streets" of New Orleans. But not only Binx: Percy finds himself in that state, as if suspended from *being* unless rescued through the magic (the *science*) of signs as making the nameless self actual: through signs activating selves as it were into selves not actual until acted upon by sign. Sign, Percy begins to argue, proves mediator to a possible wholeness of the self, as if sign were the necessary active agent to the existence of the self. The concern has implications in Percy's mode as artist, a most conspicuous evidence being the dialactical form of his *Lancelot* (1977).

For Percy, then, sign effects a community between two selves suggestive of a wholeness. What is thus certified (and Binx is hungrily anxious for this self-certification) is the special nature of human consciousness as distinct from other creatures which that consciousness may encounter. Percy says emphatically in *Lost in the Cosmos*: "You—Betty, Dick—are like other items in my world [in that Betty and Dick exist only in a *dyadic* mode separate from that "world"]—cats, dogs, and apples. But you have a unique property. You are also a co-namer, co-discoverer, co-sustainer of my world—whether you are Kafka whom I read or Betty who reads this. Without you—Franz, Betty—I would have no world." We note the term *world* here as distinct from *cosmos*. Percy is careful to set these apart. The *world* of the self exists in this perspective in a relation to the *cosmic-environment* as experienced in a *dyadic* mode, in which respect that self feels set aside from the cosmic-environment as the maze containing the self. That is, the world called the *self* is distinct from the cosmic environment. "For the sign-user," Percy says, "a world is imposed upon the Cosmos—to which he still responds like any other organism"—that is, responds in a *dyadic* mode to the cosmos. But there is a significant difference between that thing called the "signal-using organism" within the cosmic environment, acting in a *dyadic* mode toward the cosmos by imposing a world upon it, and the "sign-user" become a self by using signs in relation to co-namers, co-sustainers, co-discoverers of the imposed world. The "sign-user has an environment, but ... also has a *world*." Specifically, that world is the world of *selves* as *imposed* upon the cosmos through sign. (How fascinated Stephen Dedalus of Joyce's *Portrait of the Artist as a Young Man* would be by this argument, though wary of co-participants.)

This unique dimension of the self as sign-user is certified by signs as a difference between the dog's response to the sign *ball* and the child's response to that sign. It is a difference between the dyadic signal relation of *term* to *thing* (dog-ball, the *signal* aspect revealed by the dog's fetching the ball when the signal is given) and the triadic relation in the term whereby intellect enters into a community of intellect with some other "sign-receiver." The sign-giver and sign-receiver thus exist on the same plane of response to sign, but in a dimension of the triadic. Thereby the sign-using self is certified in its "unique property" by the sign-receiving self, certified in its existence as a self by that separate self receiving projected sign.

A limited truth lies buried here, but it is one which may require a clarification, and perhaps as well a statement of a position regarding the nature of sign with which Percy might or might not agree. For instance, one is uncomfortable with the use of the term *imposed*, which suggests an action whereby a *world* is established as an extension of the self by the action of sign, commanding consent of both the sign-giver and the sign-receiver. The use of the term, indeed, seems to have lingering in it a faint residue of Nominalist thought, in which address to reality the sign becomes the manipulator of being. There seems implicit as well the Existentialist principle that willed action is the cause of being, in this instance the *being* of that world termed the *self*. Perhaps there is an excess of assertion in Percy's framing of his argument traceable to the lingering influence of his early encounter of Existentialism. Put bluntly, there is a sense of the presence of Jean-Paul Sartre in the formulation.

If Chesterton were putting the point from his position of Thomistic "orthodoxy," he might say that the world of the self is *recovered* as hallowed, but through its recognition of being already included in a community antecedent to it. The reality of this experience is the recognition of participation as being antecedent to recognition in concept or the formulation of concept by sign. This, rather than that a world is *imposed* upon the cosmos. For Percy, the world of the self is rather hollowed out of the cosmos as a dyadic and raised to a triadic whole by the sign. Percy's address to the sign becomes problematic, then, if considered in relation to the position Chesterton advances, or in relation to the position advanced by Chesterton's mentor, Thomas Aquinas. We see what Percy is led to. For in this marvelous world of the self, seen as set aside from the cosmos by its triadic mode of existence in the sign, Percy concludes that "all triadic behavior is *social* in origin." For him, then, Adam requires Eve before it is possible to enter upon a triadic world, and it would seem to follow that it is only that triadic world which makes Adam unique—makes him in Percy's phrase a possessor of a "unique property," the self. Sign, in which the sign-maker is made a self *within itself*, also transmutes the signified. Within the sign "the signifier becomes, in a sense, transformed by the signified." The signifier is "transformed."

What seems uncertain in such a formulation is whether being *transformed by the signified* means that the signifier (the sign-projector) is transformed by a thing itself as existing antecedently in a dyadic mode to consciousness or not. If so, there lies buried in the formulation, by implication, a possible Thomistic principle, but one which for Thomas does not depend upon the sign itself to mediate transformation. Nor is it to be understood in such a concept of active confluence of things as signified by *dyadic*. It is rather a grounding common to things existing in the ground of *being*, the initiating cause of which is the Creator. Additionally uncertain in some of Percy's argument, the sign as mediator to a transformation of the self seems to depend crucially upon a *receiver* of the sign other than the self, who makes the sign toward some other self a co-signifier of a world. Thomas on this point would argue instead a relation existing between the thing signified and the signifier which has been mediated to the self through the senses, effecting a *becoming* of intellect to the act of knowing, not through sign. A communion exists already in a triadic mode, effected by intellect's perception of the thing through the senses. If Chesterton were to modify Percy's position out of St. Thomas, he would speak directly of grace as effecting the transformation through the body's senses, in consequence of the person's open response to the antecedent world's (cosmos's) real things—an openness (Thomas would say) removing obstacles to grace. The transformation precedes both concept and sign. For sign is a witness *to*, not causal agent *of*, the transformation. It is subsequent to a "triadic" experience of a thing in itself through the intuitive mode of intellect.

What we seem to have in Percy's address to the sign as a reality holding reality (and Percy cites the semiotic scientist Saussure as authority to his point) is a power of transubstantiation in the word, in the sign. That the word is in itself so transubstantiated may be demonstrated, Percy suggests, by a simple expedient, its desubstantiation. If we "repeat the word *apple* aloud fifty times," somewhere in the process the word "will suddenly lose its magic transformation into appleness and like Cinderella at midnight become the drab little vocable it really is." Etienne Gilson, who in his *Linguistics and Philosophy* (1988) also pays limited tribute to Saussure, might admonish us to consider that what has occurred is not a desubstantiation of the sign but rather a shifting of our attention from the sign itself to its accidents, namely to its "drab little vocable" aspect. For in respect to the sign, Gilson makes the important point that what is a word for one self is but a noise for another. "The meaning that is attributed to [a word] does not partake in any way in the nature of the noise, and inversely. It is in the hearer, not in the sound."

The point in contention turns on our being instructed by Percy to repeat the vocable *aloud* fifty times. To reflect on *apple* for a comparable duration might yield quite other effect, for in such reflection we may discover ourselves closer to the apple than to its name, being less distracted by sound. The mystery at issue in the sign is that the immaterial dimension is borne in a material dimension, *meaning* in *sound*. Sound must, in the end, be concluded an accident of the essential nature of sign. In turning by reflection from that vocable as drab and little as it "really is"—a sound in the realm of physics—we turn more directly to the actual center of the mystery engaged by sign: to the apple as a thing in itself. Thus our activities as sign-makers may be seen in a different perspective. That is, we will be turned to the consciousness, to the self, as holding a likeness of apple which is not "held" by its name. For the substantive nature occasioning the insubstantial sign, the apple in itself, is held imagistically as a truth quite separate from the imposed accident, vocalized or inscribed. The inherent accidents to the essence of the apple yield a sign *in* the hearer, and *in* the speaker. Thus it is the consciousness, the central self, the existing soul—the *person* as sign-user—that is, the intellectual soul—which has been "transubstantiated" intellectually by a reception of likeness into intellect through the senses, effecting an intellectual change not attributable to *sign* in Percy's sense. Thus the exercise of verbal repetition of the name until it becomes mere noise does not demonstrate a reduction of sign from its magic but rather an exorcism of the mystery of a being already held in intellect itself given an association with the spoken term *apple*.

The mystery is not in actuality a transubstantiation of the self, whereby the self *is*—exists—in consequence of the event experienced to which a name is subsequently given. Rather, there is a transformation (*trans-formation*) through actual sensual experience of an existing, an antecedent thing (the apple). The act of knowing the apple through an intuitive openness is a "natural" response of the intuitive intellect, through which intellect itself is *in-formed* as knowing. There has occurred a *becoming* toward intellectual potentialities, now made actual to a created nature as itself one of the things of God. This, from Thomistic epistemology which understands intellect as formal to *soul* in constituting that singular creation this *person*: This intellectual soul incarnate is more accurately said therefore to have been actualized, not transformed. From this perspective, we must say that the "self" *is* before its intellectual actions. Therefore, from this perspective, the "self" is already embarked as *homo viator* upon its journey of fulfillment of potentiality through its unique gift as a being, through its existence as a created intellectual soul. And it is so embarked out of an initial givenness within which rises, out of experience of things, a self-awareness. Such is the nature of the secret to our journey in the cosmos. It is self-evident, we have said, that at the earliest point of a recognition of itself the "self" finds itself already possessing knowledge—possessing an aspect of specific beings as experienced before any sign is made, under the rubric attached to that self-evident reality of the self subsequently: It knows some *truth* of some *thing* which is actual in itself. The self is a self from inception, we contend here. If this point is not granted, then Percy himself must have difficulty justifying his fervent opposition to abortion. To declare the existence of the self as dependent upon the sign, in other words, would deny the existence of a self prior to that self's existing through the enjoining of a sign as transmuting a dyadic "animal" into that "person" too vaguely termed a "self."[6]

If St. Thomas were putting the argument—and we remember that Percy is not only beholden to the Existentialists from Kierkegaard and Marcel to Camus and Sartre but to Thomas and St. Augustine as well— if Thomas were putting the argument, he would insist that the *appleness* which so fascinates Percy in relation to the sign *apple* is not in the sign. It is first of all in the thing itself by its given nature—in the particular apple which one takes up and perhaps treasures by munching it. *Appleness* is *secondarily* in the intellect, and as such through cumulative effects in the intellectual experience, through the senses as initiator—becomes a *concept* in intellect, the concept we call *appleness* as a universal arrived at by reason through intuitive knowings by discrete experiences. But *appleness* is in the thing itself as an actuality, for which reality we use the rubric *essence*. It is *in* intellect, as possible to the nature of intellect in its encounter with things, as a *truth* held out of experiences. It is in intellect as the *truth* of the thing, Thomas declares, lest we confuse that truth as but synonym for the *essence* of the thing which resides in the thing itself. The analogous realities are *essence* in apple according to its nature as apple and the *truth* of essence possessed in intellect by its nature as intellect.

There is a consideration by Thomas in a work left incomplete by his death, his *Compendium of Theology*, which speaks to the mystery of the *word* itself in relation to this mystery of *essence* and *truth*. Thomas's concern is the principle of proportionality between the Word (Christ) and man's word. In Chapter 38, "The Word as Conception," Thomas says that what is contained in intellect as response to the experience of a thing through the medium of the senses is an "interior word," which by common usage is said "to be a conception of the intellect." (He will say in another context that intellect is *in-formed* by truth, as if the truth were the seed of essence of the thing effecting conception.) Thomas develops, as if poet, the correspondences of the *word* born in intellect to the *animal* born to natural creatures. Analogously both come to exist out of an "active" male function in relation to a "passive" female function. In his analogy, intellect is, initially, the passive female function in its "receiving" the seed called truth intuitively—the consequence of which becomes an interior word, the concept. Here then *word* is used in the sense of *concept*, not of *sign*, for it has not reached an outward birth by sign as midwife as it were.

Thus Thomas explicates his metaphor: "What the intellect comprehends is formed in the intellect, the intelligible object [the thing from which the truth is received] being ... the active principle, and the intellect the passive principle." In a figurative argument he continues: "That which is thus comprehended by intellect [by its *receptive* openness to the thing actual in itself, from which the seed of *truth* about that thing is gathered to intellect] is conformed both to the moving intelligible object (of which it is a certain likeness) and to the quasi-passive intellect [which confers on it an intelligible existence]. Hence what is comprehended by the intellect is not unfittingly called the conception of the intellect." He follows with comment on "The Relation of the Word to the Father," saying that "when the intellect understands something other than itself, the thing understood is, so to speak, the father of the word conceived in the intellect, and the intellect resembles rather a mother, whose function is such that conception takes place in her." That is the relation of concept as already a word waiting articulation, its initiating origin the thing perceived out of perception embraced as truth by intellect. The effect then is of a conception not yet arrived, as sign, at a "full term," at a birth through an intellectual project in surrendering concept into the arena of the creation, out of which has come the initiating "seed," a truth of a thing, received by the mothering intellect. In that surrender lies the prospect of community consent to truth as engendering concept. In this respect then, "the word conceived is related to the understanding person as offspring to father." Or as Gerard Manley Hopkins might put it as poet, the sign is an effect of a "mothering forth" by intellect whose ultimate Cause is God the Father. It is in this relation of man as maker (as poet, for instance) to God as Creator that man shares providentially with God in a well-ordered community of man's stewardship.

St. Thomas's "metaphysical poem" about *concept* is perhaps more simply dramatized in that passage of St. Augustine's *Confessions* in which he reenacts his own turning out of Manichaean closure of his "self" against things declared evil, turning back into the world as real and full of real things which because real are good in themselves. It occurs in Chapter 7 of Book 10, his "Philosophy of Memory." In the moment, St. Augustine coming to himself in the cosmos as in a dark wood, his deportment is not initially as a passive intellect but a deportment as if intellect were the active agent projecting creation. Thus he demands an answer of things, though wavering in an uncertainty of his autonomy: "To all the things that stand around the doors of my flesh I said, 'Tell me of my God!'" To which demand comes an answer "with a mighty voice ... 'He made us.'" It is then that Augustine as intellect turns the more receptive: "I, the inner man, know these things; I, I, the mind, by means of my bodily senses." "My question," he says, "was the gaze I turned on them; the answer was their beauty." It is an experience that Percy would already have encountered in Gerard Manley Hopkins as we have anticipated, though Percy will also come to St. Augustine reflectively, after having written his *Moviegoer*. As *homo viator*, after the discovery, he understands part of his journey—one of whose significant signposts is *The Moviegoer*. He discovers that not simply Binx Bolling but the novelist himself has been changed—"almost by accident—or was it accident?" The novelist has "landed squarely in the oldest tradition of Western letters: the pilgrim's search outside himself, rather than the guru's search within. All this happened to the novelist and his character without the slightest consciousness of a debt to St. Augustine or Dante." This, from Percy's "Physician as Novelist," speaking a recovery beyond science's theories that endanger the "self" with temptation to scientism.

The point of our visiting Thomas and his metaphorical argument in relation to Percy's concern with his semiotic theory is to suggest that, in the actuality of our experiences as intellectual soul incarnate, intellect discovers and holds truth before turning to signs. There already exists a triadic relation: The person as intellectual soul incarnate, experiencing an "object"—a thing in itself—knows that object in the active witness not only of its own existence but of the existence of the "self." The passive intellect (that is, intellect in its potentialities to receptivity of the truth of things) has known a thing—in Thomas's figure, has known it metaphorically "in the Biblical sense" by analogy in his metaphor of "conception." There has occurred an action of grace, disproportionate to that visitation of the Virgin Mary by the Holy Ghost, but nevertheless (when seen proportionately) an action which draws the person closer in understanding to the Virgin Mother. The *thing* so known *is* through the sustaining grace of the Holy Spirit, the Lord and Giver of *being* to things, through which the action of grace occurs, a conception "fathered" by the reality of a thing in itself. In this union (a *communion*) of intellect and thing, made through the senses, the effect is a conception of the word in Thomas's sense of *word*, and not a sign in the usual sense of sign. If we view the possible fulfillment of the intellectual soul in this manner—as an *in-forming* of the intellectual soul by things fathering concepts by truth of themselves—we may be somewhat more cautious about Percy's insistence upon the necessity of a separate person from the sign-user in order that the sign-user may become a self through sign. Indeed, one might even suggest that *homo viator*, on his way, is seeking a true "word" for the actuality of himself as effected out of his limited potentialities: He seeks his own true name, implicit in himself, and will not be content with a Nominalistic ruse, a name given intellectual soul incarnate by gnostic will at play through its reason, at the expense of intuitive knowing. Indeed, that is a game through which the self is destined to lose itself in the cosmos through Cartesian shell-games, played by the self with itself.

This being said, if agreed to, makes one hesitant to agree with Percy that "triadic behavior is *social* in origin," if by *social* Percy means, as he says he does, that his own existence is dependent at a primary level upon "Franz or Betty." And one remembers to the point that ancient parable about man as name-giver. Adam, naming the creatures under the auspices of God, is not naming them through a participation with Eve. Of course, Adam's is a "triadic" encounter, but the mysterious third presence is the Cause of being in things, of which Adam is one creature peculiarly created in distinction from the tiger or lamb or other things. Each exists in its peculiar nature, a complication to any Adam's conceptions of truth.

8

The intent in summoning ancient "mythical" Adam to our concern with the sign is that the mystery of sign is addressed by Percy out of semiotics—out of a science of signs. It is also in part to recover the mystery of names from the Nominalistic appropriation of signs to gnostic intentionalities, which in recent centuries has empowered various species of Modernist ideology. That is, through Nominalistic assumption pressed to extremity, the delusion grows that while names themselves are absolutely arbitrary, the Nominalistic use of an arbitrary name creates a medium through which to confer essence upon the thing itself. By the act of naming it with intentionality, it *is*. That is the gnostic delusion which would presume that power over can be gained by declaration of autonomous intellect's absolute freedom, intellectual autonomy arbitrary as an act self-divine. Intentionality becomes the only law to this new giver of being though seldom acknowledged when stated as bluntly as here stated. That is the delusion which Eric Voegelin engages so forcefully in much of his work, most famously in his *Science, Politics & Gnosticism* (1968, 1977).[7] Contrary to Nominalism as a technique to gnostic ideology to serve Positivistic science, there is that moral responsibility to sign which we heard O'Connor subscribe to: "The moral basis of Poetry is the accurate naming of the things of God."

In our present concern, that accurate naming requires the poet's consent to the thing named as existing in itself, his naming understood to be a sacramental consent to the named thing as already existing and, by its existing, honoring the Cause of that thing. The "accuracy" we might say is that of an accord through recognition, and the naming itself a sort of contract through intellectual consent to the Cause of that thing. It is a recognition within the "self" of its providential responsibility toward that thing as shared by delegation with the Cause of both poet as leaseholder of Creation and God as Absolute Providence. St. Thomas Aquinas speaks to this relation of the self as Adam, as providential agent in creation, when he says (*Summa Theologica*, I–II, q 91, an 2) that "Among all others, the rational creature [man] is subject to divine providence in the most excellent way, insofar as it partakes of a share of providence, being provident both for itself and for others. Thus it has a share of the Eternal Reason, whereby it has a natural inclination to its proper act and end." Thomas makes this argument as an adaptation of Aristotelian argument as completed through his own faith in Revelation. In this respect, then, Thomas's next sentence of the quoted passage follows as necessary conclusion: "The participation of the eternal law in the rational creature is called natural law."

We might, as poet, suggest in this context that Adam's naming of all particular creatures in the presence of his own Creator is a parable of a "home schooling" in moral responsibility of intellect to the truth of things, to be remembered to us as always undertaken in the presence of God despite any gnostic intentionality to deny Divine Providence. It is by this denial nevertheless that *science* as properly serving intellect decays into a *scientism* serving the intellectual "self" in its presumption of autonomy. Whether the reductionism of things in themselves thus attempted is of things proper to the disciplines of cellular biology or to semiotics (actual creatures or signs), the intellectual manner of intellect as a proper "science" is compromised. Science ordinate to intellect, when prudentially employed in the light of the limit of intellect, pursues truth according to its interior purchase of natural law to divine law. (Natural law, Thomas says, is "*in* the rational creature" man.) In its pursuit of the "accurate naming of the things of God" (the poet's responsibility, O'Connor says) is the implication that moral responsibility to naming requires a prudential humility in recognizing intellectual limit, since finite intellect is insufficient to *comprehensive* naming. It is a deportment that remembers that the initial *name* derives from *concept* in reason's responsible keep. The difficulty that follows (which the poet might say is inherited from Adam through his fall) is a measured—a proportionate—*making* of signs as devolved from the Thomistic "word" (the concept) through the agency of signs. What seems necessary to the prudential making is the maker's remembering that his signs can never be comprehensive. What he usually discovers is that his signs even prove insufficient to his own word-concept, let alone comprehensive of the thing or things themselves initiating (*conceiving* in intellect) his concept. Hence the timeless lament, used by Eliot's Prufrock in justifying a turning aside from the risks in the action of love itself: "It is impossible to say just what I mean." From one impossibility to the next: from the impossibility of comprehensiveness of the thing itself by intellect through concept; to the impossibility of signs sufficiently serving his concept. And out of that doubled challenge to intellect: How conspicuous (because so rare) become witnesses of the intellectual deportment of prudential humility—the action of openness to creation in recognition of the inadequacy of intellectual action of openness to creation in recognition of the inadequacy of intellectual actions as a self-sufficiency. Percy, as well as others, has observed such a deportment in Albert Einstein, which perhaps makes Einstein apt reference for Percy in his juxtaposition of Einstein to Newton. For more is involved in Percy's illustration than whether Newton or Einstein is the closer to absolute truth about the physics of matter.

In the attempt to "call out" a suitable sign as naming an intellectual conjunction with a particular thing there is witnessed intellect-as-Adam, attempting a praise. It is an attempt to hallow intellect's own changed relation as active intellect within the company of beings as well, accepting the moral responsibility to an accuracy of consent to a created thing. That manner proves a sacramental deportment, a lifting up of things in acknowledging their Providential Cause. Articulation, a deployment of signs in a devolution of concept, becomes a long labor, especially for the poet in "purifying the dialect of the tribe" as Eliot characterizes it. It is a celebration proportionate as a lifting up of things, each as itself, of which ritual of sign the poet David Jones calls it summarily in a great poem, "Anathemata." It requires of the celebrant the moral responsibility of accurate naming, under that pressure upon him, his knowing that his naming is never sufficiently a *comprehensive* naming, that fullness possible only to Omniscience. Thus the complex of signs, those inherited and those refashioned in response to actual things in the light of inheritance, proves insufficient to any fixity of the particular intellect itself or to the social community which is always a continuing body which sign can never fix.

Our signs decay—an old lament more ancient than Eric Voegelin's reminders. They do so in part because they are inadequate to a fixed-certainty effected by finite intellect. That is, though in the thing made of signs (a poem, an argument) there be a fixed certainty—the poem or story or argument committed by sign to a "textual" arrest—intellect is itself of a primary creation and not fixed. It moves within the confluence of created things, all in a mutual *becoming* within the limits of each's particular being, which becoming includes decay. Indeed, it is in this distinction that Nominalism is itself at last given the lie, because it is inadequate as technique to the Modernist intentionality of sign as "angelistic" instrument beyond nature occupying a point of fixity. No sign is absolute in its power to *comprehend* being, even if pronounced "transcendentally" by its angelistic agency. To assume that agency to be beyond nature and therefore empowered over nature is to deny the limits of being in the person as *homo viator*. The Nominalist gnostic himself is the origin of such a presumption, projecting illusion as truth. That is a cautionary note struck in Percy's late essay, "The Holiness of the Ordinary," when he says that we are "man in a predicament and on the move" but "in a real world of real things, a world which is a sacrament and a mystery." Man is "a pilgrim whose life is a searching and a finding," but within limits prescribed by that "real world." That, he adds, is a recognition giving rise to "a recipe for the best novel-writing from Dante to Dostoevsky."

Community in the real world proves for such a writer as Dante or Dostoevsky or Percy to be his circumstantial matter, particular to each by its proximity to the writer as journeyman of this sacramental world at *this* time in *this* place. Such is a recognition to the novelist as Adam, a recognition Percy comes to more and more as a mystery not to be resolved by science but by faith in response to that Reality of realities, the Incarnation. Underlying his attempt from the beginning, as the necessary foundation of any social community, is an initiated *community* between *a thing* and *a discrete intellect*. That is the circumstance to Adam as namer, under the auspices of God Himself. This is to suggest, then, that a communion (a *con-union*) occurs, calling intellect to its providential participation in existential reality as antecedent to the intellectual person's own awareness of himself as actual. Hence in the moment of self-awareness the "self" discovers that it already possesses knowledge of things—has experienced some things and knows them—a knowing which has awakened it to self-awareness, as St. Thomas says. This con-union (this union *with*) of intellect and thing occurs before the effect in intellect called *concept*, even as concept is an effect preceding the act of naming a concept intellectually *conceived* (to recall Thomas's metaphor). The act of con-union is through intellectual openness to impinging reality, in a receptiveness to the actuality of a thing as necessarily antecedent to the receptiveness itself, since intellect is not the creator of the thing perceived. Such is a moment of an intellectual consent to existing things—an openness to things which we call love, however embarrassing that term to sophisticated intellect. It is an openness of love in that there has been a movement of consent allowing the senses their response to actual things. This is to suggest that it is love as *agape*, out of which may devolve *eros*—an extension of agape which rational intellect is responsible to keep ordinate.

If Percy in his borrowing from the Gesell Institute's studies of the child singles out the four-year-old in relation to the seven-year-old in respect to their responses to experiencing the world around them, we might rather emphasize the child much earlier as revealing to us this action of love as native to man. (Professor Lejeune, out of his understanding of genetics, might conceivably find origin of this love as agape in the grace of conception.) There are in such a child's responses (remembered when older in a vagueness of nostalgia for lost moments) what we recognize as self-evident: an openness to things. As a response of love, a receptive openness to things as actual to experience, it is not a response measurable by science except at the level of spectacle. Recall the infant's response to color and movement—prompting entrepreneurs inevitably to market mobiles to be hung over cribs.

Such things speak to the infant at his waking. It is a waking of intellect to things themselves, as St. Augustine might suggest. And this before the child possesses any word suited to his experience of waking. (Remember our own later experiences, watching a small child respond to some small thing alive—to a kitten or young rabbit.) Along his journeying way thereafter, the child will attempt to distinguish rabbit from cat, with concepts in intellect raising wonder out of the mystery of the actualities of such creatures as specific things within the confluence of things with each other. He must come to some *terms* with confusions within that confluence of things as each itself, within which confluence cats eat rabbits and scratch children. How challenging to intellect in its initial inclination to an openness of love—a growing mystery for the child becoming youth, becoming an old man: There is good, and there is evil, seemingly confluent in life in a becoming. And the most astonishing becoming of all: that of the person as intellectual soul incarnate. Most troubling, that journeying wonder, though it may at last come to a truth Percy speaks late in his life: The "world ... is a sacrament and a mystery," the implication of which vision is the obligation of the person to a sacramental deportment to things in themselves.

We are attempting to describe a relation of intellect as a property of our existence as person, but at the level which Percy addresses as *dyadic* in his early and into his later reflections. But we are suggesting that this so-called dyadic arena is more profoundly complex in its implications about our *becoming* this particular *person* than Percy seems to allow. Something has happened to the "self" *before* it possesses either concept or a word for concept. It is a change in intellect from a potential to an actuality as a "self," as a knowing intellectual soul. What Thomas argues to this point is that the relation between the soul and the thing has been certified by a truth already effected in intellect itself: that is (in another of his arguments) there has occurred in intellect an imaging of the essence of a thing in itself—which exists antecedently. Thomas will speak of this effect as an "in-forming" of intellect itself. (Observe once more, in relation to such esoteric argument, the small child responding to a kitten on a first encounter.) Here, Thomas would remind us against a confusion: Truth and essence are not interchangeable realities but separate, neither of them to be comprehensively measured at last by science, though science *as science* has a responsibility to a pursuit of measure as governed in its conclusions by providential humility—lest science presume to absolute comprehension. Truth, Thomas argues, is a property of essence made congenial by Providence Itself (by God) to man's given intellectual property of perception according to its finite limit. In that act of perception occurs a bonding—a communion—of intellect and thing, so that intellect holds a truth of the thing itself, bequeathed it by the essence of the thing perceived. It is in this complex of intellectual action that Thomas argues our first movements toward God. It is a movement made through our senses in response to existential reality. In such an orientation of the self, truth certifies the self to itself, through intellect's initial consent to the reality of that which is not itself. It is in the loss of this orientation that self-consciousness becomes deracinated, most proximately in our intellectual inheritance through disorienting signs inherited from Descartes—at least that is the source pervasive of Modernist dislocation in Percy's judgment. Out of that inheritance Modernist ideologies grow dominant through the Nominalistic advantage taken of Cartesian uncertainties about the self. It will lead Percy to that argument already introduced, his "The Fateful Rift: The San Andreas Fault in the Modern Mind," and to his "Diagnosing the Modern Malaise" and "The Coming Crises in Psychiatry," and in others of his essays.

Our own concern here is a partial demurrer to Percy's address to the sign in attempting rescue from Cartesian confusion. *Naming*, we suggest, is a ritual celebrating the recognition of a community *in* being, already effected before the act of naming. That is, Percy's "triadic" concern (we contend) is already effected and is not dependent upon the sign shared with another self-consciousness, another person. By that ritual of naming, when once initiated, there occurs an opening upon a larger and more complex recognition of the (complex) nature of the self's (the intellectual soul's) relation to all that is not itself, including both things and other persons. But this is not a transformation but an enlargement. (Here one is reminded of Flannery O'Connor's observation that "The longer you look at one object, the more of the world you see in it.") Such, then, is the initial movement of a *communion* with a thing, a joining with reality participated in by a "self" through a sacramental deportment. That is the beginning of the journey of the self into the possible fullness of the person's becoming, a fulfillment of the self in its diverse potentialities. The perfect fulfillment of those potentialities, a coincident replacement of the potential by the actual through grace, is that fulfillment which the saints and mystics and theological philosophers call Beatitude.

Such a transformation of the self from its actual beginning to its fulfilled end—that unity spoken of in theological discourse on dimension of the self—is the issue. The self's relationship to a community of selves thus proves to be a crucial corollary responsibility, though that is not the determinate necessity to the existence of a self. In that relationship, the self discovers membership in a body. This distinction, if not clearly understood, leads to possible confusions that eventually distort the nature of the self. For the intellect is easily tempted to presumptuous excesses by knowledge unmodified by an understanding of its limits to knowing. On the one hand, it may be tempted to an excessive centering upon itself, the effect being an isolation of itself as an *autonomous world*, set apart by intention from all existence else, that fatal rift of self from creation. On the other hand, it may succumb to an excessive centering upon its social nature as if the social arena contained the person's ultimate end. Neither orientation of the inherent desire for fulfillment within the self—of what Thomas calls "a natural inclination" of reason "to its proper act and end"—is necessarily improper, though each is susceptible to disproportionate excesses of action which obscure its proper end. It becomes improper as an obsession by an extremity on either hand—either that of self-love or that of a worship of existential reality by a reduction of the self in making creation itself an idol. For at either extremity, mediate ends to fulfillment are taken as ultimate end.

Such distinctions as we have here attempted to make are not foreign to Percy, though they may not be at the center of his thought as they are for St. Thomas—or, closer home, not so central to Percy as they are for Flannery O'Connor. Percy engages a common problem, which Eliot engaged in similar intellectual agony. Eliot's resolution of his own struggle is celebrated at last in his "Ash-Wednesday," in which a prayer is uttered: "Teach us to care and not to care." It is a prayer concerned with an *ordinate* address to *mediate* ends as the soul's providential responsibility, which address must nevertheless not be changed to the inordinate by excessiveness. We must learn, that is, a balance between caring responsibility within mediate concerns for the self as steward to existential reality within the existential world, and the seduction of excessive concern at the expense of the self's final end. That final end requires that we not "care" excessively for mediate ends. Excessive "care" for the proximate too easily tempts *homo viator* to a presumption of himself as savior of creation. At the same time a proper caring for the "self" must not be perverted to a self-love whose end becomes the self lost in the cosmos by estrangement from it. Eliot's prayer is an utterance made within an enlarged triadic conception of the self, effected within a community of the living and the dead out of several millennia of *homo viator* responding to existential reality as a "self." Eliot comes to an accommodation with that *tradition* by the time of his signal poem "Ash-Wednesday." By then Eliot concludes that the tradition is not to be rejected but made ordinate through *orthodoxy*, whereby finite intellect's inheritance of a tradition may be sorted. And in a kinship to Eliot, we are suggesting, Percy does this most evidently in his *Thanatos Syndrome*, to which accommodation to reality his essay "The Holiness of the Ordinary" is a sort of codicil.

T. S. Eliot published "Ash-Wednesday" as a whole in 1930, beginning with separate sections of it in periodicals in 1928. The dates are of interest here, since Eliot's principal American friend among the Fugitive-Agrarians published his "Ode to the Confederate Dead" in 1928. Both Allen Tate and Eliot are concerned with the intellectual Narcissism we may trace to a proximate origin in Western philosophy back to Descartes, as Walker Percy will do in recognizing a fault in the Modernist mind. It is worth noting that Percy's friends, the Tates, celebrated that turning by entering the Catholic Church, Allen Tate himself only at mid-century, at about the time Walker did. (Percy at this time was in correspondence with Caroline Gorden, Tate's wife.) Footnotes to that turning of Tate himself would have been of particular interest to Percy at the point of his own turning, especially perhaps Tate's essay on his most famous poem, given Percy's uneasiness about his own Southern origins. Before entering the Church, in 1938, Tate wrote an exposition of his own poem, in response to what he saw as critical misunderstandings of it, under the title "Narcissus as Narcissus." In his essay he asserts that the "poem is 'about' solipsism, a philosophical doctrine which says that we create the world in the act of perceiving it." As Walker Percy would respond to it, Tate argues his concern with "the failure of the human personality to function objectively in nature and society."

In 1945, Tate published his "The New Provincialism," an analysis of the Modernist mind in its progress toward Narcissism now become dominant doctrine among intellectuals in the post–World War II world, an end implicit in Descartes, entering literature through Edgar Allen Poe and Poe's influence on French letters that led to French Symbolism, the movement fascinating to the younger Eliot. (That is an "American" influence as well upon Sartrean Existentialism.) In 1951 Tate gave two lectures, "The Angelic Imagination: Poe as God" and "The Symbolic Imagination: The Mirrors of Dante," both relevant to Percy's current circumstances in the intellectual desert. This, just as Tate was becoming Roman under the auspices of Jacques and Raisa Maritain, a coincidence of pilgrims, of *homo viator* as critic or poet, as Percy could but be aware. (The Maritains together translate Tate's "Ode to the Confederate Dead" into French at this time.)

Such then are recognitions of intellectual Narcissism that Walker

Percy shares with Eliot and Tate which allow, though gradually, his accommodation to his Southern tradition. He will subsequently become more comfortable in his Southern "place," Covington, Louisiana, with a new appreciation of Eudora Welty's early and comfortable accommodation that required of her no intellectual engagement of the larger Western tradition such as he seemed forced to make. She differs as a writer in this respect from Eliot or Tate or Walker himself, a recognition evidenced in several of Percy's comments on his neighbor up there in Mississippi. Celebrating her as being "alive and well in Jackson," he anticipates a time when the "American novelist will tire of his angelism" and will "wonder how to get back into a body, live in a place, at a street address. Eudora Welty will be a valuable clue."

Eliot's recognition is of himself as a *soul*, not a psychological "self," in consequence of which recognition he becomes comfortable in a place at last, at an address far removed from the likes of Covington or Jackson, but nevertheless a place allowing some sharing with Welty a sense of being at home, his "home" London by then. It is a recognition Eliot came to, but in a journey for which neither a Betty nor a Franz proved sufficient authenticators of his arrival. The enlarged "triadic" arena Eliot recognizes has as its third point of the self's reference the Cause of the self and of Betty and Franz and of cats and dogs and apples. In the 1920s Eliot had begun to read Thomas Aquinas in his recovery from the "nervous-breakdown" which Thomas reveals as a spiritual crisis. It is in relation to that ultimate Point, which in its transcendent mystery is inclusive of all points in the Cosmos-environment, that the self and each thing *in itself* are authenticated beyond the powers of any certification by intellect alone through its complex but limited signs. So Eliot will conclude. With the guidance of St. Thomas, we may consider, then, that the initiating movement of the self is precedent to the sign announcing that movement with the desert as backdrop. It is located by intellect as an event effecting reasoned reflection on the event within intellect itself, affecting its becoming.

A complex of such events, which we speak of as our experiences of *being* through encounter with discretely existing *beings*, allows reason its movement toward universals, Thomas argues. There is an initiating movement of intellect consequent to that consenting grace whereby we *are* a "self" existing, self-recognized as existing through our actual encounter of things. It is experience, not signs, that certifies our existence. In response to encounter, consciousness (the self becoming self-aware) wakes to the mystery of its own nature as already inhabiting a "triadic" world by virtue of its very created nature. It already is a little world which does not at last exist by being hollowed out *from* the Cosmos *through* signs, nor is it imposed *upon* the "Cosmos-environment" which holds the self in its initial journeying toward its proper end. The initiating movement is the intellectual soul's encounter with discrete things in themselves. The essence of discrete things—whether of a *dog* or *water* or *apple* or *Betty* or *Franz*—is to be held as known truth of actually existing things—however partially held by intellect. When truly encountered, things' effect *in* intellect is of a gained possession of a truth, borne to it through the senses, of the essenced thing—which possession is antecedent to any concept thus consequential to experience or to any sign assigned to concept. No wonder then that O'Connor testifies of her own experiences of things that the longer we look at a thing, the more of the whole world we see in it. The point is implicit in the example Percy himself uses of Helen Keller's discovery of a correspondence of the letters "w-a-t-e-r" to her sensation of water as a thing in itself.

Percy refers to that famous event, quoting Miss Sullivan's account of the miraculous entry of Helen Keller into a new dimension of the self through sign; though from our perspective as here argued, Percy makes Miss Sullivan too centrally a causal agent to the event in her role as sign-giver. Not that that role is not important certainly. Miss Sullivan is a part of that dramatic moment. But it does not follow that her presence as sign-maker is determinate, a necessity to the existence of Helen Keller as a *self* transformed triadically by responding to her sensation of water through sign. It cannot be that without Miss Sullivan, Helen Keller would not be herself a *world*, nor have that world which Percy calls the *self*. It seems evident to the contrary that Helen Keller already possesses a world of the self, is self-aware, in a fundamental way—a world within which the drama is then played out as an enlargement, not a transformation; Helen Keller becomes *more fully* the person she already is. She is not so radically transformed as to allow us to say that as a self she only comes to exist subsequent to her association of a sign with her experienced communion with actual water.

The concern for certainty here is crucial. For if the self does not exist save through communal participation in sign, both abortion and euthanasia become the more easily acceptable actions in pursuit of a "quality of life." The "pre-self" may be reduced to an inconvenient mistake of nature; the self demented and reduced to the dyadic by incapacity of sign becomes but a dying animal suitably "put out of its misery." Such is the "rational" excuse for the convenience of the living sign-users. And so we must affirm, on the evidence of our personal experiences of becoming, that Helen Keller is already possessed of a sense of community with actual water as with other things she encounters intellectually through her senses' responses to things, though sense response to things is naturally limited for her. She demands names *subsequent* to the signaling event of experience of an actual thing, water. The marvel of sign-mak-

ing (in this event w-a-t-e-r) opens her to other sign-makings and mag-
nifies both her receiving of communion within an enlarged body of communion with Miss Sullivan, and her being received reciprocally into an
enlarged community of intellect. It need not follow that the sign *makes*
the world of Miss Keller's self, nor does it make the community with her
teacher. Very obviously, before this celebrated event Miss Sullivan already
bears witness of a community of love with Helen Keller. Both already
are, and Helen Keller is in an "intelligent" and active participation with
things beyond the limits prescribed by the consent of the *dyadic*. The
evidence of her existence is, in fact, her hunger for a new magnified relation of her self to things, a sharing of that relation through names. Names
may enhance her *seeing*, but do not cause seeing.

Miss Sullivan spells out in Miss Keller's hand "w-a-t-e-r," as water
pours over Miss Keller's other hand. What we assert as true, on reflection,
is that Miss Keller is already considerably advanced into the world and
even into the world of signs before this event. Through the sense of
touch she has learned letters and principles of association of letters reaching a compact sign unit, *water* in the association of sensation known to
sign proposed. What seems suddenly revealed to her is not a first recognition of existence as a self in a triadic relation, out of a dyadic one with
Miss Sullivan. Is it not rather a recognition that the already perceived
existence of the self as a world allows, through the material sign (the
spelling out of *water*), an enlarged and more subtle relation with other
such worlds as that of Miss Sullivan? What Helen Keller already knows,
among the many things she knows, is water in itself as desirable and as
separate from the common sign "w-a-t-e-r." In that knowing, without
which there could be no public association of sign to thing as at last
occurs in the exchange with Miss Sullivan, there nevertheless lies already
a *concept* in Helen Keller as an active presence to her intellect. There
already exists that bonding which St. Thomas speaks of in his metaphor
of conception, an action we have spoken of as receptive love. The self
we call by name Helen Keller has undergone no radical transformation,
no change of the self in kind, certainly, but rather a change in a degree
of understanding of sign as a means of communion of intellects within
that unique body within creation, humankind.

A suggestion that such a conclusion seems at least probable is in Miss
Keller's immediate acquisition of a term suitable to the relation she has
with Miss Sullivan as companion, friend, teacher. But there already exists
before this addition of names a real and intimately known relationship.
What happens in the event of naming, then, is that Helen Keller experiences a growing understanding of a relationship, founded in a prior
knowledge of a relationship already possessed *with* a thing not herself;
namely, an enlarged relationship with Miss Sullivan. Through Miss Sul-

livan's report to us of the historic event, we see Miss Keller initially ravenous for the names of things—the pump at hand as *pump*, whence flows the water which is named *water*, the trellis as *trellis*, door as *door*, and so on. We observe here a passage into "elfland," as it were, such as Chesterton distinguishes as separating the three-year-old's and seven-year-old's response to existential reality. Helen Keller's passage is with a joyful wonder which is already more sophisticated than that of the child of three but akin to it, while the seven-year-old's experience (according to Gesell) is marked by a withdrawal which, decayed to Narcissism, becomes a deportment of sullenness to things—especially to persons. A woman many years in the world, struggling with a three-year-old's wonder against her severe natural deprivation as deaf, dumb, blind: She responds with a joy in this enlarged relation of intellect to reality, enabled by sign to share that relationship already existing at a "triadic" level.

In the midst of her joyful seizing upon signs, upon names, Helen Keller "suddenly turning round" demands of Miss Sullivan *her* name. "I spelled 'Teacher.'" Indeed, that is the name for Miss Sullivan's crucial relation to Helen Keller in this particular encounter with the principle of naming as a specialized intellectual action. One notices Miss Sullivan's typography in her report, the ascribing of a capital letter for her term. As Teacher and as Pupil in relation to the names of things, they share a limited community of intellectual deportment toward reality though differing in degree of sharing. The point here is that it is a restricted, circumscribed deportment of a relation of two intellectual selves to each other as already known to each other, though lacking a name for that relationship. It is dependent, we must say, upon a prior community of those two selves, now become limited by a precision of thought under the aspect of Teacher and Pupil. That prior community depends *in* the prior existence of discrete and separate selves, Miss Keller and Miss Sullivan. Each of these discrete selves *as a self* has moved more and more into a community with things as a consequence of encounter as *self* with the other as person: the *substantial* existence of the self, by its very existence in limit ranging from the finitudes of its potentialities down to the accidents of its existential particularities. Through those limits occurs a *becoming* of separate selves within a confluence with the *other* self whereby each self becomes the more *this* person by virtue of response to the discrete givenness of the self. Miss Keller does not dissolve into Miss Sullivan nor she into Miss Keller. Each *is*, already a self—an intellectual soul incarnate.

Intellects, in their potentialities, we remember, differ from each other self-evidently, as experience of other selves reveals to us. So too do trees differ from rocks self-evidently, or persons from trees, though poets play at kinships. Some ensouled creatures differ from others in the limits of their incarnate, existential actualities of body in time and place. And so Helen Keller's address to sign understandably differs in its difficulties from the address of the "normal," physically able three-year-old or seven-year-old. Within such differentiations of discretely existing persons lies our concern for the marvelous potentials of signs to community—a challenge fraught with error for intellect since signs themselves are *incomprehensible* of things. The limited omnipotence of signs to establish relation to discrete existences may not be ignored. As we have already suggested, it is an error of gnostic intellect to deny the limitation of sign in relation to being. But only by that denial is the gnostic intellect confident of its power to its transgressions upon being. Such transgression affects the body of the world with inevitable consequence, the sum of those transgressions having reduced us so largely, as Percy suggests, to that strange "new" creature at large in the body of community, the theorist-consumer—become the gnostic ravager of things.

It is in this respect that signs liturgically ordered in service to community may regain for us both a recovery of con-unity with community itself and through that recovery a con-union with the Cause of all things. We discover the ritual of name already implicit to the four-year-old's reaching out to a thing with a name, whether a name given to a toy or to a puppy or kitten. We know it in the festive response of a Helen Keller to a name, w-a-t-e-r. It is a sacramental response both to and through things in that they are holy by virtue of existing as caused by Love and sustained in their existence by grace. We need only recall or observe the signing gesture of infant, child, adolescent, adult—especially in speaking the sign Mother or Father—to know whether the sign is used sacramentally or not. Through such recovered vision, Percy comes at last to his moving affirmation in his "The Holiness of the Ordinary": "The sacraments, especially the Eucharist, ... whatever else they do, confer the highest significance upon the ordinary things of this world, bread, wine, water, touch, breath, words, talking, listening...."

9

The commerce of signs and through signs makes intellectual community possible. But we know how complex are the problems to community through shared signs. The variety of tongues—Greek, Latin, French, English; or within the same tongue, contexts spawning divisive traditions suited to diverging "tribes." How multiple our languages within the tribal specializations that exist even within a common "tongue": for the astronomer, the neurosurgeon, the mathematician, on and on. We risk as person becoming a sectarian in tribal loyalties, the tribe of the moment itself discovered as splitting into sub-tribes in the deconstructions of community. The extremity of sectarianism is the self isolated from all else, a tendency occurring in ironic manifestations. At the end of World War II, in a prophetic essay, Allen Tate argued that we are moving to that end through a "new provincialism" quite different from that associated with a local place, the latter in that paradox appearing to Percy as represented by his friend Eudora, a *writer* in a *place*, with an actual street address. Tate defined the new provincialism as a "state of mind in which regional men lose their origins in the past and its continuity into the present, and begin every day as if there had been no yesterday."

We become by that provincialism, he says, "committed to chance solutions of 'problems' that seem unique because we have forgotten the nature of man." As new provincials, we suggest, we specialize in signs, reducing signs to formulae, replacing the older concern for the Thomistic universal as binding us to creation in its particularities. If we recall Eliot's concern for the "dissociation of sensibilities," the disjunction of "thought and feeling," seen by Eliot as occurring at about the time of Milton (not long after Descartes), we might see as well a certain irony in Milton's conflicted callings as poet and as statesman. As poet, his concern in his great epic *Paradise Lost* is to measure the ways of God to man to recover man to God. Meanwhile he serves Cromwell as "Latin Secretary," Latin already arrested as a tribal language among tribes mediating political upheavals in which were emerging nationalistic intentions to power of nations over nations.

How strange, that unfolding separation into our own day, into ever new provincialisms of formulae as the dialects empowering tribes as they are increasingly disjoined from the actualities of place. Consider the random commerce of intellect whose universal language is genetic code. There grows a tribal universalism more and more suggestive of intellectual angelism over being itself such as that against which Tate warned the poet to take a stand in his essay "Poe as God."

How inevitable, in hindsight, was the increasing detachment from reality through tribalism, a detachment from what Percy declares the real world—in which real things exist requiring a sacramental deportment—the disjunction effected by the ever-new "tribalisms" existing within an "inner space," occupied fleetingly by diverse tribes. We embrace, with an alarmed enthusiasm, the Internet for instance as capable of seining us as a self from the threatening void to our self. *This* person in relation to *this* person, each real things in a real world, seem to grow more distant from each other than the fading star that occupies the excited astronomer as he cruises the void as a "self" through instruments more real to him than himself as person. How symptomatic, the emerging spectacle called "virtual reality," in respect to which there appears increasingly alarmed reaction, symptomatic of disjunction of each "self" from reality as actual. How excitedly disturbing this "virtual reality." Such symptoms led Percy to his *Lost in the Cosmos: The Last Self-Help Book*.

And so we seem to need more and more, to the healing of specialized isolations into tribes whose "place" seems the vacuum of the Internet, the services of philosopher and of poet. That service is pressingly needed to the task at hand: in Eliot's phrase, the task of purifying "the dialect of the tribe" called humanity. This is a need, but in an age in which philosopher and poet are tolerated at the suburbs of disintegrating community. Waiting their possible rescue of us, we as deracinated tribal members struggle with the variousness of our memberships in competing tribal "orthodoxies," each under the diversity of Modernist ideologies. *Homo viator* struggles with signs received and signs projected, attempting to recover a common recognition of the limits and range of his own membership, having lost the grounding of his own reality in the real world at hand, out of which are to be gained credentials to membership. The rules of membership seem always shifting under the pressures of random contingencies. Man as pilgrim, Percy suggests, is thus suspended between two extremes in his quest for "place." Shall he settle in Lost Cove, Tennessee, to "wait for whatever he is waiting for?" Or should he set out under the auspices of the latest technology for that imagined Eden, "Copernicus 4" by its imagined name? Those are the extreme alternatives offered in the "Last Self-Help Book."

Walker Percy's attempt to recover a grounding as poet, we have seen, is through semiotics, a science of signs, in relation to which possible recovery the philosopher might well encourage science's attempt to "purify the dialect of the tribe"—though suggesting perhaps that science itself needs to recognize its point of departure as shared with the philosopher and poet. It is the point of recognition of the self-evident through common sense, requiring no "scientific" measure. A suspension of scientific disbelief in the self-evident, accepting the gifts of the self-evident such as Descartes could not grant out of uncertainty of his own actual existence: That is a point of relocation in reality. We intend here the most fundamental of all self-evidents: The recognition that *I* exist beyond all assaults of skepticism about my own existence which prove, not original, but to have been reintroduced into the Western intellectual community by Descartes out of an ancient Sophistry such as Socrates engaged. Long ago, St. Augustine also rejected that erosive skepticism of which he was first a disciple, saying that the "academic skeptic" (as he called the gnostic intellect of his day) presents no threat by subtle Sophist doubt: Though you *say* you exist, what if that is but an illusion, a delusion? To which St. Augustine: I cannot be deluded, cannot project illusion, if I do not first exist. Therefore I exist, however much inclined I may be to distortions of that reality of my "self" by a waywardness of my intellect. It is to recover from that waywardness that St. Augustine turns from his skeptical Manichaeanism, which he practiced as hypocritical Sophist in submerging himself in the "evils" of the body itself as if that action were a rejection of the evil world by the actions of consuming it.

By the time Percy writes his "Why Are You a Catholic?" published the last year of his life, he sees beneath the marvels of spectacle as now complicating and disorienting both the self and community life through technological "progress." How close we now are to that crucial moment St. Augustine engaged. But in a new provincialism using spectacle, the old position of the Manichaean as Sophist—or the Sophist appropriating Manichaean "reasonableness" to his destructive intent—has been turned on its head. Yet it reveals nevertheless the same self-centered rejection of reality. St. Augustine at his waking at last confronts and condemns his own false intellectualism, his perverse self-love. Percy, looking back on *The Moviegoer*, discovers himself in that work as having been unknowingly an incipient Augustinian. In a late essay, he declares that the "present age is demented. It is possessed by a sense of dislocation, a loss of personal identity, an alternating sentimentality and rage which, in an individual patient, could be characterized as dementia."

This is a statement which (could we but engage him on the point) seems to modify his earlier reluctance to agree to Flannery O'Connor's insistence that the Devil is a real contender for man's soul within the arena of the "self." Percy's drift in such phrases as *possessed by*, followed by the clinical description leading to that "possession" as characterized by *dementia* in the *individual patient*, suggests his old hesitation about the Devil. He is nevertheless very carefully concerned with a moral responsibility as poet to name accurately the things of God, here the most valued thing of God spawned "bodily" in nature, *community*. As much poet as scientist now, he isolates instance by the particular of metaphor: the "dementia" of the "individual patient." Dementia: *de* plus *ment*, a falling away from *mind* toward *madness*—but toward a madness of rejection which neither psychology can fully account for nor psychiatry restore. The possession is a studied, an intentional, rejection of ordered mind in the interest of an absolute freedom of intellect, whose motto is understood anciently as Satan's *non servium*, the rejection Milton dramatizes in his poem. Milton's Satan declares the mind its own place and its intention sufficient to make a Heaven of Hell, a Hell of Heaven—whichever serves the intentionality to an absolute freedom. To this passage from Percy's "Why Are You a Catholic?" and in reaction to a dementia become the climate of mind suited to pursuit of angelism, Percy remarks of the twentieth century as it draws to a close that it does "not yet have a name, but it can be described. It is the most scientifically advanced, savage, democratic, inhuman, sentimental, murderous century in human history."

That last sentence is set for emphasis as a paragraph unto itself, after which he ventures a name for the age: "I would call it the age of the theorist-consumer." The characterization combines in the singular person, as it were in the patient suffering dementia, the principles possessing an age bent on its own self-destruction. Each person, this suggests, partakes as both theorist and consumer: The fascination of theory is devoted to proximate ends of consumption of the world's body as the ultimate end of human desire. It is a description, then, of an age *possessed* by a "Thanatos Syndrome" such as he dramatized in his recent and last novel. He finds symptomatic evidences to his point in a "New Age" mentality, the more popular designation of later decades of the century. That is the mentality of "an amorphous group ranging from California loonies like Shirley MacLaine to the classier Joseph Campbell," the extremes of stylistic manifestations in consort, joined not by a concern for the truth of things but by a "mythical liveliness" which finds its most lively expression (since lacking intellectual justifications because of dementia) in the excesses of sexual destructions as if the sexual act were the ultimate beatitude. The response of such a New Age religionist to Walker Percy? "So you are a Catholic? How odd and interesting!" From that antagonist's position Percy concludes, "single things and events" are "assigned significance," but "only insofar as they are exemplars of theory or items for consumption." Such is the presumption *possessing* intellect, signifying intellect's decay into "an inflation of a method of knowing" which is "unwarranted" by reality itself. And so his answer to the question put to him by this New Age small inquisitor, now further fallen from the precisions of Ivan Karamazov's Grand Inquisitor: "The reasons for my conversion to the Catholic Church, this side of grace, can be described as Roman, Arthurian, Semitic, and semiotic." Roman—see Marcus Aurelius. Arthurian—see Richard I and Robert E. Lee. Semitic—see the Old Testament activist heroes and prophets struggling with the mystery of the one God, whose service alone may order mind and body. Semiotic—see Charles Peirce as philosopher with a scientific bent.

What is of particular interest here is Percy's expressing his having come at last to an accommodation to his own "Southernness," after long uneasiness with that inheritance that at first appeared to be forced upon him by circumstances—his birth into a family long associated with a place. Now he is prepared to say that "If one wished to depict the beau ideal of the South, it would not be the crucified Christ but rather the stoic knight at parade rest, both hands folded on the hilt of his broadsword, his face grave and impassive as the Emperor's [Aurelius's]. In the South ... he came to be, not the Emperor or Richard, but R. E. Lee, the two in one." To which, in respect to cultural becomings, Percy discovers the saving recovery to such a beau ideal, the crucified Christ. But Percy himself? Such a Southerner reluctant to renounce Lee and King Richard and Aurelius? "After all, the pagans converted by St. Paul did not cease to be what they were. One does not cease to be Roman, Arthurian, Alabamian" [remembering having been born in that affluent suburb of Birmingham]." But to become much more through that saving grace—that is a recognition allowing him to be "at home" in Covington. For "the European knight with his broadsword at Mont-St.-Michel" would make no sense "without the crucified Jew above him." Percy then quotes John Paul II to the point of his own "self" as a Southerner rescued in Covington, Louisiana: "Whatever else we are, we are first of all spiritual Semites." The *self* as *Semite*, whatever the place: the *person* as *homo viator*. And so, as O'Connor says and Percy echoes through his fictions (at first not realizing how much he does so), we are all "Christ-haunted," though some are more evidently so—i.e., evidently so in spectacles of action within cultural community—in the "South" which sustains both these writers as Southern and Catholic.

How various our membership within the body of any community proximate to us—in city or suburb or country. Variety itself reminds us, if we are not hopelessly demented, of the necessity of submission in *place* as *member*—the action of participation that we name as *manners*. Manners evolve in recognition of our limits as *this* person in *this* place—of our existing as person by virtue of limits in ourselves required for participation in community as member. That is self-evident, though not always easily recognized, or accepted upon the recognition. Jacques Maritain engages this conundrum to *homo viator* in his *The Person and the Common Good* (1947), reminding us that as person we "enter society" as "a part whose proper good is inferior to the good of the whole." But the *whole* itself exists in response to the person as *person*, who in his "spiritual totality" is to be "referred to the transcendent whole" which "*surpasses* and is superior to all temporal societies." And so with respect to "the eternal destiny of the soul, society exists for each person and is subordinate to it" in respect to that transcendent whole. That is a self-evident reality, to be served by signs purified as the "dialect of the tribe," the dialect itself in service to the tribe in ordering the membership of the person to the particular proximate body called "society." That is in the best interest of that member's ultimate end, common manners as a consent to the relation of *person* to community, the solvent to civil friction.

Signs bonding members in community are effectively common through recognition, in consent of the person to this self-evident relation of his person to family, of family to community—the relationship of membership as known by the person intuitively through an openness of love. The ordering of love as proportionate to membership is the principal burden of signs themselves, requiring reason's service to the self-evident. Such reason in action is larger than merely a deployment as *rationalism* toward imposing order, the letter of the law divorced from natural law. Rationalism, reason dehumanized, proves increasingly disregardful of the mystery of the person's membership in either community or nature. Such then are prior limitations upon sign as ultimate authority, in that sign must be submissive to the reality of things as discretely existing. Hence names require a sacramental office in lifting things in tribute to their ultimate Cause, whether in lifting up a person or a dog or an apple, or water on the palm—or Dame Julian of Norwich's hazelnut on her palm, which she recognizes as held in being, and so not falling to nothingness, by a sustaining Love. That is a sacramental ground not to be ignored, even by the scientist no less than by philosopher or poet. Such a relation of name to thing cannot at last be sufficiently served by "pure" science, then, whether directed at the stars overhead on a clear night or through the formulae of the astronomer's seeing under the auspices of a Newton or Einstein with the aid of the latest technology. Thus it proves again and again that the point of departure of the discrete "self" is that of a self in relation to a thing—thus self-evidently known. The thing itself submits to measure when sign is understood as a limited measure, as the action of a limited intellect to be governed by love. And so sign is never *comprehensive* of the thing known, nor is it ever the cause of the thing known. And at the beginning, a mystery: The first thing of which there is a conscious knowing proves to be "self" as already existing in response to a thing.

One need not, of course, deny the importance of that communal enjoining of Miss Sullivan and Miss Keller as Teacher and Pupil, the dramatic event of Miss Keller's action of wedding name to thing. But caution is required against the temptation to conclude from that reported experience that either person in the "enjoinment" therefore, consequently, *is* a self—is a person as an effect of the sign. That would be to come perilously close to the extreme Sartrean position, in which the action of making (here the making of sign) is supposed the cause of the being of the maker himself. In this concern, we recall that Walker Percy, like Dante before him and like St. Augustine before Dante in the middle of their lives, comes to himself in a dark wood, under the sudden shadow of tuberculosis. He does so in circumstances in which occur a self-recognition: He is already a physician in a professional progress far from home. It is then that he discovers St. Thomas and Kierkegaard as he begins slowly to respond to a new calling, that of becoming a Physician as Novelist, he tells us. Given his dedication as scientist in pursuit of his medical calling at that point of his turning, he brings with him into his discovered calling the intellectual deportment of scientist. He finds an initial encouragement in writing his first published novel in Jean-Paul Sartre, an empiricist of signs who would command sign to his own rescue. It is only after having published *The Moviegoer*, looking back on that experience as physician-novelist, that Percy is awed by what has occurred to him.

It is a discovery analogous to that moment for Helen Keller of discovering *water* as the name of a known thing. We have heard Percy affirm his discovery:

> The novel, again by accident—or was it accident?—landed squarely in the oldest tradition of Western letters: the pilgrim's search outside himself, rather than the guru's search within. All this happened to the novelist and his character without the slightest consciousness of a debt to St. Augustine or Dante. Indeed, the character [Binx] creates within himself and within the confines of a single weekend in New Orleans a microcosm, the spiritual history of the West, from the Roman patrician reading his Greek philosophers to the thirteenth century pilgrim who leaves home and takes to the road.

By this point of his turning as novelist, Percy has engaged the mystery of signs as issuing into an almost "scientific" clarity in his "Delta" theory, his "triadic" theory of the transformation of the self effected by sign. It is a theory he never quite abandons, though he will encompass it more largely within a sacramental vision in that last brief essay, "The Holiness of the Ordinary" (1989). The emerging "self" Percy has discovered, and affirms with his own signs worth repeating. We have heard him testify that "the sacraments, especially the Eucharist ... confer the highest significance upon the ordinary things of this world, bread, wine, water, touch, breath, words, talking, listening—and what do you have? You have man in a predicament and on the move in a real world of real things, a world which is a sacrament and a mystery; a pilgrim whose life is a searching and a finding." But such a recognition is possible only in a discovery that the "self" is already antecedently holy in having been "spoken" by Love and so existing as *this* journeyman now newly committed to a sacramental deportment to things already known.

That is why we noted as a parable to our concern that Adam in the Garden did not require Eve's presence for his naming of created things. And we should note as well that it is not easy to determine at what point in the enlargement—the actualization of potentialities through intellectual actions—that a "self" comes to possess signs, the names of holy

things. The self's journey of becoming, within the limits of its potentialities, begins long before any words are spoken by mouth or eye or
hand, though from the beginning the self is already *as itself* a word spoken. By that speaking by Love, it *is*. Percy would insist, as does St.
Thomas, that this word spoken, *this* person, *is* consequent to the proximate world as a biological conception. Such is a mystery of personhood
as effected by grace. And we are emphasizing, as Percy no doubt would
within our present context of signs, that the self thus exists at a triadic
moment, conception. Dr. Jerome Lejeune, in his *The Concentration Can*
as we have seen, brings the poet to service in his witness, seeking a word
more difficult to utter at last than "w-a-t-e-r" for a Helen Keller. His is
a pressing concern to accurately name this miraculous creation of a *thing*
of God, this new entity which by that miracle is a *person*. In the moment
of conception (effected by grace, he and Percy would agree, to which we
add that presence effecting a triadic nature) the "cell splits in two in an
exchange of information from one cell to the other one." Then "When
it's split in three it receives information: we are an individual." And yet
the "first cell knew more than the three cells stage, and the three cell stage
knew more than the morula, than the gastrula, than the primitive streak,
and the primitive nervous system." This is Dr. Lejeune's testimony before
a civil judge in defense of those persons confined to a "concentration
can" by our technology.

At what point of this miracle of life, of the "self's" initiated existence, is that self communally bound to the things of God under the auspices of sign? We remarked that Percy's insistence upon sign, at least
theoretically, as *substantively* first known between two selves makes each
self to *be*, transforming the signifier to a triadic nature. And we cautioned
that such a position makes a consistent defense of the unborn at least
problematic, if we allow that the self *as self* is determined only by a mutual
becoming between the sign-maker and the sign-receiver. Even so, the
whole mystery of communion among created things (but most especially
among those created things called *persons*) is discovered to be a deepening mystery through the explorations of existence with the "science"
of signs as used by persons: not only articulated formulae, however, but
with experimental instruments of genetic science pursued back to a
grounding in an initial cell.

There is at this moment considerable "research" interest in the
fetus's attunement to community language per se before it is born as we
observed, discovering in the fetus's response to language, to sign which
continues after it is born from an initial bonding before birth. It is not
the three-year-old but the infant just emerging from the womb, for
instance, who differs significantly in his response to geometric figures or
to a face drawn simply and starkly on a sheet of paper. *Science News*

reports (February 8, 1992) that current evidence suggests that two-month-old infants "discern differences between speech sounds of many languages, including those never heard at home." Before they utter any word, they seem attuned to phonemes, but more acutely attuned to those of their native language, so much so that after several months, it becomes almost impossible for the growing child to appropriate sounds peculiar to languages other than its own, no longer clearly hearing distinctions sufficient to its own repetition of peculiar signs.

It has long been argued that the younger the child, the more adept at learning a foreign language, a supposition which leads to many attempts to move the study of foreign languages to the grammar-school level. Dr. Mel Levine, in his recent (2002) *A Mind at a Time*, suggests this to be a myth. For "several recent studies have shown that fourteen-year-olds learn foreign languages much faster and more effectively than do five- or six-year-olds." Generalizations in such speculative concerns for the mind, as Dr. Levine repeatedly reminds us in his book, require careful attention. Proficiency of *a* child in his own language may say much of his prospects of acquiring a second language, whether observed in him at age six or fourteen or thirty-five. How proficient the particular mind? Has *this* person at *this* point "fully managed to absorb completely the phonology, semantics, or sentence structure of his native language?"

From his considerable experience with children, and from his study of the experiences of other like professionals, Dr. Levine observes that "Most often children who fare poorly with a second language harbor (knowingly or unknowingly) neuro-developmental dysfunctions in their first language." Such possibilities to the controlled understanding (the scientific understanding) are points of departure into the problem. They are both self-evidently and necessarily to be reckoned with. But so reckoned, it may yet prove true that the child learning French by playing with French boys and girls in the garden—while his parents respond to a tutor or learn phonology and semantics and sentence structure from grammars of French in their library—may prove disparate in their acquisition of a mutually unfamiliar language. The immediacy of *things to words in relation to things and actions*—testings and protesting in a game of soccer—might show one dimension of the mind's acclimatization to French in the child distinct from his parents' dimension. There is an additional factor in a formal address to the new language, in which the fourteen-year-old and the adult as "minds" have an advantage of intellectual sophistication over the six-year-old. They may set down sentences on paper or read such "foreign" signs with a facility lacking in the six- or eight-year-old. We might, then, observe the parent fetching the child in to dinner from the loud game in progress. The parent in the circumstances may discover himself dependent upon the six-year-old in talking to French six-year-olds to persuade the child to dinner or his companions to let him go. There might then arise a question of which—the child or his parent—is more proficient in French.

And so, in respect to the nature of sign as used by a sign-giver and sign-receiver, there arise questions fascinating in themselves, perhaps even complications to any conclusions about the uses of signs. There is certainly required of such answers, that caution voiced by Dr. Levine: It is always necessary to engage *a* mind, at *a* time. Composite studies toward answering such questions require always a truth recognized and articulated by Percy concerning science as "applied" to questions such as these, especially science in pursuit of theories. We have heard him say that "the scientist, in practicing the scientific method, cannot utter a single word about an individual thing or creature insofar as it is an individual but only insofar as it resembles other individuals." He suggests as well, as we have noted, that in such a scientist as Freud, concerned with the "mind," Freudian science seems able to explain everything—but Freud himself.

It is in respect to the mystery of the existence of this particular thing that we have argued a fundamental concern, not for a mind but for *this* mind, to be sacramentally responded to according to its specifically given nature underlying the accidents of any confluence with things. Out of that confluence of already existing things rises our formal attempt to order the actual through signs. Such an attempt—especially to be made *of this self* and *by this self*—may clarify the coordinates of *this* self in creation—at *this* place at *this* time. At issue is the particularity of a being (*this* person) in relation to particularities of discretely other persons and things, in movements toward a community within the common nature binding persons—each as a specific intellectual soul incarnate. And, we are arguing further, such a particular intellectual soul is incarnated at conception, a recognition of a truth increasingly troubling to Percy as he sees the world of the theorist-consumer violating that truth.

Some of the questions rising out of this fundamental principle, a belief which is itself fundamental to Christian metaphysics, may prove perhaps discomforting to Percy's semiotic theory as he has argued it— according to his signs but not to his intuitive sacramental deportment to things. For instance the deconstruction of the sign *apple* as perceived by the sign-maker in repeating the drab vocable is one thing. But what of that deconstruction in the repetition as heard by the sign-receiver? There occurs, we suggested, a shifting of attention by intellect in both the sign-giver and sign-receiver. Is it not a shifting of attention to a new event separated from the question of *appleness* in apple, an event in the physical dimension of actually experiencing apples in themselves? With an attention upon physical manifestation of sound, the attention is quite radically shifted from what the sound signified, the apple. Thus to repeat our caveat is to be reminded—as Percy was again and again—of the necessity to return to the ground zero of actual experience for a new beginning.

Another question: What, we may ask, is the effect of nonsense syllables upon a hearer, the deliberate distortion of sound from meaning by a sign-maker? That is a technique of parody with a significant intention to metaphor or a rhyming of correspondences between sounds or signs imagistically echoing other like signs. Lewis Carroll, the mathematician of sound as separated from sense, is adept and delightful to us in his distortions of language rhythm played against nonsense sound. He is delightful largely because, disrupting phonemes from significations, he plays a music of signification peculiar to our language. What is the possible response of sign-receiver, however, to drab vocables disjoined from the music of our tuned speech patterns? What is signified in our response to cacophony? What is signified of the nature of sign itself by our hearing Arabic or Finnish discourse with our alien ears? Do we nevertheless perceive a content in such sound, a sense of ordered sound suggesting commonly assumed significations? At the least, we recognize a reality of person at play with sound.

Even if we could answer such questions, as I cannot, the problem at hand is itself an evidence of the existence of the self as prior to a *developing* communal existence as oriented by signs when signs are given a common consent. By this observation, we must call in question the sign as transforming a self. It would rather seem to be a social certification of the self as already existing within social circumstances, and as such a certification of the formal cause of the self's existence as antecedent to sign. That has necessitated the ruse of Modernist ideology in appropriating Nominalistic sign in order to separate positive law from natural law, or in Flannery O'Connor's version of the disjunction, to separate grace from nature. Percy's "Holiness of the Ordinary" is his own rejection of what he long explored with satiric irony, that same Modernist reduction of being as effected through scientism and at the expense of honorable science, justified in the name of *imposed* social unity. His final novel has been an affirmation of *life* as opposed to our devotion to *death* as the enveloping syndrome of Modernist doctrine as engineered through scientism's systems: the reduction of pre-existing selves—persons— toward a deadening unity, in violation of the self's inherent nature as person from its very conception.

The mystery of the *natural* existence of the self is the fundamental concern on which all such questions depend, the *nature* of person as person, of cow as cow, ball as ball. And for that reason we may consider how

arresting to our understanding of existing things is that secret knowledge between fetus and mother, a mystery of increasing interest to scientific explorations of the mystery of life itself. We address this concern
in honoring Percy's heroic insistence on the sacredness of things and of
his unrelenting concern for the uses of sign to that end. Between the
mother and the growing fetus there exists the most immediate and fundamental community of selves. What are the signs of this community in
being, signifying existential selves? We are familiar with the mother-to-
be, crooning to her unborn child, singing the fetus to sleep. It is touching, or it may touch a sentimental chord in us without our taking such
an event seriously. We even know the impulse of the father in speaking
to his unborn child, no doubt patting the squirming presence. But we
should be mistaken in our sentimental response if we conclude these to
be actions predictive of a family unity only *yet to be*, rather than signifying a communion of family already existing.

Dr. F. Rene Van de Carr, in "Perinatal Psychology: Birth of a Field"
(*Brain/Mind Bulletin*, September 30, 1985), reports on his work with
expectant parents at his Prenatal University in California. At five months
into a pregnancy, he introduces the parent to the "kick game," "played"
twice a day. When the baby kicks in the womb, the parent pats the spot
and waits for another kick. After two months, a response pattern has
been established, after which six basic words associated with physical
sensations are introduced into the game: *pat, rub, squeeze, shake, stroke,
tap*. The parent also begins talking to the baby in sentences, and playing music, restricted to a single soothing song. One study of 150 mothers in the program showed that the infants so treated developed after birth
with "a significantly higher incidence of pre-speech and early speech"
and even with the use of "compound words." Is there then a communion of selves through signs in that prenatal relationship, rather than, as
some might insist, merely a Percyian dyadic relation of mother to child?
Mothers would seldom consent to their reduction to the dyadic, and
theirs is a knowledge we must defend against the distortions of the merely
biological relation of fetus to female body.

Consider additionally Joan Lunden's experience with her daughter,
reported in "Connecting Early" (*Health*, March 1985). Her husband, in
the third trimester, would "talk to my tummy. 'Hello there, this is your
father speaking,' and then he'd sing a musical scale. He always did the
same thing. When Jamie was born, she cried endlessly. Then Michael
held her. he said, 'Hello, this is your father speaking.' And he sang the
scale. The baby looked up at him and stopped crying." (The research
here cited, and the anecdote of Joan Lunden, are given in Francis and
Judith MacNutt's *Praying for Your Unborn Child*, Doubleday Image Book,
1989.) Not exhaustive, but suggestive, evidence—these testimonies by

Dr. Van de Carr and Joan Lunden—that a triadic dimension of the "self" as already existing, through which signs bond in a community of persons. The suggestiveness of such testimony must give us pause before the mystery of community of selves as we approach that mystery through signs, but especially with signs tainted by intentions of *scientism*.

Given this pause, let us introduce the relatively new discipline called "prenatal psychology." Dr. Thomas Verny, a psychiatrist concerned with the relation of the fetus to the enlarging cosmos, details the status of current research in the then-emerging discipline in his *The Secret Life of the Unborn Child* (Summit Books, 1981). What the research shows is the early development of consciousness *in utero*, leading us, not to discoveries about the fetus but to "rediscoveries," as Dr. Verny puts it. For much of what science now establishes was intuitively known centuries ago. With the application of new technology to such concerns, it seems now well-established that the fetus at four to five months "responds to sound and melody—and responds in very discriminating ways." For if we put "Vivaldi on the phonograph ... even the most agitated baby relaxes. Put Beethoven on and even the calmest child starts kicking and moving." In relation to the role of speech, recent studies show that the "fetus hears clearly from the sixth month in utero, and, even more startling, that he moves his body in rhythm to his mother's speech." Perhaps most startling is the considerable evidence accumulating that the relation of mother to fetus involves a bonding or, in unfortunate relations of mother to child, a failure of bonding long before that capacity to respond to speech patterns develops in the third trimester. The "feelings" of the mother toward her unborn child significantly affect the fetus, who "knows" whether it is wanted or unwanted. Laboratory evidence for such a proposition is presented in Dr. Verny's book in some detail. There is even this remarkable demonstration of that closeness. Dr. Michael Lieberman, measuring the fetus's heartbeat, seems to have established that a smoking mother, merely by thinking of smoking a cigarette, agitates the fetus. "She doesn't even have to put it to her lips or light a match; just her *idea* of having a cigarette is enough to upset him."

Now what emerges from this new concern for the life of the fetus as a person, established by scientific techniques, is that consciousness develops before birth, that a sense of the "I"—of the self as self—is already present to the person in the womb. And an important part of that relationship of the self to the other, establishing self-identity, is knowledge already held in intellect by the fetus. It knows, for instance, the ill-effects upon its comfort of his mother's smoking. (So convinced is Dr. Verny from his researches that he does not refer to the fetus as an *it*, but as *he*, explaining at the outset that his using *he* is "solely to avoid reader confusion" such as the awkwardness of "he or she" or the inac-

curacy of "it.") That the fetus brings some knowledge already held into
the world is indicated by a considerable evidence as well, for which one
witness may suffice here. Boris Brott, conductor of the Hamilton
(Ontario) Philharmonic Orchestra, reports the experience of conduct-
ing scores for the first time, when "suddenly, the cello line would jump
out at me; I'd know the flow of the piece even before I turned the page
of the scores." He mentioned the experience to his mother, a professional cellist, as a curiosity, but in their talking of the events it developed
that "All the scores I knew sight unseen were ones she had played while
she was pregnant with me."[8] From such studies, we may easily understand that Percy would pursue his concern further toward conception
than in the Gesell Institute's concerns for the four-year-old and the seven-
year-old. We encounter a point of mystery in doing so, arresting in a
delight of wonder to which any signs seem insufficient.

Dr. Verny as both medical doctor and psychiatrist pays careful attention to both the physiological and behavioral communications between
the child in utero and the mother. But out of his long experience as prac-
titioner and as scholar of the accumulating evidence which shows the
fetus to be a person, he suggests a third relation, "sympathetic communication." This is that arena of engagement of two persons, the child in
the womb and the mother. There appears an inescapable relation between
two *persons* in the sense in which we use the term, the Thomistic sense.
The child, he says, is affected by fear or anxiety in the mother or by her
ambivalence toward the child she carries, or even a smoldering hostility
toward the child. But on the other hand, the child is also affected demonstrably by the mother's active love and acceptance.

Verny says, "Nothing we know about the human body can explain
why these feelings affect the unborn child. Yet study after study shows that
happy, contented women are far more likely to have bright, outgoing infants."
It is interesting that when this man of science comes to the necessity of
naming this desirable relation of the mother to her child, he uses two
words, usually together: *love* and *acceptance*. *Acceptance* suits that deportment of the scientific mind as it is concerned with the physiological and
behavioral relationships, which concerns seem to fit more easily those
traumatic events between these two persons, the rejection or ambivalence
of the mother toward her child, for instance. But there intrudes again and
again the inexplicable: the child's *knowing* beyond the more primitive
levels of our knowledge of life which physiological and behavioral sciences restrict themselves to. What intrudes is the mystery of a love that
binds, or an absence of love which by its absence disjoins. An instance
from the considerable body of evidence deals with a new infant, "Kristina,"
who repeatedly refused her mother's breast at birth. Her doctor tried
giving the child to another patient, and Kristina began nursing hungrily.

That Kristina's hunger appears to have been for more than food at the physiological level of her well-being seemed indicated to her doctor when, questioning Kristina's mother, he learned that the mother all along in her pregnancy had wanted an abortion. Her husband insisted on her bearing the child, which was the only reason she had (apparently) for going through with her pregnancy. Dr. Verny's concern for the existence of "sympathetic communication, or its absence"—that is, for a dimension of the "extrasensory" through which in this case Kristina knew herself unwanted—speaks directly to our continuing theme of *personhood* as distinctive of human existence. It also speaks toward personhood as wisely understood in relation to love, but most particularly to that relation of *person* to the *Causing Love* of all existing things. It is a concern that was sufficient to make Walker Percy write two letters to the New York *Times* (one ignored) arguing a parallel between the Weimar Republic and post–1960s America, such an audacious comparison no doubt leading the "Newspaper of Record" to ignore this letter by a prominent American intellectual. The unpublished letter (available in Percy's collected essays, *Signposts in a Strange Land*) reminds us that it was "democratic Germany in the 1920s" that prepared the way for Hitler, through such influential arguments as those of a jurist and a psychiatrist in their book *The Justification of the Destruction of Life Devoid of Value*. Percy's letter was sent on the fifteenth anniversary of *Roe v. Wade,* and in it he remarks a parallel between American democracy in his own day, in the post–*Roe v. Wade* era—and the Weimar Republic.

That unpublished letter (dated January 22, 1988) is a footnote to a theme pursued by Percy for many years, a theme reaching concentrated attention in his *Thanatos Syndrome*, published a few months before the letter was sent. It is Tom More in that novel who allows Percy a drawing-together of his argument. Dr. More remembers his prison days (earned in the actions of *Love in the Ruins*—Percy's novel published just before the *Roe v. Wade* ruling). He remembers sitting in the prison library reading about "the Battle of the Somme, a battle which, with the concurrent Battle of Verdun, seemed to me to be events marking the beginning of a new age, an age not yet named. In the course of those two battles, two million young men were killed toward no discernible end. As Dr. Freud might have said, the age of thanatos had begun." It is in relation to this gnawing suspicion that Tom More is drawn more and more to Father Smith, who in the section of *The Thanatos Syndrome* entitled "Father Smith's Confession" gives a long account of his own experiences in Germany in that emerging post–World War I world in which convenience to political and social "life" allows redefinitions of lives "devoid of values" and so to be eradicated.

Father Smith will speak to Tom More of his "colleagues," the

"Louisiana Weimar psychiatrists." Now out of prison, drawn into Father Smith's orbit, Tom More finds himself beginning "to think like Father Smith," with a growing "sensation that the world really ended in 1916." The emerging age without a name, Percy himself will suggest we call the "Age of the Theorist-Consumer," as we have heard him say. In this late account, after Tom More's experiences with his old colleagues back in Louisiana following his prison experience, what is his conclusion at novel's end? Tom More, totaling destructions beginning with the Battle of the Somme down to his century's close, concludes: "We did it. Reason warred with faith. Science triumphed. The upshot: One hundred million dead." A conservative estimate of the effects of the thanatos syndrome underlying an increasingly frenzied race called "life" whose only end seems to be death—in contrast to life as Chesterton's dance. Still, there emerge new signs in this strange land, undeniable registers of realities for which theory restricted to convenience is insufficient as measure, the very technology used in a pursuit of convenience raising grave questions.

Hence a cautionary note about Dr. Verny's discovery of the relation of *love* and *acceptance* as bonding child and parent. For Dr. Verny is, in his own conclusions about this arresting relation, rather more given to psychological and behavioral explanations of human nature than to an enlargement upon that given nature offered by his "sympathetic communication" conclusions. It leads to somewhat embarrassing simplifications of character formation (Chapter Six) which seem leftovers from popular Freudianism. Thus the "adult who thrills at the magician's ability to pull a rabbit from a hat is responding" to unconscious recollections of birth, the magician's trick "symbolic re-creation of man's magical emergence from the womb." And those people who refuse, "no matter how nasty the weather," to wear "turtle-neck sweaters, scarves or other restricting clothing around their necks" probably had "a painful delivery."

The simplistic dimension lies in a careless transgression upon grounds more suited to the philosopher, in that Dr. Verny's unexamined assertions bearing philosophical import are made as if demonstrated by science. (But then, as Tom More laments, as scientist himself, "Science triumphed.") Thus, "Birth and prenatal experiences form the foundations of human personality," Dr. Verny contends. In addition, "Both the distinctions between Heaven and Hell and the expulsion of Adam and Eve from the Garden can be read as birth parables," connected with sexuality. And no less an authority than the late Carl Sagan is summoned to support speculative conclusions which are given a more than speculative assertion. Presumably the "cosmologist" Sagan, one of Walker Percy's satiric targets in *Lost in the Cosmos*, seems authoritative to Dr.

Verny on the grounds that Sagan is a "scientist-author," as he says. In justifying personality as the foundation of human *personality*, over our position that the nature of *person* is the foundation, Dr. Verny falls back to a "primal anger" or "fury," or primal content out of well-adjusted fetal relationship to the mother, as the cause which accounts for personality.

The nagging question, however, is whether such primal emotions explain the actualities of personality. For implicit in the reaction or acceptance by the fetus of the conditions of its development, its responses to the cosmos of the womb, are expectations which Dr. Verny has stated early and emphatically cannot be fully explained by either physiological or behavioral principles. While Sagan operates in an intellectually exploding way, as if intellect might thus fill the universe with its own wonder, Dr. Verny is engaged in the more limited sphere of the particular person whose "personality" is the foundation of that little world within parameters dictated by the "synaptic self" as argued by Joseph LeDoux in the book by that name, who is more comfortable in that confined theory which eschews ultimate questions. As the "promo" for LeDoux's book puts it: "Ultimately, it is at the level of the synapse that psychology, culture, and even spirituality meet, where memory joins with genes to create the ineffable essence of personality." Memory and genes, joined interspace and contained by that three-pound universe, the human brain: that, too, becomes a "concentration can" of scientism in its rigorous stance as guard over being.

Much more is involved in the meaning of *love* or *rejection* than is accounted for by the underlying commitment to chemistry and evolutionary behavior that keeps Dr. Verny from his recognitions of any larger dimension to "personality." It is as if he came to the threshold of a recognition of personhood, of the reality of the soul which flourishes or diminishes in relation to love or its absence, but cannot himself break free of his own intellectual conditioning by a Modernist thought committed to the denial of the soul as a reality. We have already remarked this hesitancy in that emerging discipline of "psychoneuroimmunology," to which this corollary discipline of prenatal psychology seems related. Questions raised about the "3-Pound Universe" and the unity of the fetus in developing toward this "3-poundness" are complementary of each other, though such questions require more than speculative science—that is, more than empirical experimentation. Otherwise, science reduced to scientism will transform theory into "scientific" myth. We shall then have such new scholastics arguing myth as the reality, as in the confident insistence that personality is an accident of larger deterministic accidents—the cosmos as seen by Carl Sagan. That is the buried principle of Dr. Verny's and Dr. LeDoux's confident resolutions of the mystery of existence.

Dr. Verny pays considerable attention to the relation of heartbeat as a communicator to the fetus from the mother. Thus, "Because the human mind, even the human mind in utero, is a symbol-making entity, the fetus gradually attaches a metaphorical meaning to it. Its steady *thump-thump* comes to symbolize tranquility, security and love to him. In its presence, he usually flourishes." If *metaphorical* and *symbolize* here do not carry the technical implications we engage in semiotics, we nevertheless recognize that those signs point toward evidence of an experience of *knowing realities* by the gift of intellect itself—a knowledge precedent to the formal symbolisms elaborated in our social contexts, whether between mother and child after his birth or between the child and other persons. In the light of such evidence, we may better understand as well Walker Percy's position on the questions of abortion and euthanasia as he came to that position through his concern for the nature of the sign in relation to the "triadic" experience of reality. (Our argument with Percy's triadic theory is not with its reality but with the point of its inception in the person.) It might even help us with the discomfort occasioned by a Mother Teresa's charge to our worldly existing self that by consent to abortion any murder must be at last justified. That is a consent now universalized in the popular spirit (see the latest polls), in accord with the philosophical sentimentality of Dostoevsky's Raskolnikov and Ivan Karamazov.

We may be left suspended in bemusement by our confrontation by sign from Mother Teresa, finding ourselves (one suspects) in a state like that described in the old Baptist hymn, "Almost Persuaded." For in a common world in which our terms pretend to transmute reality—dulling the effects upon us of our experiences of reality by our presumptions of power through signs—how shall we say whether we are persuaded, amused, startled, or confounded by her words? Our world is one which translates the reality of marriage to *arrangement*. Man is a *donor*, woman an *incubator*, the child a *going property* in which several parties hold an invested *consumer interest*. Such the convenience of theory in service to the consumer. We might well find ourselves in the uncomfortable position of another French geneticist, Dr. Jacques Monod, who obviously sees the genetic world quite differently from Dr. Lejeune. He appeared on a talk show on a Canadian channel with Mother Teresa, for which the topic was the meaning of life. Dr. Monod was heard to say, as he was leaving the studio afterward, "If I see much more of that woman, I shall be in very bad trouble." This geneticist's reductions of life in the presence of Mother Teresa, his insistence that the *dyadic* dimension of reality (to apply Percy's term) is the only reality, left him discomfited by Mother Teresa's very presence as much as by her arguments—arguments he had surely heard before.

And so we in turn may stand bemused or amused or confused by such a presence, a presence more terrible than sign alone can demonstrate. It is as if in Mother Teresa we are confronted by a Jonathan Swift, but a Swift in whom there is no profound disappointment over what current theory would make of humanity. Compare Swift's "Modest Proposal" for the consumer exploitation of Irish children, based in the theory dominant in an English address to the "Irish problem," as Swift puts it, to which problem the economic convenience of cannibalism is the logical solution. But there is a most disturbing difference in Swift's circumstances and ours in this Age of Theorist-Consumer. Ours is a relation of *us* against *them* from our perspective as denizens of this age as named by Percy. The *them* is *vague* as the *Irish* were not vague. For we would have it that our *them* names the *not-yet*, the fetus as if at most an *it*, at best for consumer concern, mere tissue suited to experimental uses in the name of the "common good." A certain *something* threatens our present purchase upon the world's body in its unrelenting presence nevertheless. *They* threaten us at least as potential *persons*. But so long as we can maintain that they are *not*, we can contain *them* in our signs as *nonpersons*, the term itself a "concentration can" as term. Our very sign *nonpersons*, justifying our actions, belies the reality. We are burdened by a residual sense of personhood even in the negative term, discomforting to our intent to an unbridled conquest of existing persons. Those *nonpersons* are expendable tissue and so if by the magic of sign we may exorcise moral baggage in conscience, the named things can be turned to serve consumerist interests—justified by a theory of signs divorced from reality. The self-absolution is put succinctly by Magda Denes, in her *In Necessity and Sorrow* (1976): "Abortion is murder of a most necessary sort." Again, Jeffner Allen in her "Motherhood: The Annihilation of Woman": "I am endangered by motherhood. In evacuation from motherhood, I claim my life, body, world, as an end in itself."[9]

We must not from such testimony make the mistake of attributing the position formulated by Denes and Allen merely to a radical feminism. *Fatherhood* is as suitable a term as Allen's when we consider the narcissistic position she advocates as *motherhood*, judging from the evidence we exhibit through our signs in society. Walker Percy was acutely aware of the disease of our "demented" age as general among us. The disease is a perversion of love, whereby the self becomes "an end in itself," as Miss Allen would have it. That is the very point Percy is pursuing in his characterizations of our age. He sees that thereby we end up isolated as theorist-consumer, and not only isolated from any community with existential reality beyond the self, but isolated most particularly from our own personhood as *this* discrete "self." And so we are thrown into radical competition with each other over advantage to the isolated self. Ours is a Hobbsean reductionism, operative as the condition of social "interaction," which in its nature is opposed to this kinder, more gentle word *interaction*. We feel comfort in such a term as *interaction* to name a relationship which in its reality is a cannibalism of self-interest, however justified with the veneer of signs that attempt to exorcise conscience in pursuit of unlimited, infinite political and social pluralism.[10] What Percy knew, as a Catholic, as others before him have known—Dante and St. Thomas and St. Augustine among them—is the deepest horror of this cannibalism. As we have said, by that perversion of reality the self devours itself. For that is the aspect of perverted love that is the most terrible of all, even as (because it is so terrible) it is the most difficult reality for our world to either recognize or (when recognized) to deal with.

10

Our concern has been to explore, as a possible preliminary to a rereading of Walker Percy's fiction, his engagement with the mystery of the sign. It is a mystery he first engages as scientist, but with a philosophical concern, a combination of "ideas" about the manner of intellectual response to reality which he entertains, which ideas tilt more to Kierkegaard than to Thomas Aquinas, though he reads both in coming to himself (as Dante might have put it) in the world as a dark wood—in the middle of his life.[11] Much further along that way, in 1980, Percy was interviewed by the Danish scholar Jan Nordby Gretlund, who gives as perceptive title to his interview "Laying the Ghost of Marcus Aurelius?" Gretlund asks whether Sutter Vaught in *The Last Gentleman* is a Stoic. No, Percy says, echoing Kierkegaard, he is rather "desperate," because he has "exhausted the aesthetic sphere." And then an elaboration on the "idea" as dramatized in the convergence of the two characters, somewhat to Will Barrett's bafflement in responding to Sutter. Percy says, "I would go further than Kierkegaard, I would combine the aesthetic with the scientific. I think the two parallel. I think Mozart and Einstein are on the same plane."

Percy respects St. Thomas Aquinas, but is not at last very comfortable with him, in contrast to Flannery O'Connor. His discomfort seems almost a "social" incompatibility. (He will reject "scholastic mumbo-jumbo.") It emerges in his response to Gretlund's next concern, the function of knowledge in attaining faith. That is a question of interest to Percy, though no doubt he would rather discuss it with Kierkegaard than with Thomas, perhaps remembering Thomas's own somewhat awkward social presence as reported in Chesterton's engaging, celebratory

portrait of St. Thomas as *The Dumb Ox*. At a court gathering about King
Louis IX (St. Louis), the party underway and Thomas Aquinas a guest,
the friar is withdrawn from the social fun, into himself in the midst of
court spectacle, but suddenly bangs his fist on the table and cries out
("like a man in a dream," Chesterton puts it): "And *that* will settle the
Manichees!" Had one rather be at a party, even so select a party as that
at St. Louis's court, with Kierkegaard or with the friar Thomas Aquinas?
And so to that question lying between the two philosophers, the one
"Protestant," the other "Catholic," the question of faith as knowledge sep-
arates them decisively, leaving Percy in something of a quandary. It is a
quandry Percy remarks in passing in his "Diagnosing the Modern
Malaise": "Christendom began to crumble, perhaps most noticeably
under the onslaught of a Christian, Søren Kierkegaard, in the last century," an observation perhaps in considering Camus and Sartre as finding
Kierkegaard a philosophical father.

To Gretlund's question, Percy responds: "Well, it is a classic dispute
between Catholics and Protestants.... I thought it was very nice opposition to have Kierkegaard making a clear statement that faith is not a form
of knowledge." It is a leap into the absurd, into which leap Percy has earlier followed, from Kierkegaard into Jean-Paul Sartre. "St. Thomas
Aquinas [says] in his classical thirteenth-century way that faith is a form
of knowledge. It is different from a scientific knowing, but it is a form of
knowledge. I tend to agree with Aquinas there, even though I am more
sympathetic with Kierkegaard. I am on his wave length, I understand his
phenomenology, his analysis of the existential predicament of modern
man. Aquinas did not have that, but I think Aquinas was right about
faith. It is not a leap into the absurd, it is an act of faith, which is a form
of knowledge." Faith is not absurd for Flannery O'Connor, evident to
us in her letters and talks and implicitly in her fiction, though her characters themselves appear "absurd" to man in his modern predicament
of removal from faith. She might, indeed, argue with Percy that it is
Thomas, through his epistemology sounder than Kierkegaard's, who
makes clear the nature of that plane on which Percy finds both Mozart
and Einstein fellow pilgrims. For that is the plane of a common intellectual nature, through which the person as person and not as mere "personality" journeys. He does so not as the Modernist "self" but as an
intellectual soul incarnate.

On that common plane, Thomas argues, the person is guided by the
gift of the simple intellect manifest as peculiar to each person but shared
with all persons as common to human nature. And, though simple (undivided), it operates in the complementary modes of the *intuitive* and the
rational—properties of intellect suited to its action and as such common
to Mozart and Einstein, though specific and distinct in them as persons

and varying by degree. That is, intellect is *specific* to each (i.e., as *species* particular to *this* person as unique). It is *specific* according to the grace of limit to each whereby each is *this* person, signaled—signed—by particularities inherent to the essence peculiar to *this* person. The hidden drama in Percy's fiction, we might suggest—the tensional action out of and toward faith—lies in the intuitive intellectual desire for faith as complicated by the rational "scientific" suspicion of intuition itself by rational intellect. Out of such suspicion internal to intellect, the rational may be subverted by the will into a rationalism triumphant over the person. It is a subversion under the pride of intellectual autonomy. Thereby through willfulness there is effected a diminution of intellect itself. That turning of reason by will (a submission of reason to will as consequence of Original Sin, the theologian might say) is radical in recent history of intellect (O'Connor suggests) evidenced in the 18th-century Enlightenment. For it is by this turning that "the popular spirit of each succeeding age" is persuaded "to the view that the ills and mysteries of life will eventually fall before the scientific advances of man."

O'Connor and Percy share in a common dramatic ground in their fictions here, but a difference lies between them. It is a difference more clearly seen by her, she believes, as a "prophet of distances" through St. Thomas. Beginning as scientist (a point Percy returns to often in reflections upon his "self"), Percy is wary of the intuitive mode of intellect. (Reason is an *extension* of the intuitive in Thomas's argument, not discrete.) Not entirely comfortable—not certain—Percy finds himself more comfortable in his writing of fiction to approach it indirectly, an indirection wittily deployed which affords some protective cover as it were. Not surprisingly, then, we encounter Percy's self-reflection in an interview in the *New York Times* a year before the Gretlund interview: "It's been said that all novelists write the same novel over and over again. And since the kind of fiction I write is an exploration to begin with, all I can hope to do is push the boundaries back. I'm convinced that in 'The Second Coming' there's a definite advance, a resolution of the ambiguity with which some of my other novels end: the victory, in Freudian terms, of Eros over thanatos, life over death." A complaint about ambiguity had been raised critically about his *Love in the Ruins* (1971), whose subtitle is "The Adventures of a Bad Catholic at a Time Near the End of the World," that "bad Catholic" being Tom More. But it is in the further engagement of Tom More that, at last, Percy pushes the boundaries beyond the Freudian term for love, Eros, in his *Thanatos Syndrome*. In his final perspective on Modernist man's end of the world, effected through "losangelization" of place, there emerges in Tom More love as *agape*. (The contemplated novel Percy did not live to write he spoke of in his last days as to be located at "the end of the world.")

We considered and expressed reservations about Percy's initial engagement of the sign, the fascination which never leaves him. His *Thanatos Syndrome* just out, he writes Jan Gretlund from Covington, June 13, 1987, that he is "fed up with the book, and the interviews and can't stand to read it. I find myself turning to semiotics as usual, contemplating a book elucidating Peirce's 'triadic theory' (which I consider probably as important as Quantum Theory) toward end of reconciling it with people like Wittgenstein, John Poinsot (John of St. Thomas)...." (This letter is in Gretlund's *Frames of Southern Mind*, Odense University Press, 1998.) The "scientific" point of departure occasioned by tuberculosis, through Kierkegaard-Peirce-Sartre—to end with Wittgenstein. Intellect on the edge of the absurd, but with a fascination for the absurd which logic perhaps may accommodate. It continues nevertheless an intellect yet conflicted with an intuitive discomfort, brought along the way to the earlier dialectical engagement in *Lancelot* which could not resolve the concern. There continues that fascination with triadic theory, though now somewhat modified. How account, by logic, for this distinction between the "dyadic" and the "triadic" nature of experience as subject to sign, issuing in that "Delta" theory known by experience? How may the self be accounted for? Perhaps as effected by sign itself; almost as if, by the sign, person has personhood conferred upon it.

We heard him early remark the emptying of sign through an endless repetition of *apple*. But in his last essay, not long before his death, he closes with words affirming a new dimension in his own concern for the word, a concern grown out of his increasing devotion to the Word. In "The Holiness of the Ordinary," he concludes that "In the end, ten boring Hail Marys are worth more to the novelist than ten hours of Joseph Campbell on TV." Percy is amused by his own venture into comparative signs in his last sentence: "the notion of saying one's beads while watching Joseph Campbell is funny enough as it is," an amusement hardly requiring explication.[12] But it does bring into focus for us Percy at the end (almost) of his quest in the Modernist desert, the long journey made from that point where he was arrested by "the best disease I ever had" to his settling on Old Landing Road in Covington, Louisiana, where "I stay put. I don't get in trouble." That was the journey begun in 1942, Percy having spent almost half his life in this dark world and wide, to summon Milton to the point (in deference to Percy's wit of playing Protestant intellect against Catholic intellect in *The Last Gentleman*). Looking back from the late perspective of "The Holiness of the Ordinary," Percy himself would probably put the turning in Dante's rather than Milton's metaphor, as he does in his "Physician as Novelist." Lying abed, felled by the best disease he ever had, that experience is better understood through his gradual recovery as a journey. In his *Moviegoer* then, "almost by accident—or was it accident?" he asks—the making of that novel "landed" him in "the oldest tradition of letters: the pilgrim's search outside himself...." Thus, it proves by hindsight that he arrives in a new country "without the slightest consciousness to the novelist and his character [Binx] of a debt to St. Augustine or Dante." It is Dante, then, in a comparable moment of looking back, who begins his "memoir" of a spiritual recovery with the words:

> Midway upon the journey of our life
> I woke to find me astray in a dark wood,
> confused by ways with the straight way at strife.

So begins that great "autobiographical" poem about "our" common circumstance as intellectual soul incarnate, *The Divine Comedy*. By the poem's end, Dante the Pilgrim has risen to a level of understanding we recognize as already held by Dante the Poet as he begins those opening lines, enabling him to write an account of his journey. With close attention to Percy's novels, we discover them as well to be Percy's dramatizing of his own spiritual and intellectual journey, made through his exploration of ideas as the mapping of the territory through which he *is* journeying.[13] Such characters as Binx Bolling, Will Barrett, Tom More reveal something of the comic agony of that journey. By indirection—by humor and witty detachment—the kinship of Percy to his protagonists is delayed to our recognition. Even in *Lancelot*, with its violence as unusual to Percy's fiction, the focused intensity of the dialectical engagement of *ideas* in conflict suggests Percy's loss of patience with some of us as fellow travelers in the Modernist swamps.

Percy had been born in Birmingham, Alabama, near the No. 6 hole of a new country club, he reminds us, thus beginning life as a suburbanite of the middle class in the "city" of his social origins. Except for that good fortune waiting him in his internship at Bellevue Hospital, pulmonary tuberculosis (he says much later), "I might be a second-rate shrink practicing in Birmingham, at best." He began recuperation in sanitariums in New York State, at Saranac Lake (his longest stint). Then to Connecticut and thence to New Mexico—a route approximating that of his protagonist of *The Last Gentleman*. (It is interesting coincidence—or is it grace?—that Flannery O'Connor a little later—at Yaddo in New York, then with the Fitzgeralds in Connecticut—discovers her lupus. In response she returns to Milledgeville, Georgia, afterward counting her disease a fortunate gift as does Percy.) There, at Saranac Lake in the Adirondacks, Percy began for the first time to read extensively in philosophy and fiction, especially 19th-century Russian fiction, and more especially Dostoevsky.

He read Dostoevsky's *Notes from Underground*, he tells us, and that

turned him to Kierkegaard and then to the French Existentialists, especially Sartre and Camus, along his intellectual way. And in that portion
of his journey, he encountered as well Edmund Husserl's Phenomenology, as Husserl develops it at about the time Henri Bergson also bursts
upon the scene. Both attempt through philosophy to recover from
Descartes' dislocation of the intellectual "self" which has occasioned the
Modern mind's malaise. Then there was that special species of Phenomenology encountered in Charles Peirce, rising out of Harvard as the
center of a gathering intelligentsia at the close of the 19th century, becoming intellectually influential (in government and academy) in the first
decade of the new century. This was the intellectual climate just as Eliot
was engaged upon his own philosophical studies, reflected in his disser-
tation on *Knowledge and Experience in the Philosophy of F. H. Bradley*—
drawing Eliot toward the despair of solipsism, from which he withdraws
into a clever skepticism that will bring upon him his own "best disease,"
the spiritual crisis contemporary to his editing and publishing his *Waste
Land.*[14]

As for the lingering lesson from Dostoevsky's unsympathetic version of Eliot's Prufrock, his protagonist of *Notes from Underground*, that
renegade Russian's lesson emerges once more in Percy's last years. He
celebrates Mother Teresa's words of rebuke to the Modernist mentality
within which Ivan Karamazov crafts by logic his principle of action: In
a "good" cause (for Ivan, revenge against God for the suffering of children) anything is allowable. Answering a question put to him about the
pervasive "cultural privatization of values," we have heard Percy say: "I
can't do better than quote Mother Teresa. She said about abortion: 'If a
mother can kill her unborn child, I can kill you, and you can kill me.'
The privatization of values could lead to that, couldn't it." The convenience of a private vendetta against God can be used to justify both the
killing of Ivan's father, Old Karamazov, or the killing of a child to save
it from death, either by birth as death or, after birth if defective, then a
"life" which is "devoid of value." Both in that perspective could be
claimed "mercy" killings. A shocking declaration, but then Percy also
says: "Nothing offends the American liberal more than being compared
to the German liberals of the Weimar Republic," which, as Percy often
points out, made a way for Nazi atrocities. By the Weimar liberals' beginnings, the public spirit accepts positive law according to privatized values, in the name of the common good. That made the Nazi way more
acceptable to the German "public spirit."

Before his turning point into fiction, Percy at first ventures into
essays concerned with psychology and philosophy, collected later in his
The Message in the Bottle (1975). These essays issue from his recuperation. In them Percy is yet but tentative, even timid, about being a novel-

ist. He was absorbed by ideas in that moment. But he discovers he need
not abandon ideas in order to write novels. Rather he brings ideas to dramatic issue in the novels, a procedure setting him apart from his close
friend Eudora Welty, for instance, and from that other Southern writer
he so much admired, Flannery O'Connor. But in neither Welty nor
O'Connor could he discover the accommodation to his own South.
Meanwhile, he continued to pursue idea, even as he turned to fiction.
There accompanied his thinking, nevertheless, a certain disquiet in
respect to the relation of "place" to "idea," especially stirred by the necessity in fiction of a concrete setting, a place. Across the literary landscape
by the 1950s there were lectures and essays devoted to Welty and then
to O'Connor as "Southern" writers, made Southern as if by geographical place in which lay a thick cultural residue commonly termed "provincialism." And increasingly there were attempts to incorporate Percy into
that "Southern" perspective—the attempts sometimes requiring a considerable critical struggle, given Percy's differences as a displaced person in his own South. Though he admired both Welty and O'Connor,
somehow they were very unlike him when examined with *idea* turned into
an instrument probing *place*. For a long time he was uncomfortable with
the critical shibboleths applied to him as a "Southerner," yet knowing
that his Southernness was more than a mere convenience to his writing
novels.

But place as *determinate* to fiction, over *ideas*? What role has place
to the wanderer, to *homo viator*, as he moves from a Birmingham suburb, a country club "environment," to a University at which there is at
that moment a strong antipathy to the concerns for place being raised
by those Fugitive-Agrarians at Vanderbilt? Some of those Vanderbilt
poets and essayists would eventually become Percy's close friends. *I'll
Take My Stand* was a reaction to the recent comedy of the Scopes Trial,
held in what Menckin labeled "The Sahara of the Beaux-arts," a consideration not at first given them by Percy. The reaction of those Vanderbilt poets was against the Darwinian theory declared the science of
reality overriding all other "theories" of human nature. (Whether Percy
at North Carolina as a chemistry major was very much aware of the
debates going on at the time between the Fugitive-Agrarians and the
variety of responses to their concern, including some from his University is uncertain.) Their opposition reduced the concern as evidence of
the provincialism of the "South." It would be a concern, nevertheless, of
some relevance to what Percy experienced in Germany, where the call
for "room to live" rose as a battle cry, summoning the survival of the
Germans as the fittest. The destruction of persons that followed is
addressed by Father Smith in *Thanatos Syndrome*, in that tower above
the Louisiana swamps, in a novel in which one might discover Fugitive-

Agrarian kinships in retrospect, as Percy discovered kinship to St. Augustine and Dante in his *Moviegoer* after having written it.

Before that first novel, however, Percy travels to New York, goes through medical school and then encounters what had been a dread disease in Dostoevsky's world: a wide intellectual ranging for him after his undergraduate chemistry. In such circumstances, it may not be easy to distinguish spiritual deracination from geographical deracination, the sense of place perhaps only vaguely residual to the wanderer. Such nevertheless becomes a haunting concern out of an intuitive response to his wanderings in geography. As a Southerner, Percy had no store of front porch stories shared, as he remarks in contrasting himself to his friend Welty. He came to himself nevertheless on that removed patio of the shotgun cottage in New Orleans—hardly a place imbued with personal or family history for him. In an interview titled "Reentry Option" (*Southern Review*, 1984) Jo Gulledge puts the tedious question to Percy once more: "You have the traditional southern heritage in the strictest sense and always tend to steer away. Why?" He is now in the last decade of his life, confronted by that perennial question. But his answer suggests that it is a question not yet fully resolved though much considered. First a playful response: "I did my 'southern apprentice' novels, but they were imitations of Thomas Wolfe and Thomas Mann." Two novels unpublished, and in imitation of two novelists who found that they could not "go home again," Wolfe to North Carolina, Mann to Germany.

As he began to come to public attention, the myth of the "Southern writer" had already been established, formalized in academic courses that dealt especially with Faulkner and with the Fugitive-Agrarians, even touching upon his beloved Uncle Will by virtue of *Lanterns on the Levee*. And so he had to deal constantly with the insistent questions about himself, about whether he was a Southern or an American writer. Often boring questions as put to him superficially, and so sometimes irritating because speaking a naïveté in the questioner about the role of *place* in fiction. Given that pressure as steady, however, but especially given his own sense of a difference recognized between himself and Faulkner and Welty and O'Connor, he engages *place* itself as an idea, often as if he were an outsider to place. Then he might call himself sharply back to the importance of place to pursue its significance at a personal level. He discovers that *place* speaks of more than a geography or cultural history, though that seems the relation of place to Faulkner and to Welty. It is a sense of place important as well to his old friend Shelby Foote, the celebrated historian of the three-volume account of the "recent war" of 1861 to 1865. Foote, also a novelist, is more impressed by Marcel Proust than by Jean-Paul Sartre, bringing up Proust's stylistic mastery in letters to Percy again and again. (See their correspondence, edited by Jay

Tolson, 1997.) But what has place to do with a Binx Bolling or Will Barrett or Tom More? A concern, a backdrop certainly. But a concern not unique to the Southern writer, otherwise making Thomas Mann also a "Southern" writer in Percy's teasing yoking to Thomas Wolfe. To an interviewer he responds sharply: "My God, what about Camus? Who had a better sense of place than Camus in Algeria?" And what of Saul Bellow? To another interviewer: Nobody "calls Saul Bellow a Midwestern writer." And yet the idea of place is unavoidable in the consciousness of a "self"—that idea binding consciousness unavoidably to something peculiar to place, whether a response of feeling at home or of feeling in exile in a present place. Indeed by that correspondence there arises the idea of *provincialism*, of *regionalism*, as significant aspects of a given culture. Yet place is somehow known as important to the specific consciousness in relation to a something *beyond* limited geography and history. How is one to be at home with such a continuing sense of exile?

The conundrum of place to consciousness, then, seems somehow local and perhaps in somewise peculiarly resonant when it is the "Southern" local. Percy will repeat on occasion that remark of Flannery O'Connor that we introduced earlier: Though the Southerner is not Christ-centered, he is rather certainly Christ-haunted. She will assert as well that "the present reality is the Incarnation." Perhaps *place* then has to do with a sense of spiritual dislocation. The disquiet recalls a "self" to this present reality, to this place within which there is to be rediscovered a known but forgotten truth: A Presence is manifest in proximity to consciousness itself, through the senses in response to things that speak that Presence to ears that can hear, *now* and in this *place*. Thus if one comes home again, as Percy did, there may lie in wait for that returned pilgrim a sense exacerbated by a familiar place—seen in cultural things and heard in cultural signs, in talk of a certain cultural manner. Thus this place may bear an immediacy of experiences, new and recovered, a burden of history difficult to sort in relation to history alone, let alone in relation to the "history" of the returning pilgrim who like some latter-day Odysseus has come home after some wanderings of the world.

The consciousness in such circumstances—the "self" made the more self-aware—may feel like a ghost. The familiar seems also strange, but whether so because the place is changed or only the self—that proves ambiguous. Such is a theme developed through a fictional return of Percy's "last gentleman" to his native South, a character who echoes Percy's own history. The remembered *here* is not that here *remembered* by the spiritually restless Will Barrett. He had been in New York. Now returned to the South, he muses that it had been "possible for him to be at home in the North because the North was homeless." That seems at first a desirable circumstance to the pilgrim as spiritually disoriented. The "one condition of being at home," Will muses, is that "you are yourself homeless." And yet how difficult for that pilgrim to feel at home in a place called home, even though in his residual history he shares culturally in the local? Will knows that "The South [itself] was at home," but he as Southerner now returned is made miserable by a sense of homelessness, though reluctant to flee that home country again.

The sense of being in exile at home! Will experiences it without recognizing that it is occasioned by a spiritual restlessness preventing his settling in any place, North or South. He lacks a recognition of what is happening to him, a change underway in him which Percy signals in his epigraph to the novel quoted from Romano Guardini's *The End of the Modern World*: "The unbeliever will emerge from the fogs of secularism," Guardini says, endangered by having lost "benefit from the values and forces developed by the very Revelation he denies." If he should discover that his rescue from loneliness in that "Modern World" depends upon love, he may discover as well that "Love will disappear from the face of the public world" so that it will prove therefore "the more precious" as a "love which flows from one lonely person to another." Meanwhile the "world to come will be filled with animosity and danger, but it will be a world open and clean" as well, in that the actual world is much deeper than errors in surface perception of it. The world in its realities deeper than spectacle stands in unchanging defiance of the distortion of "values and forces developed by the very Revelation" which secularized man denies. Confusing circumstances to such a naïve spirit as Will, who is seeking "home" in a "place."

Seek he must, and no doubt (if grace allows) discovering himself to be one of those Percy will characterize as an "ex-suicide," once Will finds the right way of accommodation to the world. Such is the necessity to the pilgrim which Percy's fellow Southern Catholic Flannery O'Connor affirms, and for reasons clarified for her in the metaphysical vision of St. Thomas. She, returned to Milledgeville and to that small cattle farm on the outskirts she called Andalusia, bears lupus as a secret paradoxical blessing. She will say, in "The Fiction Writer and His Country," that "To know oneself is to know one's region. It is also to know the world, and it is also, paradoxically, a form of exile from that world." It is out of this understanding of herself as pilgrim that she comes to recognize as well a lingering, residual sense of a truth still extant in her "Georgia types," though they lack gifts sufficient to sophisticated testimony to the vague recognition. She brings out that understanding in her fiction, out of her Thomistic understanding of place, that truth about such local persons. The residents of her South, close at hand, reveal themselves (some of them certainly) as Christ-haunted, though not Christ-centered.

Thomas, in his treatise *Questiones disputatae de veritate* (which Flannery had at hand), says that "Nobody perceives himself to know except from the fact that he knows some object, because knowledge of some object is prior to knowledge of oneself in such a way that it immediately apprehends itself, but it arrives at knowledge of itself by the fact that it perceives other things." Such is an aperçu to that epiphany experienced by Tom More in Percy's last novel, *Thanatos Syndrome*. In a Louisiana swamp, in a small boat, he is arrested by the beauty of the sunfish flapping on the boat floor. Though More might not articulate that moment, it is one of a recognition such as Gerard Manley Hopkins might celebrate. It speaks here-and-now, a moment in a place but more than the complications of culture or geography can explain. It is a moment at a ground zero to spiritual recovery—in a Louisiana swamp with Dr. More's experience in Father Smith's firetower yet ahead of him. It is to this possibility that Thomas speaks in the *Summa Theologica* (I, 14, 8 ad 3) when he reminds us that "Created things are midway between God's knowledge and our knowledge, for we receive our knowledge from things that are caused by God's knowledge. Hence ... things that can be known are prior to our knowledge and are its measure," while "God's knowledge" is "the measure of created things and prior to them"—even that ordinary flapping sunfish. Hence Thomas will as well remind us that our first movement toward God as an intellectual soul is through the body's senses.

That is a movement to be effected in us only in *this* place at *this* moment. And it follows from it that some *place* affords a moment of recovery to consciousness—a recognition of itself as more than a ghost, despite that modern malady Percy engages all along his way, that San Andreas Fault in human consciousness made into a philosophical movement as Cartesian Idealism. The answer must lie, not in that attempt to acquire rescue through angelism, which can only offer a reduction of the "self" as dislocated and so the more a ghost hovering over and beyond place. For the Cartesian angelism is a willed presumption of autonomy in reaction against a real world of real things. Those things, St. Thomas argues, mediate and bond the person to his Creator God, through the self-recognition of having been created in the image of God. By angelism occurs a refusal of dependence upon creation itself, and so a refusal of dependence toward God. A significant form of that refusal is a Kantian projection of an intellectual "platform," above and removed from reality, thus making reality subordinate to the self. It is a platform built by "pure" reason. To extend the metaphorical point: The self turns its intellectual back on God in order to focus its intentionality upon things as thus reduced from any possible mediation as objects relating the self to its Cause. Thus things as mere objects are made subservient to the apotheosis of the autonomous self.

When Percy remarks Camus as actually "Southern" with himself in respect to Camus's love of Algiers or Paris as places, he is surely right. For Camus is haunted by place, in consequence of which there accrues to his signs a sense of melancholy, reminding one of John Keats in this respect. Both desire a joy denied by a sadness out of having supposed themselves intellectually entrapped in a world where (in Keats's words) "but to think is to be full of sorrow/ And leaden-eyed despairs." There is a poignant Keatsian moment for Camus, reported by Julian Green (*Diary: 1928–1957*). World War II just over, Green goes to hear Camus lecture at a Paris convent. Camus is talking about "what is expected of Catholics in the France of 1946," says Green. Camus speaks rapidly, "his eyes sad, his smile is sad." The talk finished, he is confronted by "an ex-revolutionary with an ingenuous face": "Monsieur Camus, I tell you very humbly that you are not in a state of grace." As response, Green reports, at first there was only that sad smile, but a little later, returning to that ex-revolutionary, Camus says, "I am your Augustine, before his conversion, I am struggling with the problem of evil and can't get to the end of it." It is an anecdote which distinguishes Camus from Sartre as "existentialists" and somewhat explains (among other things) why Faulkner was more drawn to Camus than to Sartre. Percy as well, gradually coming to himself in place, is perhaps much closer in his own intellectual deportment to Camus than to Sartre, though he speaks often of Sartre as revealing to him that ideas are legitimate in fiction. There is not much sense of a sadness of dislocation in Sartre as contrasted to Camus— Sartre striking one in his deportment as so intensely arrogant as to reject pathos as a weakness of will.

Thus a troubling conundrum yet to be resolved in Percy's early thinking as novelist, under his growing fascination with Peirce and his "Delta" theory that at first seems to lead to the radical program of intellectual action as propounded by Jean-Paul Sartre. Sartre himself turns through a conquering of and reduction of the body as it were to consciousness as omega, to be self-made and therefore "transcendent" by willed intention. And yet, place continues a haunting, a teasing, affront to consciousness; no one will talk more of the relation of the South to his own writing than Percy himself. And if an interviewer doesn't raise the question, he will do so. When the relation of place to fiction is put to him by a questioner—usually one skating on the surface of the idea— he reacts variously. Sometimes he does so not as if irritated, but as if concerned that this is a serious question which might receive an insufficient and misleading answer if not carefully addressed. There is a mystery buried within the idea of the *South*, he knows, which he has not yet accommodated by idea itself. But *mystery* buried in *idea*, affecting *sign*? It is the mystery that he tends to steer away from, more so early than late in his active life as novelist. He concentrates upon *idea*, upon *concept*, as signaling a progress to be made more surely out of science than faith, into philosophy but not a philosophy pursued too far into theology as O'Connor does in reading her St. Thomas nightly. Still, the question will not lie low: the unresolved question of place. Percy will raise the question to himself, a self-challenge, as he does in his "self-interview," "Questions They Never Asked Me So He Asked Them Himself," in which he assumes the roles of both interviewer and novelist. It is a play in dialectics, echoing perhaps that manner of his novel, published the same year as the self-interview in 1977, *Lancelot*.

If he is not a "Southern" novelist as the term is used superficially, then what kind of Southerner is he? Over the years, through questions put to him by fans and scholars, he reflects upon that question in relation to his first published novel, *The Moviegoer* of 1960—the year before O'Connor's *The Violent Bear It Away*. O'Connor's novel is out before Percy begins to engage so intensely this mystery of place as it affects him, as both he and O'Connor stir new interest in Southern fiction through their two novels. As early as the 1960s, in an interview with Ashley Brown, the question of place and "Southerness" is raised. Percy responds to it: "Eudora Welty said the other day that most Southern writers were produced by a society in which people talk into the night and tell stories. My literary career came about in a different way. My education up to the age of thirty was almost entirely scientific. When I went to the University of North Carolina I majored in chemistry." This is also the time when he spent some days with a Nazi family in a very foreign place, even spending some time alone as wanderer through the Black Forest—then visiting towns and cities at the time Hitler was becoming widely celebrated. There was evident a new German enthusiasm, a new public spirit, waking from the seeming arrest of the Weimar Republic. It rose feverishly.

Returned home, then to medical college in New York, then the internship and the disease, the arrest in recuperation, and a final return to his "South." Meanwhile, essays in periodicals—like *Psychiatry*, *The Modern Schoolman*, *The Journal of Philosophy*, *Philosophy and Phenomenological Research*, along with writing the two "unpublished novels." And then a discovery, an epiphany opening a possibility, through signs, of an intellectual accommodation of consciousness through *idea* in fictional drama. Out of that discovery, *The Moviegoer*. In an interview for *The New York Times Magazine* (March 22, 1987), he recalls the moment. "I can remember sitting on that back porch of that little shotgun cottage in New Orleans with a little rank patio grown up behind it [observe the recognition of *place* here], after two failed novels. I didn't feel bad, I felt all right." And then it "crossed my mind." After all of his reading in phenomenology as a philosophy affecting the larger intellectual community become more remote to him when he came home to the South: "What if I did something that American writers never do, which seems to be the custom in France: Namely, that when someone writes about ideas, they can translate the same ideas to fiction and plays, like Mauriac, Malraux, Sartre." (He might have added one of his earlier interests, the writer of plays as well as of philosophy, Gabriel Marcel.) "So," he goes on, "why not take these ideas I'd been trying to write about, in psychiatry and philosophy, and translate them into a fictional setting in New Orleans, where I was living."[15]

It is the complication occasioned by that setting, New Orleans, that raises increasingly the question about place—about whether, beginning with *The Moviegoer*, he is emerging as an "American" novelist or but a "Southern" novelist, both designations unsatisfactory to him. He will engage the question with good humor before a Louisiana audience under the rubric "How to Be an American Novelist in Spite of Being Southern and Catholic." This is a talk in the last decade of his life, some twenty-five years after *The Moviegoer*, made by a physician turned novelist through an intellectual journey that had taken him early to Sartre and Camus. And still place proves inescapable to both psychology and philosophy, despite an emphatic commitment to ideas in fiction. What proves inescapable is that always art is an "incarnating" discipline which cannot avoid the actuality to the consciousness of the artist of his own presence at *this* place, required to use objects known as actual—wherever the place in which he encounters those objects or however he may wish to use them as mere backdrop for ideas. Located on science's various mappings of existential reality, they resonate beyond the certainties of science.

"You do not think of yourself as a Southern writer," W. Kenneth Holditch observes in an interview (May 1980, included in *More Conversations with Walker Percy*). Percy this time responds somewhat testily, "I am a Southern writer. I could not possibly write the way I write unless I was born and raised and living in the South." But then, a difference in him from Faulkner, Welty, O'Connor, "who I think are more Southern in one sense than I am, who depend more on the Southern scene than I do." Faulkner and Welty as writers use "Southern legend, Southern story, Southern history. O'Connor, of course, uses her Georgia types. I think I have more of a distance than they do. My scenes are middle-class, more urban or suburban, and therefore closer to American suburbia." The distinction is one Percy has engaged dramatically in *The Last Gentleman*, in which he dramatizes what may be "the last *Southern* gentleman" just before that pilgrim becomes lost in the cosmos, his possible rescue lying (Percy will suggest) in his becoming an "ex-suicide." Will Barrett, forced home from New York, makes the disturbing discovery we have heard: "The South he came home to was different from the South he had left. It was happy, victorious, Christian, rich, patriotic and Republican." He comes to a sad conclusion: "[I]t is much worse to be homeless and then to go home where everyone is at home and then still to be homeless.... Therefore his homelessness was much worse in the South because he had expected to find himself at home there." How close Will's thought to Percy himself. Will Barrett, out of upper middle-class circumstances, has not likely heard that old hymn popular among Southern Baptists, most of whom (in the South) feel rather at home: "The world is not my home,/ I'm only passing through./ If Heaven's not my home,/ then Lord what will I do." That touches upon the abiding Southernness to which O'Connor seems attuned from the beginning.

There is, then, an inescapable clash in Percy's peculiar Southerness with that losangelized suburban middle class upon whom he turns a satiric wit. It is a conflict within a lingering cultural ambiance of the South increasingly dissipated by the suburban milieu, a reduced "place" in which love itself is reduced to self-love under the idol of Eros, as Percy sees it. But at the same time his is never a sense of reassurance of place like that he recognizes in Faulkner and Welty and O'Connor. It will lead Percy to see himself as closer to Saul Bellow than to Faulkner. For Bellow as Midwesterner also deals with a species of Percy's losangelization of a cultural place—Bellow's Chicago Jewish culture paralleling Percy's Southern suburban culture as "backdrop," conspicuous to him in New Orleans.

We have argued a journey by Percy which brings him much closer nevertheless to Faulkner, Welty, and O'Connor as Southern writers, though differing from their responses. Welty is open to the cultural immediacy of Jackson, Mississippi, and its environs. She is not as writer drawn to a pursuit of the *idea* of Southernness, which idea perhaps ties Faulkner more closely to Percy than Percy acknowledges. Percy is wary of "Southern tradition" as he takes it to be limited to geography and local history. That South "doesn't interest me in the slightest, except as a backdrop to something more important.... I'm kind of a maverick; that is, I don't fit into the southern pattern." But then a complication not yet resolved for him, though it is as if in stating the nature of himself as maverick he does not fully recognize the South in relation to the measure of his maverick nature. He says, "All my characters, whether from Binx Bolling to Will Barrett to Thomas More and the others, find themselves in a here-and-now predicament. And the whole backdrop is this historical scene. It's there all right, but my character is looking in the other direction; he's not looking back."

For Percy as novelist it is against this backdrop that he "sees" his

characters into a fictional existence. But that backdrop limits his characters willingly, whether they look back or not. Though here-and-now,
each brings a history in relation to that backdrop, against which they
appear to us as convincing presences—as if made incarnate by rising out
of the local here-and-now. They are drawn convincingly, but they are so
drawn in a dependence upon the Southern backdrop as more than a convenient stage setting. It is at this point that Percy makes a confession of
his maverick nature as Southerner. He is himself very like his characters,
attempting not to look back. "[T]hat is why I've always felt more akin to
Faulkner's Quentin Compson than to anybody else in his fiction because
he is trying to get away from it." He knows that experience of Quentin,
"wandering ... around this godforsaken Boston suburb, and the last place
he wants to go is back to Mississippi, to time and history. When he says
to his Canadian friend, 'I don't hate the South, I don't,' he protests too
much."

What is at least hinted here is Percy's own love-hate relation to the
South that is akin to Quentin's. "I would like to think of starting where
Faulkner left off, starting with the Quentin Compson who *didn't* commit suicide. Suicide is easy." At such moments we can but be reminded
of Percy's father, whose suicide hovers about his concern for place as it
does about the idea of Stoicism to which Percy clung though recognizing it as an insufficient "idea." Only gradually does he release that idea
in coming to terms with the South. It is not only his Uncle Will that he
sees as Stoic, but Robert E. Lee. "How immediately we recognize the
best of the South in the words of the Emperor: 'Every moment think
steadily, as a Roman and a man, to do what thou hast in hand with perfect and simple dignity, and a feeling of affection, and freedom, and justice.'" That is the South at its best, though a South now under rapid decay
through what Percy calls the *losangelization* of America. Percy recognizes
in Faulkner's Sartoris a nobility, and adds that in the South there were
"a great many Sartorises." It is "the nobility of the natural perfection of
the Stoics, the stern inner summons to man's full estate, to duty, to honor,
to generosity toward his fellow men and above all to his inferiors." That
is a natural nobility, not a perfection pursued in consequence of man's
having been created "in the image of God and therefore loveable in themselves, but because to do them an injustice would be to defile the inner
fortress which was oneself."

Admirable, that nobility, but not sufficient to reconcile the Stoic to
either this place or in itself to turn him to his intended, ultimate end
which requires surrendering the fortress of his "self." In the struggle to
recover a possible vision, the steadying service of Stoicism helps Percy
in the tensional moment, so that he is reluctant to surrender that deportment. These words above are from that early essay, "Stoicism in the

South" (1956). But at the end of his life, in his "Why Are You a Catholic?" (1990), he can at last locate Southern Stoicism, suggesting an image: "the stoic knight at parade rest, both hands folded on the hilt of his broadsword, his face as grave and impassive as the Emperor's." Here is the Southerner—the Emperor Aurelius and King Richard, combined in one figure, Robert E. Lee. But it is a figure requiring for Percy "the crucified Jew above him." Only through an opening of that fortress of the self is Stoicism at last to be set aside. It does not preclude a Stoical endurance such as Percy was reluctant to deny as admirable, since in it and through it he had come to discover himself accommodated to a place and its history, the South. His is an enlarged manner, gained in the recognition of Stoicism as insufficient. If one is Percy, that allows his Stoical wit to be moderated by a humor acknowledging his participation in place as a "self" fallen; but through an openness within such closing circumstances (even those of the losangelization of New Orleans) he is recovered by grace, through that "crucified Jew."

How, then, is one to confront that destruction, that pervasive losangelization of the South? Certainly not by abandoning the battle through suicide as with Quentin, though one may discover himself very near that nadir. In his *Lost in the Cosmos*, Percy engages this danger in a St. Thomas–like proposition: "THE DEPRESSED SELF: *Whether the Self is Depressed because there is Something Wrong with it or whether Depression is a Normal Response to a Deranged World.*" Not suicide, then, but not abiding despair as "a non-suicide" either. The difference is evident as we observe each—the *non* and the *ex*—"leave the house for work, at eight o'clock on an ordinary morning." Leave the *house*, the *place* let us add, which is already located in a losangelized suburb that has become inescapable and so inescapably depressing. The two thus seen:

> The nonsuicide is a little traveling suck of care, sucking care with him from the past and being sucked toward care in the future. His breath is high in his chest. The ex-suicide opens his front door, sits down on the steps, and laughs. Since he has the option of being dead, he has nothing to lose by being alive. It is good to be alive. He goes to work because he doesn't have to.

The ex-suicide is no longer intimidated by the here-and-now as in decay. He is, as Percy suggests to Jo Gulledge in the *Southern Review* interview, a Binx Bolling as a "Quentin Compson who didn't commit suicide." We begin to discover perhaps that Percy is indeed himself rather like Quentin Compson, protesting his neutrality too much. He doesn't love or hate the South, as novelist, using it as a convenient "backdrop" to his play of ideas. In an interview given a little earlier, "The Study of Consciousness" (*Georgia Review*, Spring 1981), he has insisted that he is not "interested in the particular mythos and mystique of the South," being "simply stuck with [his] place." Hence, "I'm not a Southern writer in the same way as Faulkner or Welty and maybe even Flannery O'Connor" (his *maybe* presumably because he and Flannery are not only Southern but Catholic). He is not interested in New Orleans as a place in his *Moviegoer*. "What I was interested in was having a conflict, a confrontation of two cultures—the Greco-Roman Stoicism of Binx's father's family and the Roman Catholicism of Binx's mother's family—and seeing what happened when these two met." There is an implicit drama in the dialectical positing of two "ideas" against each other, ideas which (as O'Connor might argue in defense of what she calls "natural Catholics" such as her Old Tarwater) speak a Southern ambivalence that requires orthodoxy as a rescue of what is viable in the inherited Southern tradition. A very "Southern" theme, haunting Percy with its irresolution from the beginning of his quest for the Word in his own word. Binx himself is given pause, encountering the man coming out of Church with the cross in ashes on his forehead. Binx goes on his way to an encounter with our version of Plato's Allegory of the Cave, the movie—an encounter with "idea" in the movie as a primitive version of the "virtual reality" we have since pursued with more sophisticated technology.

The South as an idea for Faulkner is still operative in the present—in Percy's *here-and-now*. But the present moment in this place (for Faulkner) is haunted largely by history—by a tradition still alive "in the blood," in Eliot's phrase for that condition of mind called *traditionalist*. Percy's concern for the here-and-now recognizes as well, in the present circumstances of his cultural moment, a relation to history though he is wary of that "tradition." Better deal with it in relation to the history of *idea*—in an intellectual address to idea lest the "self" become entrapped by cultural history. This is to suggest that Percy would enlarge history's parameters beyond Faulkner's. He knows Faulkner's history nevertheless somehow included within his own postage-stamp country, his Yoknapatawpha Country of Ideas. If Faulkner reaches back to the Battle of Culloden Moor in old Scotland, Percy reaches back as well, but to Pascal. Not that Faulkner does not know something of the "history of ideas," of course. But Percy's has been a more pure pursuit of the idea in its history, finding it issuing in Existentialism out of Phenomenology—out of Descartes through Kant to Husserl, thence to Sartre. Faulkner knows something of Sartre as his contemporary at least. (Sartre knows Faulkner as well, and would gather him into his Existentialist camp, as Sartre's literary arguments about Faulkner show.)

We might similarly suggest that Percy does not recognize the intellectual range of Flannery O'Connor, nor notice that in her "Georgia types" as he calls them with slight deprecation, she proves devastating on pseudo-intellectualism such as that celebrated by Sartre and Marx and Hegel and Descartes. In his "Ferdinand Phinizy Lecture" at the University of Georgia in Athens in 1978, Percy talks about "Going Back to Georgia," not coming back to Georgia, where he lived in Athens as a boy, a refugee from the Birmingham of his early life and a traumatic destruction of his immediate family. What he observes are people far removed from the "Georgia types" of Flannery O'Connor, and it is of that removal that he speaks. For Atlanta and Athens prove inescapably losangelized. Georgia has now drawn "Georgia-Arab banking alliances from which Louisiana is altogether excluded," though he suggests that "we in Louisiana have been trying for years to sell the Superdome to the Arabs, with a singular lack of success."

Meanwhile, away from the suburbs, even at the opening of this new millennium, O'Connor's country folk (and perhaps even some of the suburban folk of New Orleans and Atlanta) come upon opportunities for willful rejections of the truth of things on their own through a natively perverse will, requiring no influence from the losangelization now become world-wide. O'Connor's Bible salesman proves not remote and antique in this respect. In "Good Country People," having stolen Hulga's wooden leg (Louisianians and Arabs beware), the Bible salesman tells Hulga she is not so smart: He has been believing in nothing ever since he was born, in contrast to Hulga, who had to go off to college to learn unbelief. And O'Connor's Haze Motes of *Wise Blood* proves a "natural" Nietzschean, preaching his Church of God without God, arguing himself (and foolish believing persons) to be beyond good and evil. One might even argue that her Misfit of "A Good Man Is Hard to Find" is blood kin to Percy's Lancelot, though the Misfit is no sophisticated intellectual. Both resort to a violence, defending good by the indirection of their own undeniable acts of evil. A Polish interviewer remarks Lancelot's violence as exceptional in Percy's work. Yes, Percy responds, but Lancelot is "a different kind of rebel." As Southerner, Lancelot is an outsider like those other Southerners Binx Bolling, Will Barrett, Tom More. "But they are Pascalian. They had hope and they had embarked on various kinds of quests. The only quest that Lancelot is embarked on is what he called the quest for the unholy grail. He is also an alienated Southerner" who does not "like what he sees about American civilization." Unlike the Misfit however, Lancelot "is not interested in God."

Percy, addressing his uncharacteristic use of violence in *Lancelot*, distinguishes Lancelot as protagonist from those others of his characters who are "Pascalian." Pascal as philosopher held a certain fascination for Percy. The French scientist as philosopher had set out (in the 17th century) as mathematician and physicist, but moved beyond science toward a mystical resolution of questions that would not submit to logic. He is now largely remembered for his association with the Jansenists and still held suspect by the Church, so that Percy no doubt felt a kinship with Pascal as (seemingly) something of a "renegade," as Percy felt himself to be. He is renegade as Southern novelist in relation to Faulkner, Welty, O'Connor. But there is more: Pascal, suffering ill-health, in a confused state of mind and spirit, on the night of November 23, 1654 (in the middle of his life), had a vision. (The account is in Pascal's *Memorial.*) He encountered the "hidden God" in the person of Jesus Christ as immediately present to him. He writes an account, at the moment of his experience on a scrap of paper, later inscribed on parchment. He carries that parchment with him always, on his person, lest doubt stirred by his rational mind need stilling by that old experience, the parchment certifying his memory.

Thenceforth, Pascal brought the considerable virtues of his rational, logical mind to bear upon questions held by reason's skepticism, a skepticism which would become an obsession to the intelligentsia in the next century's "Enlightenment." (Percy would not have overlooked that among Pascal's "scientific" concerns he had invented a calculating machine, at least metaphorically corresponding to that modern machine almost worshipped in Percy's day, the computer.) Hence, to counter skepticism, that essay in Pascal's *Pensées* to which Percy alludes, the famous "Wager" which is concerned with the alternatives of two "infinities." Man, infinitely small, is suspended between the void (nothingness) as one infinity and the divine (the other infinity). He must choose to move toward one or the other (as Augustine moved, though Camus could not). And so, since *nothingness* would not be lost if one "bet" on the infinity called God and the infinity nothingness should prove the reality, logic requires that one bet in favor of God. If one choose nothingness, he loses either way. For if God should be the True Infinity against whom one chose nothingness, it is nothingness that will consume the bettor under God's judgment. Remembering that Descartes and Pascal are contemporaries, and that Percy remarks the 17th century as initiating that "Fateful Rift" in the Modern mind, we observe that Pascal's "midway" is that between Love and Nothingness. That century is a point after which increasingly we are at the point of becoming lost in the cosmos. It is a tendency to deracination as a "self" which is consequent upon intellect's turning away from creation as understood by St. Thomas, through willful angelism. For Thomas this "real world of real things" (as Percy calls it in his "Holiness of the Ordinary") is a world of "Created things … midway between God's knowledge and our knowledge," requiring intellect's recognition by a sacramental witness of stewardship toward created things mediated by finite reason in obeisance to that Absolute Cause of things. In the turning away that begins with Descartes to accelerate toward the Enlightenment's rationalism (as Percy sees it), there begins a wider wandering in the woods whose very darkness seems increasingly fascinating to intellect, as if by will receptive to finite intellect's "light." *Homo viator* becomes pathetically lost. (Pathos, we have suggested, becomes the incipient mood of Romanticism in its reaction to Enlightenment rationalism.)

Not that one escapes the wonder of this choosing creature, man. Percy declares man by nature "looney." Pascal puts it more colorfully: "What kind of chimera is man? What novelty, what monster, what chaos, what subject of contradictions, what prodigy? Judge of all things, imbecile worm of the earth, depository of truth, sink of uncertainty and error, glory and scum of the world.... Who will unravel this tangle?" Perhaps the scientist as novelist has the best prospect of unraveling this wonder, man. And so the gamble of hope, made out of the quest as suspended, such as that dramatized in Binx Bolling or Will Barrett or Tom More. They are in quest of the Holy Grail, not of Lancelot's "unholy grail." Not "interested in God," Lancelot's "solution for his alienation is a kind of fascism, or nazism," Percy says, though Lancelot finds the Nazis of the 1930s "stupid," he adds. One might take Lancelot in the light of Gabriel Marcel's observation about the enthusiasm stirred in the public spirit by Nazi élan. Marcel says that "what people overlook is the excitement and the fact that mass movements answer an emptiness in a Western soul." To hear this from Marcel, who was French, Jew, Catholic, existentialist, is to hear him "praising" the excitement of nazism as "extraordinary."

One might demur at the conclusion, and no doubt Percy might rephrase it, since Marcel is finding *hope* of *soul* still alive despite "nazism," though a hope misled. In the midst of World War II, in the midst of Vichy, France, Marcel is not praising the excitement stirred in the triumphant Germans except insofar as it speaks a possibility of recovery from the emptiness of the Western soul. O'Connor's Misfit seems hardly stirred to excitement, of course, but he reacts in a defense of evil as it were against the Modernist spirit, the American civilization which denies both good and evil, the good denied as absolute through the strategies of relativism. This American civilization does not recognize its likeness to the Weimar Republic as prelude to the rise of Hitler out of the German "liberalism" of the 1920s, Percy reminds us on several occasions. We hear Percy say, a few months before his death, that "Nothing offends the American liberal more than being compared to the German liberal of the Weimar Republic." If Lancelot as "nazi" is in reaction to the *losangelization* of the American spirit, and in reaction seeks the "unholy grail" as his way of rejecting that Modernist spirit, O'Connor's Misfit is on a similar quest, at the surface of his actions. He lacks the intellectual sophistication afforded Lancelot by his middle-class origins. The Misfit affirms his own evil, though he cannot yet consent to the ultimate Good (though O'Connor suggests that he desires that Good). His actions are his "signs" of rebuke to those who rationalize his evil away in denying the existence of both good and evil. That Modernist intellect prides itself in having moved beyond those old signs.

The differences between the visions held by O'Connor from her beginning and Percy after considerable intellectual journeying have to do with the limits perceived in the Southern backdrop each deploys as a fiction writer. What they hold in common is a recognition that by nature we are each an intellectual soul incarnate. Percy, as he reminds us, is a middle-class intellectual, scientific in his formal training. Given the intellectual sophistication of his characters and their affluent circumstances, they seem rather upper–middle class, occupying a social stratum that might be envied by Ivan Karamazov's devil, whose ambition is to appear as "a little Russian gentleman," an appearance well-suited to his "devilish" ends. Perhaps one might encounter them as well in the suburbs of O'Connor's Taulkingham, living in a suburban house beyond the wall of such an upper-class estate as that which Mr. Head and Nelson encounter on their descent into the city. (On its lawn they are arrested by that decoration of "folk art," that "artificial nigger" of O'Connor's much-misunderstood story.)

One might even wonder whether Percy's Lancelot, like O'Connor's Misfit, may not at last as person, through grace, be possibly rescued by grace. We see the Misfit, in a moment of terror in response to the old grandmother's gesture of love, shooting the old woman dead. But O'Connor speculates that perhaps the old woman's gesture of love (all other signs and gestures she makes up to that point being dictated by the Modernist spirit [excusing evil] which is hers by cultural osmosis) might yet turn the Misfit toward his calling. However unlikely this may seem, O'Connor argues, "the old lady's gesture, like the mustard seed" might "grow to be a crow-filled tree in the Misfit's heart, and will be enough of a pain to him there to turn him into the prophet he was meant to become." "Meant to become" by his gifts as "a different breed of dog"— as the Misfit's father observed in him as a child. He is then (in O'Connor's view) an intellectual soul incarnate—a representation of that actual created creature, a person. The difference in the Southern backdrop for the fiction of O'Connor and Percy aside, in the end their visions of man as lost in a dark wood coincide. (The backdrop of "The Artificial Nigger" involves not only Taulkingham née Atlanta as a Georgia place; as an actual place it also affords the possibility of a descent analogous to Dante's descent into Hell, as O'Connor's careful images suggest.) The "self" as an arrested consciousness, responding within any dark wood

of place here-and-now, is subject to an amazing grace, a mystery of rescue possible out of that dark wood by a turning toward the true way. For
place signifies that possibility. By virtue of its actual existence as the real
world it speaks to intellect through the senses.

There is a difference yet to be remarked between Percy early in his
work and O'Connor, one that fades in the final closer coincidence of
their visions. O'Connor's faith sustains her in a confident devotion as
writer, as God's postulant almost from the beginning. Her "calling" as
writer does not obligate her to evangelical concerns for the moral rectitude of her reader, as St. Thomas assures her. That is an understanding Percy comes to, but over a period of an intellectual struggle. "What
I am trying to do," he tells Jan Gretlund, "is to figure out how a man can
come to himself, living in a place like [the South now become losange-
lized]." In pursuit of his own rescue through idea, he will return again
and again to a sense of obligation to save others as it were—an inclination through which his considerable virtues as a satirist emerge, most conspicuously in his *Lost in the Cosmos: The Last Self-Help Book*. But there
occurs at last the coincident vision shared with O'Connor. Beyond that
concern he comes to a celebration of creation itself as sacramental, even
implicitly that part of the world occupied by a popular spirit which finds
itself no longer at home in place, having become losangelized and so lost
in the cosmos in suburban wanderings. It is there in his "The Holiness of the Ordinary" and is fictionally recovered in *The Thanatos Syndrome*.

Not that a tension between Greco-Roman Stoicism and his Catholicism, first engaged in *The Moviegoer*, does not continue for Percy in some
degree, accompanying his concern to recover the Word to his word.
There continues a tension of ideas in him to the end of his life, ener-
gizing him intellectually so that he contemplates as his next novel one
about "the end of the world." Always, what he is trying to do, as we heard
him tell Jan Gretlund in that interview in 1981, "is to figure out how a
man can come to himself, living in a place like that," *that* being the suburban South as having undergone a distortion as place. "There is [that]
word for it: losangelization." How are we to humanize the "South of Los
Angeles?" For now we have here a "New South, which is not the South
of Faulkner, not the South of Eudora, it is not the South of Flannery."
It is instead "the South of Interstate 12 and Highway 190." How then
humanize it? He remarks that "at the end of *The Second Coming*, very
deliberately, I've Allie and Will leave the greenhouse, go to a motel; the
first coming together takes place in a Holiday Inn." He would no doubt
be amused that there has now been built a Holiday Inn across the road
from Flannery's Andalusia, just outside Milledgeville. In those circumstances of the novel, Will proposes that he and Allie move into "a G. E.

Gold Medallion home, a mass-produced home." Percy adds: "They could be happy there."

They could be happy there, as Percy was undoubtedly happy, most of the time, on Old Landing Road in Covington, not far from New Orleans. There he could "stay put" and not "get in trouble," as he puts it. Not be drawn into the world in such a way as to be tempted to the despair of a non-suicide found wandering *places* like a disconsolate ghost. More like Fr. Smith, whose fire tower in *Thanatos Syndrome* gives that old wayfarer a perspective upon the here-and-now, seen with the eyes of a long-wanderer now come to himself in a woods no longer dark, as "ideas" and experiences had earlier drawn him to believe of the woods now called the cosmos. Fr. Smith can know, as Percy has come to know, that the humanization of any losangelized place depends on the person's recovery of the source of tenderness from the distortions of tenderness as sentimentalized to the conveniences of the deracinated self. Fr. Smith speaks words rather directly out of Flannery O'Connor, in her "Introduction" to *A Memoir of Mary Ann*, a child who is dying of cancer but is not one of God's victims as Ivan Karamazov might insist. O'Connor recalls Ivan to us. Ivan's new tenderness, devoid of faith, is "a tenderness which, long since cut off from the person of Christ, is wrapped in theory. When tenderness is detached from the source of tenderness, its logical outcome is terror. It ends in forced-labor camps and in the fumes of the gas chamber."

Enough to make one a non-suicide through depression, unless the Source be recovered. So not only does Flannery O'Connor believe, but Walker Percy as well, having been recovered as a wanderer in company with St. Augustine and Dante, fellow figures of humanity as *homo viator*—on the way beyond any species of losangelization. Percy told an interviewer (January 1986): "I keep coming back to Mother Teresa. I wish she could be cloned 10,000 times. That would be a solution to our problems."[16] Meanwhile the novelist by indirection—with a last (or almost last) tweaking of the scientist whose religion has become scientism—must do what he can. He does so in the light of a secret he would share, having journeyed long to find it: "The sacraments, whatever else they do, confer the highest significance upon the ordinary things of this world, bread, wine, water, touch, breath, words, talking, listening—and what do you have? You have a man in a predicament and on the move in a real world of real things, a world which is a sacrament and a mystery." How like those words of Flannery O'Connor to an anxious pilgrim finding herself lost in Atlanta—in Haze's Taulkingham: "The ultimate reality is the Incarnation, the present reality is the Incarnation...." That mystery is put more cryptically by a French intellectual novelist known to both Percy and O'Connor, George Bernanos, who in his *Diary of a Country*

Priest declares, "All is grace." Creation is a sign opened to us more and more as we summon witnesses to that recovery, among those witnesses such a "Southern" writer as Flannery O'Connor. But especially, given our more kindred dislocation shared with him at his outset—Walker Percy.

Notes

Part I: The Swift Bird of Memory, the Breadboard of Art

1. This theme I develop in my *Love's Labors (Almost) Lost: Ruminations Under the Shadows of the Albigensian Heresy*, 1995, in manuscript.

2. Here I am reminded of the commentary Eric Voegelin makes on our theme, worth recalling in that his remarks enlarge upon my suggestion of the infinity of play of mind in response to tensional suspense of *love* as life and *refusal of love* as death. John H. Hallowell's "Editor's Preface" to Voegelin's *From Enlightenment to Revolution* (1975) quotes Voegelin: "Existence has the structure of the In-Between, of the Platonic *metaxy*, and if anything is constant in the history of mankind it is the language of tension between life and death, immortality and mortality, perfection and imperfection, time and timelessness, between order and disorder, truth and untruth, sense and senselessness of existence; between *amor dei* and *amor sui, l'âme ouverte* and *l'âme close*; between the virtues of openness toward the ground of being such as faith, hope, and love, and the vices of infolding closure such as hybris and revolt; between the modes of joy and despair; and between alienation in its double meaning of alienation from the world and alienation from God." Eudora Welty, so far as I know, had not read Voegelin, but very close companions in her own vision did, and comment on Voegelin's comfort to the artist; Walker Percy and Cleanth Brooks come at once to mind. The significant speculative engagement of this theme by Voegelin is his *Anamnesis* (1978), on the nature of human consciousness.

3. The danger to the critic here is that he may force-meld art and history, and in doing so both violate history and abuse art. Marxist criticism notoriously takes advantage of this confusion for ideological ends, but the abuse is more common than simply the Marxist use of art in pursuit of social goals. It is an abuse underlying instances of art's forced manipulation of sentiment in order to enslave intellect by sentimentality, whether the instance is some "docudrama" violation of art's relation to history for ideological ends, or a pandering through sensationalism as in pornography, or spectacular violence in the various modes of the entertainment media.

4. Here I have in mind a passage in Aquinas's *Collationes Credo in Deum*, to which we shall presently return. In it, Thomas with care and precision distinguished the *maker* from the *creator*.

5. Eudora Welty, unlike Laurel, knows her creatures intimately, an aspect

of her deportment of love to existential reality everywhere evident in her fiction. In her treatment of the swift, for instance, she reveals intimate observation of that creature, a pest to Missouri, who must clean up after such intrusions. There is a vivid precision here of the bird's quivering wings as it clings to a curtain, to this disappearing "tilting crescent," precise in that the bird's long thin curved wings and no tail and its erratic flight of ascent prescribe the visual image to us. As I was writing this there came to hand a puff piece on a new novel, from our regional literary editor in the Atlanta paper. ("Winter's Tale," Michael Skube. *Journal-Constitution*, April 16, 1995, on Jim Grimsley's *Winter Bird*, Algonquin Books.) To indicate how fine the writing is, the novel's opening paragraph is quoted, in part to reveal how masterfully the details are handled. In part we are told, "By the river flocks of wren, starlings and a few faded female cardinals have gathered to feed on the leavings in the cornfield...." Two of the three birds eat insects, the third can hardly manage corn kernels. Wrens don't flock, and cardinals are rather notoriously monogamous so that a gathering of females calls for comment, being unusual. The situation is for boys with a BB gun, waiting to "burst open bird skulls." Boys know better, given that uncertain gun. They would shoot at the body if they mean to hit the bird, unlikely in the case of a quick wren. Once a neighbor complained to a neighbor that his son had shot off one leg of all her robins on her lawn, not knowing (as the amused father did) the robin's habit of standing on one leg before running to a heard worm. One fears for fiction in such carelessness, not for the fiction itself, but for the ignorant praise of false observation, upon which fiction so much depends since we have lost common vision of the mystery of existence itself.

6. Eliot writes of Joyce's book in the *Dial* (November 23, 1923): "[Using myth] is simply a way of controlling, of ordering, of giving a shape and a significance to the immense panorama of futility and anarchy which is contemporary history.... Instead of the narrative method, we may now use the mythical method. It is, I believe, a step toward making a modern world possible for art." Some of the criticism of Welty's fiction—of the stories in her *Curtain of Green* or *Robber Bridegroom*—seems to follow out of Eliot's argument. Our own argument is not that such dimensions to her fiction are not important to its order and structure, but that such critical concerns bring us only to the threshold of the significance of myth in her art. We delight in the intellectual wit of such control in art, but why are we moved beyond such delight by her stories? I am contending, of course, that we are moved because our maker is attuned to the holiness and mystery of creation itself through love, and her gifts as maker affect us through her stories with that same invitation to openness. Not either/or—concerning the cleverness of her art—but rather yes, and....

7. The triumph of Cartesean Idealism, Gilson suggests in *Methodical Realism* (1936, 1990), has left the Western intellectual cursed with the insoluble problem of epistemology. What is required is that we "free ourselves from the obsession with epistemology" consequent upon an entrapment in consciousness by the presumption in Descartes' distortions of the nature of thought itself. Epistemology is not "the necessary pre-condition for philosophy. The philosopher as such has only one duty: to put himself in accord with himself and other things." That is, even as with the poet, he must turn back to the immediacy of existence itself, experienced as actual, whereby experience of the truth of things rouse thought, rather than thought prescribing the truth of things. My own engagement of this obsession with epistemology, especially in relation to intellect as at once intuitive and rational, is in my *Making: The Proper Habit of Our Being* (2000).

The festering thorn of "Romanticism" wounds intellect (I contend) through Descartes, issuing at last in the confusions to the Western intellectual community which C. P. Snow calls the splintering of that community into "Two Cultures." Fragmentation continues apace, with an accelerating spectacle of it in the academy in the 1990s.

8. Just how much Western philosophers since Descartes have exacerbated this confusion is addressed by Karl Stern in his *The Flight from Woman* (1965, 1985). See especially in it his "Womanhood," and the essays on Descartes, Schopenhauer, Sartre, and Tolstoy.

9. Concerning this participatory submission as we may focus it upon, not the poet, but his hearer: both poet and his audience are beholders of reality through the art of sign. They are alike in sharing the mystery of *making*, which by analogy is related to *creating*—which are not terms of common identity. This aspect of art, whereby the made thing is mediator of community, speaks to the formative nature of intellectual community, so chaotically addressed in our moment under the ambiguous rubric of "education." Here let us borrow and refine Coleridge's expectation of the "reader" as unlettered becoming literate—becoming educated. What is required of him, says Coleridge, is a "willing suspension of disbelief." We have cast it rather as more active, as a participatory submission through love. In this perspective we may consider the poet as imitating in sign the action of nature—i.e., the action of the *created* by his action of making. In doing so, he participates in existence in a sacramental manner, insofar as he makes through love. The aesthetic response to the made thing is properly speaking also a participatory submission: in this sense, a sacramental consent to that continuous creation (*nature*, in its popular designation) as mediated by art. That is a condition of participation we discover in formal sacraments, whose formality is that of art not science, under the limits of intellect incarnate—the soul whose response to the truth of things is mediated by bodily existence in a confluent embodiment called nature. Through sacramental consent to creation, there develops to the finite consenter his participation in making of the self through grace, as opposed to a creation of the self through will. By this "self-making" we mean the action of love's openness, whereby proximate obstacles to grace as the proximate cause of the perfection of the self are removed; thus a participation in the perfection of the self according to the limits of gift as *this* particular person, whereby a making through consent allows a creation of perfection of the person. This is the arena in personhood in which, through a sacramental submission of openness to existential reality, one enlarges love as *eros* to its inclusion as *agape*.

Welty does not speak in this manner, yet her recognition of the spiritual dimension of sacramental openness seems compatible to Thomas as we hear her talk about her "anticipation." As for our aesthetic engagement of this spiritual conditioning to love, we must add that Coleridge's concern for the willing suspension of disbelief is not a passive consent to the made thing as usually supposed. It is an active, even critical, openness, since experience resident in the memory of the beholder is an active presence in the encounter. The consent is to the making itself as analogous to creating but not an identity of creating. That inclusive action of creating *effects* beings, among them the human being (the person) who makes. Here is a distinction of the mode of making (governed by reason) proper to the active becoming of the person, as distinct from his power to "create." What is required of the maker—or so Thomas insists—is reason in consent to making, whereby failed made things are recognized as such and not consented to nor elevated as if perfect by the "sincerity" of the maker.

10. Welty's remarks are agreeable to those spoken by that explicitly Thomistic poet, Flannery O'Connor, who warns relentless questioners concerned with what she intends to "prove" with her fiction that one never "proves" anything with a story. At the same time, she also speaks to a "greater mystery" in art than its maker may know. Even that writer who may be severely affected by the Modernist spirit may *make* more largely than he knows. "If the novelist is in tune with this spirit [of Modernism], if he believes that actions are predetermined by psychic make-up or the economic situation or some other determinable factor, then he will be concerned above all with an accurate reproduction of the things that most immediately concern man, with the natural forces that he feels control his destiny. Such a writer may produce a great tragic naturalism, for by his responsibility to the things he sees, he may transcend the limitations of his narrow vision." ("Some Aspects of the Grotesque in Southern Fiction," 1960) To which we add that such a writer may himself subsequently recognize a transcendence of that narrow vision, affecting his own development as artist. I have in mind as example not only T. S. Eliot but also Alexander Solzhenitsyn.

11. I have explored Eliot's escape of such entrapment at some length in *T. S. Eliot: Our American Magus* (1970) and *Eliot's Reflective Journey to the Garden* (1979).

12. The gradual loss of faith by the poet is reflected in his growing discomfort, first with analogy and metaphor as dependable, and then with uncertainties about imagery in relation to his signs—the uncertainty of sensual perception of the *other* (real or only imagined?), which uncertainty calls in question sign itself. The loss of metaphysical faith after the English metaphysicals troubled Eliot, though at first he did not put his concern in our terms. Later, C. S. Lewis gave us his "Introduction to Medieval and Renaissance Literature," *The Discarded Image* (1964), which is a sequel to his exploration of the dislocation in Western philosophy by the reductions of concept, especially that of *love*, in which dislocation the Provincial poets have a considerable responsibility. Lewis's *Allegory of Love* (1936) opens this topic. Once more, this is a question I engage in *Love's Labors (Almost) Lost: Ruminations under the Shadows of Albigensian Heresy*, 1995, in manuscript.

13. On the inadequacy of the argument in "Tradition and the Individual Talent," which Eliot makes just before a turning reflected in his *Waste Land*, see my "T. S. Eliot circa 1930: The Recovery of the Permanent Things," *Modern Age*, Spring 1995.

14. In this work, Welty does not expand very much upon the obligation of piety toward creation and the complications that grow out of recognition of obligation, at least not through Wendell, though he is a touchstone of experience which Laurel clearly recognizes. For a fascinating enlargement, however, one might turn to Flannery O'Connor's Tarwater, in *The Violent Bear It Away*, who attempts to refuse engagement in the interest of minding his own "bidness" but is not able to maintain that detachment. Tarwater as protagonist in that novel, let us say metaphorically, is on the verge of recognizing, at the threshold of his own adulthood, what the speaker in "Ash-Wednesday" comes to recover on the threshold of death. It is, in sum, what Welty calls a recognition of the "holiness and mystery" of the creation.

15. Gabriel Marcel, in his *Man Against Mass Society* (1962, 1985), remarks this concern of the poet in relation to the uses of memory in relation to history. "Memory," he says, "consists essentially of being *within* the event, of above all not emerging *from* the event; in remaining there and going over it again and again

from within." On the other hand, "History is the elderly general, plastered with medals, brisk and impotent, who reviews the long lines of troops, laden with their heavy field-kit, on the barrack-square of some garrison town." Thus, history proves "*a way of forgetting*, or, to put it more flatly, of losing that real contact with the event for the lack of which historical narrative so often reduces itself to a simple abstracting *naming* of events." That is Laurel's temptation, the execution of which would be naming of past events by preserving artifact, turning the self into a museum of memories. Marcel adds, "The past, when it is merely known historically, ... somehow piles itself up outside our real lives; or it is fated to lose what one might be tempted to call its vitamins." Given the philosopher as poet here, one sees why he is so persuasive in his arguments to Welty's poet friend Walker Percy.

  16. J. R. R. Tolkien, in his essay "On Fairy-Stories" (1944) makes an enlightening argument of distinction between primary and secondary "creations," the secondary being the arena of the poet's making.

Part II: Walker Percy's Quest for the Word Within the Word

  1. Bernard Goldberg, a news correspondent at CBS television, addressed the question of media bias, specifically that which he had experienced in the CBS newsroom, writing in the *Wall Street Journal*. He found himself immediately ostracized at CBS, his on-air reports curtailed. Some four years later, he published *Bias: A CBS Insider Exposes How the Media Distort the News* (2001). The bias was not news, but the treatment he received as himself a "liberal" gone wrong was a shocking experience to Mr. Goldberg. He made Dan Rather (among others) "viscerally angry," as Rather informed him. The chapter-and-verse revealed in his book, published by Regnery, was sufficiently titillating to land *Bias* in the No. 1 spot on the nonfiction bestseller list of the *New York Times*, a periodical which is itself notoriously biased in its liberal stance, as Percy had occasion to discover. See Percy's letter to the *Times*, January 22, 1988, which was neither published nor acknowledged, though the paper had published an earlier letter from him, "A View of Abortion, with Something to Offend Everybody" (June 8, 1981). Percy's more emphatic position on abortion and euthanasia in his second letter was dangerous to share so publicly, given Percy's "name recognition," a media virtue which ordinarily makes the media enthusiastic patrons of names. (The letter was subsequently published in *Signposts in a Strange Land*.)

  2. That the Scopes Trial is still very much debated is indicated by the publication in 1997 of Edward J. Larsen's *Summer of the Gods: The Scopes Trial and the Continuing Debate Over Science and Religion*, a Pulitzer Prize–winning book. It is a debate even more alive at the moment in another arena than that old comic one in Tennessee: that of scientists calling the Darwinian "science" of evolution in question as but theory contradicted by evidence of "intelligent design," engaged from genes to galaxies by credentialed scientists concerned with the Darwinian theory dignified as science and elevated to a myth to be honored with piety by the public spirit, but which in reality rejects the rigors of true science argued by these Darwinian skeptics.

  3. I have considered this point at length in several works, principally in "Bells for John Stewart's Burden," *Georgia Review*, Summer 1966; *Possum, and Other Receits for the Recovery of "Southern" Being* (1987), but also in various essays

collected in *The Men I Have Chosen for Fathers* (1990). I do not mean to say, of course, that I would argue that the Fugitive-Agrarians recognized the full implications of the event of the Scopes Trial on the instant. Rather, it awakened them to the realization that something was destructively wrong in their present social, political, religious, economic circumstances that was traceable to the dominant intellectual climate established in the academy and pervasively effective on formal policy of governmental agencies. They began, each according to his gifts, to explore the problem implicit in the spectacle of that trial—that spectacle a symptom of a fundamental dislocation within community. One has only to read the introductory "Statement of Principles" in *I'll Take My Stand* to find themes developed by subsequent writers, Percy among them, but including Voegelin, Gilson, Marcel, C. S. Lewis, Eliot, and many others. The Agrarians were quite explicit in opposition to the intellectual mind-set that Voegelin would name and define as *gnostic*, already recognizing its doctrinal principle of intellectual autonomy as the source of and justification for power over nature. They recognized as well the implicit appeal of that Modernist doctrine popularized in "consumerism"—the elevation of the appetitive desire of the individual as to be so appealing that it enabled easier justification of "modern labor" in a surrender to the various systems, surrender required to the exercise of power but reducing man himself not only to a "consumer" but to the consumed. The history of the century, from World War I to century's end, records the consumption not only of the material world to dubious ends but a consumption of man in political and military confusions of antithetic pursuits of power. Robert Penn Warren, for instance, had suggested as title for the symposium, not *I'll Take My Stand* but "Tracts Against Communism." (The Fugitive-Agrarian concern here would be engaged by Marcel, in his *Man Against Mass Society*, soon after World War II.) The actual enemy, as the Fugitive-Agrarians were already recognizing in the 1930s, was the secular gnostic power over nature, which may be exercised from either the "left" or the "right," in the increasingly secularized gnostic destructions of reality itself. They objected at the outset to the attempt (whether by the left or right) to "cure the poverty of the contemporary spirit by hiring experts," as they said, to rebuild that spirit "by pouring the soft materials from the top" in the gnostic's manner. Of course, Voegelin's now-famous term *modern gnosticism* or Percy's *theorist-consumer age* were not terms spoken by them, but it is evident that they too were concerned by our spiritual dislocation as symptomatically evidenced in economic, religious, political, philosophical, and educational decay. As for their position as if restricted to the South, to a regional chauvinism, they assert at once: "Proper living as a matter of the intelligence and the will, does not depend on the local climate or geography, and is capable of a definition which is general and not Southern at all." My own principle for the recovery of "proper living" I believe encompasses their concerns and is termed *Thomistic realism*. It is a position which was pursued increasingly by some of the principals among the original Fugitive-Agrarians, most especially by Allen Tate and (I believe) Donald Davidson, Cleanth Brooks, and Andrew Lytle, as my works cited above suggest.

    4. There has become very active from within science itself, as we have suggested, a movement of intellectuals participated in by a variety of scientific disciplines, the movement called Intelligent Design. It proves discomforting to established gnostic scientists since not easily dismissed as ignorant provincialism standing in the way of *progress*—the code-word for gnostic acceleration of *theoretical* evolution. Michael J. Behe's *Darwin's Black Box* (Behe a biochemist);

William A. Dembski, a mathematician whose initiating works are *The Design Inference* and *Intelligent Design*; Stephen C. Meyer, whose field is history and the philosophy of science: these minds in their works prove formidable. The three appear in concert in *Science and Evidence for Design in the Universe* (2000), but they are a few among a growing many. There is the astrophysicist Guillermo Gonzalez, a fellow at the Discovery Institute (Seattle), as is Dr. Dean Kenyon, a biologist, and David DeWolfe, who as legal scholar engages the Darwinian theory as theory with effectiveness in exposing rhetorical manipulations by the theorists. In brief, there emerge from several sciences and intellectual disciplines formidable examiners of Darwinian "science," asking incisive questions. Their questions have occasioned an alarmist response from the Darwinian "Fundamentalists." In relation to the reaction of the Fugitive-Agrarians to the Scopes Trial and the presently emerging movement by scientists calling Darwin's theory into question, one might consider also Etienne Gilson's philosophical engagement, as a Thomistic realist, of the theory in his *D'Aristote à Darwin et retour* (1971), translated by John Lyon in 1984: *From Aristotle to Darwin and Back Again: A Journey in Final Causality, Species, and Evolution.*

5. Thomas's "principle of proper proportionality" may be engaged in his treatise *On being and essence. Being*, the Perfection (i.e., God) of all possible perfections created, cannot be conceptualized by finite intellect *comprehensively*, since then finite intellect would itself be greater than that which it has *comprehended* by its own absolutist sense. The illusion of doing so tempts gnostic intellect to presumption of absolute autonomy: that Being may be approached by finite intellect through acts of conceptualization in response to *esse*—experienced in actual things—the experience of the reality of discrete things as the things they are. That is a movement of intellect, an act of judgment dependent upon truths known by intellectual experience of actual things pre-existing the experience itself. In this movement toward actual things through the senses there is (Thomas says) a first movement toward Being, toward God—the Cause of the thing to which intellect thus responds through the body. Thus the intellectual soul turns from itself, out of a responsibility of reason in conceptualizations. It turns to what is not itself. It finds itself "on the way" toward that which transcends its powers of conceptualization. It is in this complex to a turning out of self-awareness that the *word*, naming *concept* as an effect of experiences, becomes crucial to the celebration of existence itself. The distinction here, in regard to *proportionality*, lies in the formulation by Gilson in *The Spirit of Thomism* (1964): "God *is* esse; creatures *have* esse but *are not esse*." (The intellectual danger here lies in denying this limit of proportionality between *God* and *person*.)

Thus Esse, Being (God), is discovered as the continuous uncaused action beyond finite intellect's capacity to a comprehensive conceptualization. That is the uncaused action whereby each thing *is*. We speak then (in Thomas's words) of "the perfection of all perfections." We speak of the Perfection whereby beings *are*. St. Augustine acts out, by a recovered memory, this movement as he has experienced it, sharing his and St. Monica's "Vision at Ostia" (*The Confessions*). In reflecting upon such an experience of actual things in a progress toward a visionary moment such as that experienced on a balcony at Ostia, we discover that the intellectual soul already "knows" the Perfection sustaining a limited potential perfection within this limited, created and knowing creature—the responding consciousness of an intellectual soul incarnate—St. Augustine and St. Monica. St. Thomas argues this "knowing" as accomplished in intellect by the complementary action of intellect in its modes as *intuitive* and *rational*. The *effect* of that intellectual action: *concept*, in search of a *word*. We may ourselves know, may recognize, this moment. It is in the infant's clasp of the mother to be responded to openly by the mother. It is in the moment of eyes engaged between parent and the newborn who is a person only minutes old in this world. There occurs a *confused* moment (a *con-fusing* of persons) which is celebratory of existence itself, a movement toward the celebration of the Cause of all.

In respect to *proportionality*, there is also to be recognized a secondary aspect. The distance between Being (God) and person (*this* being) is incommensurate in respect to that transcendent Cause, a distinction suggested in saying *this* person is created in the *image* of God. But it will follow that, since each created thing is *itself* in a relation to that Cause, finite intellect discovers itself incapable as well of a *comprehensive* conceptualization not only of God but (perhaps more disturbing to intellect) of any thing in itself. There is always something not "contained" in intellect's concept and so not formalized by word, despite that pride of a possession of things once *signified*—attested to by the letter naming a concept derived from thing. Only through reason's pursuit of universals, of the orders of being as created and *understood* when so ordered but not *comprehended*, does intellect come to an accommodation with the diversity of created things. To *understand* is to accept the mystery of things as at last beyond *comprehension*. Thus we come to know *this* thing in relation to things, but to know *imperfectly*. In this respect (again, Thomas) what we know of a thing is a limited *truth*, bequeathed to intellect by that *essence* inherent in the thing we experience. It is in this aspect of proportionality that a response is required of the intellectual soul, a response of piety toward things in themselves, discovering thereby the dignity proper to each thing in *proportion* to its actuality as the thing it is, within the orders of being. Thus the discovery requiring prudential humility under two aspects of *proportionality*: (1) the incommensurate one between *person* and *God*; and (2) the commensurate one between the person and created things through a participation in a mutuality as all created things—within which commensurate arena of proportionality lies the obligation of stewardship to creation.

6. That is the concern he addresses in the letter alluded to (note 1) to the *New York Times* (January 22, 1988) on the fifteenth anniversary of *Roe v. Wade*. to "call attention to an aspect of the abortion issue which is generally overlooked." The letter went unpublished by the *Times*, though rescued by Patrick as witness against that paper's position on the question in *Signposts in a Strange Land*. Percy calls attention to "democratic Germany in the 1920s" and especially to a book published there—perhaps "the most influential book published in Germany in the first quarter of this century": *The Justification of the Destruction of Life Devoid of Value*. It was an argument which "the best minds of the pre–Nazi Weimar Republic—physicians, social scientists, jurists, and the like" supported with "the best secular intentions—to improve the lot, socially and genetically, of the German people—by getting rid of the unfit and the unwanted." But, Percy says, "once the line is crossed ... innocent human life can be destroyed for whatever reason, for the most admirable socioeconomic, medical, or social reasons." Thus his warning of our having crossed that line in *Roe v. Wade*. We increasingly "favor getting rid of useless old people, retarded children, anti-social blacks, illegal Hispanics, gypsies, Jews.... Why not?—if that is what is wanted by the majority, the polled opinion, the polity of the time." His letter not published, Percy chided the *Times* (February 15), receiving neither publication nor response to the chiding.

7. See not only Voegelin's famous little book, *Science, Politics & Gnosticism* (1968) but his *The New Science of Politics* (1952) and especially his *From Enlight-*

enment to Revolution (1975). In supplement to Voegelin's arguments, see as well Gerhart Niemeyer's *Between Nothingness and Paradise* (1971).

8. The subtlety of communication between the unborn child and mother seems complex beyond our present understandings through science. But it seems probable that not only "body language" (as in the response of distinguishable movement by the fetus to specific words spoken) or that communication whereby the unborn child knows its mother's anxiety or happiness—her tacit acceptance or rejection of the person she carries—speaks to a knowledge shared, willingly or unwillingly, by the mother. Only as a knowing creature does the evidence seem understandable, as Dr. Verny holds, though he does not engage the evidence in relation to epistemology. His fascination with that kind of knowing which he calls *love*, conspicuous to his experience but somewhat beyond his science, speaks tellingly. There is that relation between the two (mother and unborn child) which is effected by intellectual communion beyond mere "conditioned" responses of the one to the other at that level which Peirce and Percy would term a *dyadic* relation. The mystery of the unspoken sign in this relationship seems of central importance to the mystery of spoken sign, especially since the discipline of pre-natal psychology turns as a discipline upon the uses of and "readings" of signs as given and received between mother and child *in utero*.

No doubt Percy would have been fascinated by this field of study. And perhaps it would make him even more wary of the assumptions of Positivistic linguistics, which in some respects appeals to him, he acknowledging it as his starting point. He gives this science credence beyond what is warranted by behaviorism alone. For while he is delighted by H. S. Terrace's book (*Nim*, 1979) "which blew upon the whole enterprise" of reductionism whereby there is created a "cult of teaching language to chimpanzees, dolphins, and gorillas," he concedes too much to that latest community of thought about the sign, as if as science it were sufficient to that mystery: "when you break through to learning things like names, which linguists recognize between the twelfth and sixteenth months of life, there's a sudden breakthrough into the human condition." Having said this, Percy recognizes in it a danger to his own pro-life position. "So it's easy to imagine a scientist saying, 'Well, what's the big deal? If a person by that definition is not properly human until he's eighteen months, what's wrong with getting rid of malformed infants or unwanted infants?'" (Phil McCombs, "Century of Thanatos: Walker Percy and His 'Subversive Message,'" interview in the *Southern Review*, Autumn 1988). The position he takes here is to reject a reduction of the concern to a "pro-choice, pro-life" engagement, since the "death syndrome as the spirit of the times" now threatens to override the whole range from decreed death for an unborn fetus to death "officially" executed upon the old or maimed or terminally ill. Our own point is that there is undeniable evidence, produced by science itself, that the unborn is already a person who is attuned to a considerable knowledge of its own being, and by a language already intellectually used between that small creature and its mother, though not by a spoken word on the part of the person we call "fetus." It responds intelligently to the spoken word of the parent by its *signifying* movement.

9. I am indebted in these paragraphs to Donald Demarco's excellent books, *In My Mother's Womb* (1987) and *Biotechnology and the Assault on Parenthood* (1991).

10. As a people, we have yet to address the extent to which our consent to the reduction of the self to its appetitive nature, the necessary operative principle of the theorist-consumer in justifying a "lifestyle," effects the social diseases

that increasingly destroy us. Such phenomena as inner-city riots or drive-by shootings or the cold-blooded execution of robbery victims to acquire a few dollars: these we address as if the effects of *poverty* or of *drugs* or of *single-parent family structure*. That is, we explain a symptom by adducing another symptom as its cause. Meanwhile, by the perversion of signs we embrace with an increasing frenzy our appetitive natures, as if the self might save itself by elevating the body as idol to be worshipped. That this solution is catered to by the intellectual community, by and large, needs only our attention to the programs advanced by science through government agencies to justify our existence. *Self-satisfaction* is posited as the ultimate end of human existence, directly or indirectly, whether managed by government programs intending a rescue of the "individual" or in the clever manipulations by TV advertising of medicines and health foods or any consumer goods as a "must" for the sake of "happiness." The success of the *dominant* self, whether that of the politician or ad-copy writer, depends on multiplying the numbers of the gullible—i.e., those who will *en-gullet* whatever is dangled enticingly. That is the exercise under way, a deconstruction of the self, whether in the name of some "Great Society" or in order to sell the latest pain pill or running shoes.

 11. Concerning a general confusion that intrudes into and arises out of Phenomenology, affecting consequently all linguistic theory as an amalgam of science and philosophy, see Etienne Gilson's 1969 *Linguistique et Philosophie*, translated by John Lyon, 1988: *Linguistics and Philosophy: An Essay on the Philosophical Constants of Language.*

 12. Joseph Campbell was famous among the academics at the time of *The Moviegoer*, and lingered into the multiprogram series on educational television, hosted by Bill Moyers, to which Percy alludes. Campbell's Jungian interest in the sign, as in his *Hero with a Thousand Faces*, placed him (in Percy's estimate) as a "New Age type," a favorite target of Percy's satire. These range "from California loonies like Shirley MacLaine to the classier Joseph Campbell," who hold all *credos* to be equal. Credos "are to be judged, not by their truth or falsity, sense or nonsense, but by their mythical liveliness." They feed feeling, this is to say, not the soul. Here, Percy is cautious of both Campbell and Jung, as is Flannery O'Connor, since these mythologizers of psychological science have as their concern for sign to induce an operative magic, not honoring mystery with a prudential piety. That is, the sign becomes instrument to power, rather than a signpost on the journey in the desert on our quest as pilgrim for our proper end. It is worth noting that Percy's juxtaposing prayer beads and Campbell's "feel-good" signs is in that last testimony of his, his answer to "Why Are You a Catholic?"

 13. There is a conspicuous difference between Dante and Percy as appropriating autobiographical material to art, as there is difference between Dante and Eliot—making Percy and Eliot more immediately kinsmen as *homo viator*. Dante was philosophically and spiritually accommodated to both *place* and *audience* in the thirteenth century, understanding a metaphysical vision out of Augustine and Aquinas as shared (not necessarily *embraced*, but commonly *known*). It enabled an order to his great work not possible to Percy or Eliot in their made things. Dante knows from the beginning the end to which the journey leads, his difficulty as poet that of making the hazards of the journey appear with an immediacy, a sense of contingency, to Dante the Pilgrim on his way. With both Percy and Eliot, where they are going is uncertain not only as they set out but along the way as well. Eliot begins as skeptical philosopher, Percy as scientist probing

steps along the way with the logic of idea, seeking the "straight way" which is at strife with a confusion of "ways" imposed upon creation by fallen intellect. The 20th century pilgrim (Percy or Eliot) does not realize at first what is happening to him. Percy as poet acts out with an immediacy which is actual to him in the moment in response to unresolved contingencies. Along that way, he has not reached the proper end or fully recovered the "straight way." Eliot recognizes this aspect of his own journeying in retrospect, as does Percy. If we take Eliot's *Collected Poems* as a single work, we discover him revisiting in his later poems a memory of himself earlier in his journey, a revisiting which begins with "Ash-Wednesday" and becomes more intense in his *Four Quartets*—those last poems retracing his steps guided by a new understanding. (I have developed this aspect of Eliot as Poet in relation to Eliot as Pilgrim in "T. S. Eliot and the Still Point of Consciousness: An Excursion into the *Four Quartets* [mss.].") Percy's revisiting of his novels we find in the variety of his essays, scattered along his journey as signposts of his progress in a strange land, perhaps of benefit to him; most certainly to us.

14. We have related kindred points of discovery between T. S. Eliot and Percy, each as *homo viator*. Here it is of interest that a decade before Percy's birth, Eliot was struggling to complete the poem we remember as "The Love Song of J. Alfred Prufrock." At Eliot's moment there was much excitement over Henri Bergson's *Creative Evolution*—so much that Eliot went to Paris to hear Bergson lecture. He was not persuaded by Bergson, but while there he was introduced to Dostoevsky's work. He then completed his "Prufrock," and one might even suspect that he did so encouraged by Dostoevsky's *Notes from Underground*, dissolving his "writer's block." There are certainly correspondences between his "Self" love song and Dostoevsky's own point of turning, dramatized in his *Notes*, after which he turns toward *The Brothers Karamazov*.

15. In an interesting coincidence, something very like this experience of a turning in *The Moviegoer* with its New Orleans setting occurred for Faulkner in residence in New Orleans. He wrote *Soldier's Pay* and several stories, published but no doubt considered "failed" by him in his subsequent reflection. Then Faulkner wrote "A Rose for Emily" (1930), discovering his "place" to be that "postage stamp" world, Yoknapatawpha County. I explored this discovery by Faulkner in the "Afterword" to my Lamar Lectures, *Possum, and Other Receits for the Recovery of "Southern" Being*. On Percy's departure as a writer from *ideas*, there is an interesting difference from O'Connor's point of departure. In her remarks on "Writing Short Stories" she says, to a gathering of neophytes at the University of Georgia—before excusing herself to go back home "to feed the chickens": "If you start with a real personality, a real character, then something is bound to happen; and you don't have to know what before you begin. In fact it may be better if you don't know what before you begin. You ought to be able to discover something from your stories. If you don't, probably nobody else will." She echoes Henry James, perhaps intentionally, since Caroline Gordon was so insistent to O'Connor that she study James. James argues that one should start with a character (derived out of *persons* known), not with a situation. The situation collects to the character in the unfolding of the fiction. Starting with idea and summoning character to it, as Percy intends in *The Moviegoer*, is closer to Joyce in the departure than to James. Joyce, too, begins with *idea* for his portrait of Stephen as "Artist"—aesthetic idea out of St. Thomas Aquinas. A possible corollary: Percy and Joyce are more dependent upon their own personal "character"—their own autobiography—in summoning characters than is O'Connor.

16. *Scientism* in a revolutionary mode: that is the aspect of the Modernist "problems" Percy engaged. The context in Charlotte Hays's interview for *The National Catholic Register* is announced by its title: "Walker Percy on the Church, Abortion, Faith, and Nuclear War." Percy has just spoken of the Nun "who shook her finger at the Holy Father" in protest for women's rights which she declares denied by the Church. The action suggests to Percy "more psychological than theological reasons for their protest." Indeed, "The way they talk about the Holy Father is nothing less than termagant hatred." How sharp a contrast in Mother Teresa: "I don't think it has ever crossed her mind that she is being persecuted by a male, monarchical Church or the Holy Father. She has better things to do.... They could be much more radical by doing what Mother Teresa does."

Index